SMALL SCALE INDUSTRIES

VOLUME TWO

Books in Series

Vol. I Problems of Small Scale Industries

Vol. II Management of Small Scale Industries

About the Editor

Mookkiah Soundarapandian is Reader in Rural Industries and Management, Gandhigram Rural Institute (Deemed University), Gandhigram. Apart from teaching and extension responsibilities at Gandhigram Rural Institute, he has been engaged in research activities. He has published many research articles in various reputed journals at national and international level and six books, namely, (i) Rural Industries in India, (ii) Women Entrepreneurship, (iii) Tribal Development in India, (iv) Industrial Resurgence in Rural India, (v) Literacy Campaign in India, and (vi) Rural Entrepreneurship. Apart from providing research guidance to a number of Ph.D. and M.Phil. students, he has directed and completed Nine minor research projects and two major research projects that were sponsored by University Grants Commission, Indian Council of Social Science Research, Bharat Gyan Vigyan Samiti, Ministry of Rural Development, New Delhi and State Resource Centre for Non-formal Education, Chennai. One major research project that is at an advanced stage of completion, are financed by University Grants Commission, New Delhi.

SMALL SCALE INDUSTRIES

VOLUME - TWO

Management of Small Scale Industries

Edited by

M. Soundarapandian

Reader in Rural Industries and Management,
Gandhigram Rural Institute (Deemed University)
Gandhigram

CONCEPT PUBLISHING COMPANY, NEW DELHI-110059

ISBN-81-7022-989-8 (Set)
ISBN-81-7022-991-X (Vol. II)

First Published 2002

Published and Printed by
Ashok Kumar Mittal
Concept Publishing Company
A/15-16, Commercial Block, Mohan Garden,
NEW DELHI-110059

Phone : 5351460, 5351794
Fax : 091-11-5357103
E-mail : publishing@conceptpub.com

PREFACE

Today, Small Scale Industries form the backbone of a developing country like India. They have become an effective weapon in bringing into existence a harmoniously balanced integrated socio-economic order in our economy. The role of small scale industries is most significant both in respect of employment and value added particularly in the developing economies. At present, the industries scene in the country is competitive by the liberalisation policy of the Government. The proper management and efficient utilisation of local resources for the development of industries provide the way for their expansion and strengthening. It is the right time to dicuss the problems and management of small scale industries in India and to find out the ways and means for the promotion of small scale industries in India. For this purpose, a seminar was conducted by the Department of Rural Industries and Management, Gandhigram Rural Institute, Gandhigram.

A few important topics are discussed in the seminar. The topics analysed in the seminar are categorized into two parts. They are :

Part - I

Problems of Small Scale Industries — Availability and Source of Raw Materials, Inventory, Production Process and Problems relating to Marketing, Advertisement, Sales Promotion, Technical Problems and New Economic Policy.

Part - II

Management of Small Scale Industries — Management of Agro based, Mineral based, Textile, Forest based, Polymer and Chemical based industries, Training for the excutives in the small scale industries, Development of Managerial skills for the rural entrepreneurs and other managerial problems.

These two categories of papers are presented in two volumes as: Small Scale Industries Vol. I and Vol. II.

I am grateful to Dr. G. Pankajam, Vice Chancellor of GRI, Gandhigram and to Dr. N. Thillainayagam, Professor and Head, Department of Rural Industries and Management, Gandhigram Rural Institute, for their encouragement and support for publishing the books. The untiring support exerted by my wife Mrs. S. Indumathy and my children Diwakaran and Vidya, helped me to enjoy the competition of this work. Finally, my sincere thanks to the Concept Publishing Company for their acceptance in publishing the book in two volumes.

Gandhigram **M. SOUNDARAPANDIAN**

CONTENTS

LIST OF CONTRIBUTORS

Anand, E., Department of Rural Industries and Management, Gandhigram Rural Institute, Gandhigram.

Aravazhi, D., Lecturer, Department of Commerce, Periyar Arts College, Cuddalore.

Chandrakantha, J., Department of Commerce, A.P.A. College of Arts and Science, Palani.

Chellathurai, G., Reader, Department of Commerce, P.M.T. College, Melaneelithanallur.

Chokalingam, S. M., Professor, Department of Commerce, DDE, Annamalai University, Annamalai Nagar.

Dhanasekaran, K., Lecturer (SG), Department of Economics, Gobi Arts & Science College, Gobichettipalayam, Erode, Tamil Nadu.

Ganesan, G., Teacher Fellow, Department of Commerce, Pondicherry University, Pondicherry.

Hasan Banu, S., Lecturer, (S.S.), Department of Commerce, H.K.R.H. College, Uthamapalayam Theni.

Jagadeswaran, R., Department of Rural Industries and Management, Gandhigram Rural Institute, Gandhigram

Jayabalan, S., Department of Commerce, A.P.A. College of Arts and Science, Palani.

Kannan Nair, N., Reader, Department of Rural Industries and Management, Gandhigram Rural Institute, Gandhigram.

Kurup, Shantha B., Dean, Faculty of Business Administration, Avinashilingam University, Coimbatore.

Lalitha, N., Reader, Department of Adult Continuing Education and Extension, Gandhigram Rural Institute, Gandhigram

Lopoyetum, Samwel Kakuko, Post-Doctoral Research Fellow, Department of Co-operation, Gandhigram Rural Institute, Gandhigram.

Mahesh, R., Alagappa Institute of Management, Alagappa University, Karaikudi

Maria John, S., Reader, Department of Commerce, C.P.A. College, Bodinayakanur

Meenakshisundaram N., Reader, Department of Rural Industries and Management, Gandhigram Rural Institute, Gandhigram.

Mukundan, N., Part-time Lecturer, Department of Economics, Madurai Kamaraj University, (Evening College), Dindigul.

Muruganandan, P., Department of Rural Industries and Management, Gandhigram Rural Institute, Gandhigram.

Nair, N. Kannan, Reader, Department of Rural Industries and Management, Gandhigram Rural Institute, Gandhigram.

Pankajam, A., Lecturer, Department of Management Studies, Avinashilingam University, Coimbatore.

Ponniah, M., Lecturer (S.S.) Department of Commerce, G.T.N. College, Dindigul.

Radhakrishnan, R., Department of Rural Industries and Management, Gandhigram Rural Institute, Gandhigram.

Rajagopalan, D., Dean & Professor, Department of Commerce, Pondicherry University, Pondicherry.

Rajkumar, C., Department of Rural Industries and Management, Gandhigram Rural Institute, Gandhigram.

Seerengarajan, R., Selction Grade Lecturer in Handloom Technology, Department of Rural Industries and Management, Gandhigram Rural Institute, Gandhigram.

Senthil, M., Alagappa Institute of Management, Alagappa University, Karaikudi

Shyamala, B., Reader and Head, PG, Department of Economics, Fatima College, Madurai

Solomon Raj, P., Lecturer, (SG) Department of Economics, Pope's College, Sawyerpuram.

Soundarapandian, M., Reader, Department of Rural Industries and Management, Gandhigram Rural Institute, Gandhigram.

Thenmozhi, G., Department of Commerce, A.P.A. College of Arts and Science, Palani.

Thillinayagam, N., Professor and Head, Department of Rural Industries and Management, Gandhigram Rural Insitute, Gandhigram.

Uma, G., Department of Political Science, Gandhigram Rural Institute, Gandhigram.

Umashankar, G., Department of Political Science, Gandhigram Rural Institute, Gandhigram.

Varadarajan, R., Professor, Department of Commerce, (DDE), Madurai Kamaraj University, Madurai.

1

AN INTEGRATED MANAGEMENT APPROACH FOR RURAL INDUSTRIALISATION

— *K. Dhanasekaran*

The Small Scale enterprises constitute a vital component in Indian economy. They provide immediate large scale employment; they offer a method of ensuring a more equitable distribution of the national income and they facilitate an effective mobilisation of resources of capital and skill which might otherwise remain unutilized. The Government of India had emphasised the importance of small scale industry for achieving socio-economic objectives like generating more employment, removal of regional disparities and reduction in economic backwardness. An interesting aspect is that, according to one estimate, it is expected that the Rural Non-Farm Sector (RNFS) at an increased employment growth rate of 8.1 per cent (growth during 1997-98 estimated at 5.4 per cent) could create about 45.2 million additional jobs by 2001 AD. The Liberalisation, Globalisation and Privatisation leading to increased investment in industrial and infrastructure sectors are likely to have wider impact on investment in small scale industries (SSI) and service sectors (Nanda, 1999).

A significant feature of the Indian economy is the rapid growth of the small industry sector and the plan outlays for village and small industries in Indian plans. The details of plan outlays for village and small industries during various plans are given in the following Table 1.1.

Table 1.1: Plan Outlays for Village and Small Industries during Different Five Year Plans

(Rs. crores)

Plan Period	Total Plan Outlay	Plan Outlay for VSI	Percentage Share of VSI
1st Plan (1951-56)	1960.0	42.1	2.1
2nd Plan (1956-91)	4671.8	186.8	4.0
3rd Plan (1961-66)	8577.0	240.0	2.8
Annual Plan (1966-69)	6525.4	126.1	1.9
4th Plan (1969-74)	15778.8	242.6	1.5
5th Plan (1974-79)	39462.2	592.5	1.5
6th Plan (1980-85)	109291.7	1945.1	1.8
7th Plan (1985-90)	180000.0	2752.7	1.5
8th Plan (1992-97)	—	7094.0	1.4

Source : Economic Survey — 1988-89 and various Plan documents.

Table 1.1 shows that the allocation for VSI has been rising gradually in successive Plans. The share of these industries in the overall outlays has, however, remained very small accounting for merely 1.5 per cent since the Fourth Plan onwards. In fact, the share has been becoming smaller and smaller after the Second Plan. In spite of its importance and potentials, this sector is now beset with various limitations and constraints. A fair assessment of the constraints in planned promotion of rural industries would also be immensely useful in carving out future plan of action for promotion of small and village industries. It is therefore necessary as a matter of national policy and strategy to make intensive efforts to promote rural industrialisation with a view to improving the overall quality of life.

Rural Industrialisation

The rural industrialisation, which received varying degrees of emphasis in successive Five Year Plans could not generate additional employment opportunities. The process of industrialisation of developing countries is hampered due to various constraints (Krishan Kumar, 1991). A picture in regard to the characteristics of rural industries helps one to indicate the possible areas where efforts can be made for the development of rural industries. Some of the characteristic features of rural industries are given below (Kotaiah, 1998).

* It is decentralised and the units are thinly and widely dispersed.
* It has enormous range of products, traditional as well as non-traditional.
* There is a vast disparity in technology employed as well as scale of production.
* The sector lacks standard and standardisation.
* There is diverse nature of markets from local, regional to national and international.
* There are serious infrastructure constraints in the rural areas for development of the sector.
* It suffers from financing, marketing and managerial constraints.
* Systematic extension efforts in use of new tools and techniques of production are lacking.
* There is a tendency to remain small.

Constraints of Rural Industries

It has been increasingly recognised through various studies that rural industries/enterprises have various constraints which inhibit their access beyond local markets. The constraints which inhibit the development of village and small industries are institutional, financial, raw material inadequacy, marketing technological and entrepreneurial (Ram, 1990).

Amarnath Bandarla divided the problems into two groups, viz., external and internal. External problems are those which result from factors beyond the control of the entrepreneurs, e.g. the availability of power. While internal problems are those which are not influenced by external forces. These relate to organisation structure, production and distribution channels, technical knowhow, training, industrial relations and inadequacy of management. These two kinds of problems are correlated (Amarnath Bandarla). Kotaiah identified some of the following major constraints faced by the rural industries.

* Lack of market information of the tastes of the consumer preference.
* Inability to scale up production and services due to inadequate capital.
* Inability to adopt technological transformation to meet the quality standard required by the market.
* Lack of standards and standardisation.
* Lack of adequate infrastructural support.
* Unaware of the various facilities offered by Central and State Governments.
* Lack of improved tools and technology.
* Lack of knowledge and adequate training facilities.
* Lack of assured and adequate supply of raw materials.

In addition to the above problems, the rural industries faced the following constraints :

1. Rigorous security norms.
2. Cumbersome procedures.
3. Lack or rural orientation among bankers .
4. Inadequate finance in relation to the requirements.

The experience of National Bank for Agriculture and Rural Development in implementation of various credit and promotional programmes/schemes has been mixed. Some of the major constraints are (Kotaiah, 1998) :

(i) Banks still perceive rural enterprises as high risk bearing and less remunerative business propositions,

(ii) Overall inadequacy of infrastructure, backward and forward linkages, market information, etc.,

(iii) There is dearth of professionally equipped, experienced NGOs to take up various credit delivery innovations and promotional projects,

(iv) There is not yet full appreciation of complexities of the rural non-farm sector enterprises,

(v) Inadequacy of skill upgradation and technology dissemination, and

(vi) Slow and painstaking process of credit delivery innovations for visible/demonstrated results.

The foregoing discussion clearly brings us to the question of evolving an appropriate framework for developing village and small industries. Needs of the small units could be summarised as under:

(i) Small industries have to be distinguished from the village industries and the latter should be promoted more vigorously through enhanced plan outlays and financial assistance.

(ii) Growth of small and village industries has to be secured by paying more attention to modernisation, technological upgradation and R&D.

(iii) Integrated marketing support through counselling, research and special studies and participation in trade fairs and exhibitions would be paramount importance.

(iv) All organisations particularly the District Industries Centres and State KVI Boards may have to be organised to make them more responsive.

(v) There should be statutory obligation, particularly on the small scale units, to furnish all requisite data. This would be extremely helpful for future planning.

Role of the Managers

1. The Managers, basing on the DIC survey decides the village where Rural Entrepreneurial Development Centre could operate.
2. He identifies the local and outside markets for the selected

activities which are pursued in the block.

3. He selects master craftsmen for providing training from the same villages.
4. He arranges for purchase of raw materials.
5. He decides on the pricing of the product, packing designing etc.
6. He arranges for sale of the products through the financing bank by means of bills drawn on the buyers.

Conclusion

In the light of the above discussion, one can say that small units can make a rich contribution to the economy. It is evident that the small and village industries have been given due recognition from the very start. In each of the Eight Five Year Plans also, their importance has been adequately emphasised. However, this sector is now beset with various constraints. The challenges cannot be met through organisation of some campaigns or the other but will require efforts made after a continual evaluation and assessment of constraints and modifying the policies and programmes to meet the entrepreneur's need. It should be quite possible to create a better perspective for rural industries by taking integrated measures/ programme packages. Hence, rural management professionals have to develop appropriate models in an integrated way and put them test before recommending the findings to policy makers.

References

Amarnath Bandarla, "Problems of Agro-based Industries", *Khadigramodyog*, February, 1992.

Kotaiah, P., "Policy on Institutional Credit to Generate Employment and Marketing Skills among the Rural Youths in Asia-Pacific Region—Indian Experience", *National Bank News Review*, Vol. 14, No.12, April-June 1998.

Krishan Kumar, "Future of Rural Industrialisation", *Khadigraomodyog* January, 1991.

Nanda, Y.C., "Employment Creation and Poverty Alleviation" *National Bank News Review*, Vol. 15, No.1, January-March 1999.

Ram, G.S., "Rural Industrialisation Perspective", *Kurukshetra,* April 1990.

Yerram Raju, "Village & Cottage Industries Sector: Integrated Systems Needed", *National Bank News Review*, Vol. 7, No. 9, November 1991.

ANNEXURE

PROMOTIONAL PROGRAMMES FOR NFS AT A GLANCE

Strengthening Credit Delivery

* PLI Training Programmes
* Orientation/Sensitation Meets for Banks, NGO's etc.
* Technical, Monitoring & Evaluation (TME) Cells (NFS) in RRBs & Cooperative Banks
* Vikas Volunteer Vahini (VVV)

Developing Entrepreneurs

* Training-cum-Production Centres (TPCs)
* Rural Entrepreneurship Development Programmes (REDP)
* Market Oriented Training (MOT)
* Other Skill Development Training
* Training of / by Master Craftsmen

Support of Promotional Organisations for Marketing and Skill/ Technology Upgradation

* Artisans guilds
* Training of trainers (VAs)
* Flexible (Catalytic) Approach
* Mother Units (MU) and Common Service Centres (CSC)

Women Development

* Assistance of Rural Women in Non-Farm Development (ARWIND)
* Marketing Assistance for Rural Women (MAHIMA)
* Women Development Cells (WDCs)

Area Programmes

* Area Plan for Rural Industrialisation (APRI)
* District Rural Industries Project (DRIP)

Research & Studies

* Product Studies
* Linkage Studies
* Utilisation/Impact/Monitoring Studies
* Research Studies
* Potential Surveys in selected districts

Miscellaneous

Other miscellaneous interventions e.g. sponsoring of workshop/ seminar for dissemination of information, rural communication, fairs/exhibitions for marketing rural NFS products, preparation of project profiles, awareness literatures, etc.

Source : Nanda, Y.C., 1999 in *National Bank News Review,* p.21.

2

ACTIVITY-BASED COST MANAGEMENT (ABCM) FOR RURAL INDUSTRIES

— *G. Ganesan* and *D. Rajagopalan*

Introduction

The global economy is characterized by greater integration, a more liberalised international trade regime following the set-up of the World Trade Organisation, a rapid pace of technological changes, especially in some high-growth areas such as information and knowledge-based industries, and intensified international competition.

India's economic policies are in the process of being restructured, through the second generation reforms, to adjust to the emerging challenges. The main emphasis of future policy will be to promote the growth of this dynamic sector through focused, sustained and wide-ranging interventions, as the SSI sector has so far been insulated to a large extent from pressures of competition both domestically and internationally. Moreover, the SSI sector is non-homogeneous in structure and includes diverse types of production units ranging from traditional crafts to high-tech industries.

Now-a-days rural industries are taking active role in rural development. Rural and village industries have immense potential to generate new jobs with relatively low direct investment by utilising local skills and resources. Development of this sector would also prevent migration of rural population to urban areas in search of employment. Rural industrialisation means value addition on local raw-materials like agriculture, forest, horticulture, chemical etc., or demand-based industries, thus making marketable products and marketing either in village and cities or exports. The concept of rural industries includes village and SSIs. Village and small-scale sector divided into eight sub-sectors, namely, khadi, village industries, handloom, sericulture, handicrafts, coir, modern SSIs. While the last two represent the modern SSIs, the other six sub-sectors constituted traditional industries which constitute a formidable part in the rural industrialisation. Hence an effective management of rural industries is essential to reduce cost of production and increase quality and value of the product.

Enhancing global competitiveness of SSIs holds the key to their future development. Effective policy interventions at the present time need to begin with the chronic and generalised problems facing the industry as a whole mainly, finance, technology, more importantly production cost and marketing. Marketing strategies, which include pricing policies, and the maintenance of international quality standards for products will be crucial in the new economic environment. With changes in demand patterns and consumer preferences and a wider range of choice for most products, pricing, and marketing is likely to become a key factor for an industry competitiveness.

In order to meet such competitive environment, rural industries need cost management exercises to find accurate costs of their products, if possible reduce costs of the individual management accounting systems tend to produce highly aggregated cost information that is allocated to products by simplistic and arbitrary methods and the allocations are often unrelated to demands made by the products on organisational resources (Swenzon, 1995). To overcome these deficiencies, ABCM was introduced a few years ago in Indian industries to calculate accurate cost, to reduce cost of production, to increase value to the product and through which they can increase profits. In rural industries also the new ABCM can be used for such purposes. The new ABCM offers a way to calculate the real costs of the products and to transform the costing exercises into Enterprise-wise process management initiatives which aimed at reduced cost in every activity.

For the present study, the following will be the hypotheses :

1. Actions constitute an activity;
2. An activity causes costs;
3. Products consume activities for their completion.
4. Control activities mean control costs.

The aim of the present study is to find :

1. the real cost of the products;
2. the way to reduce cost and improve quality and value of the product;
3. the effective management to control non-value added activities;
4. the efficient way to determine the best possible pricing for the product.

Activity-Based Cost Management (ABCM)

The essence of ABCM is the link up of the important activities that need to be performed to provide a product. It means that the cost figures along the budgetary line should be first traced to the activities before the profitability analysis of the product. It focuses mainly on managing activities that include identifying non-value added activities that can be eliminated and making sure that needed activities are carried out efficiently to improve operations, management must search out unnecessary or inefficient activities.

ABCM and Value-addition

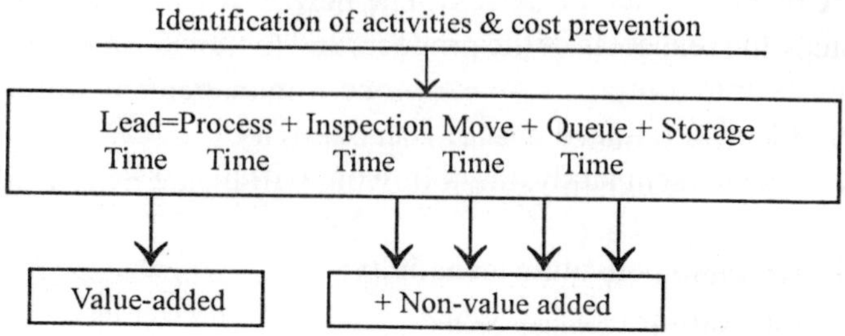

ABCM is being used in manufacturing industries for product design, development customised products and efficient management of various resources. It generates a variety of data and information that can be developed for performance measures. In face, performance measurement is regarded as a central feature of ABCM (Vehmanen,1994).

Activity-Management

Organisation performs activities that provide goods or services to their customers. A sequence of activities that create a good or service can be viewed as a value chain since each step in the chain should add something that the customer values to the product. Activity-management exactly means an improving cost performance, which requires an examination of the need, efficiency, and effectiveness of existing activities and any new activities.

In an activity-management approach to cost improvement, a manufacturer, for example, may try to reduce costs by studying its current activities and developing loans to eliminate unnecessary activities and improve the performance of necessary activities. For example, a study of activities may indicate that 50 per cent of labour costs in a factory relate to handling work in process, which adds nothing to the product attributes that customers value.

Instead, handling activities reflect organisation constraints, poor product design, and a poor factory layout. The organisation may reduce the need for handling. It would be possible to eliminate many material-handling costs permanently without affecting the value of the products to the customer. This approach would not require that employees work harder to reduce costs.

Steps in activity analysis :

1. Identify process objectives
2. Chart the existing process
3. Classify all activities
4. Continuously improve all activities and plan to eliminate non-value added activities.

The above exhibit summarises four steps in activity analysis. It is very useful in helping organisation identify opportunities to reduce cost and improve quality and processing time in a systematic way.

Uses of ABCM

1. Cooper & Kaplan (1991) pointed out that, " the activity based system shows that significant expense reduction can be achieved by reducing setup costs, making production scheduling and materials handling more efficient and reducing the number of parts required to need final customer products demands."
2. It increases the profitability by identifying and eliminating the non-value added activities.
3. It helps in process improvements and waste elimination by providing feedback on product design.
4. It is a tool for managers to determine price more precisely.
5. It generates a variety of data and information that can be developed for performance measures.
6. Shank and Kaplan (1993) provided a evidence that ABCM is a detailed tracing of resource consumed by-product output and their cost impact.

Conclusion

Thus the role of SSIs in the economy can be seen from the fact that it now accounts for 95 per cent of all industrial units in the country and 40 per cent of total output. About 7,500 products are manufactured in the small scale sector. The exports share is 35 per cent. Further, it is recognised that the potential of a sub-sector to become globally competitive will change as a result of changes in the domestic and global economy. The sub-sectors which may have a major role to play in the future are: Readymade garments, leather footwear, electronic components, processed foods, and automotive tiny industries are likely to emerge as the dynamic segment within the small industry category. Their flexibility will prove to be an advantage at the time of rapid economic change bringing about changes in demand patterns. With the help of ABCM, rural industries can get an accurate cost of a product and maximum reduction in cost by eliminating non-value added expenses and achieve maximum profits and benefits. Once rural industry moves on to ABCM, direct links with other management tools will emerge to generate information which would throw light on how to reduce wastes and prune non-value added activities (BPR), eliminating the need for checking activities (TQM), paring down inventories (Just-in-time), and changing manufacturing process (Shop Floor Re-engineering), etc., to get full benefits of ABCM.

References

Bellis, J.R., 1989, Customer Profitability Analysis, *Management Accountant.*

Birmson, J.A., (1991), *Activity Accounting,* New York.

Cooper, R. & Kaplan, R.S., *The Design of Cost Management System,* Prentice Hall.

Rural Development and Privatisation, Edited by Debendra K. Das, New Delhi.

Sara & Chandra, Panigrahi, *Rural Sector and Development,* Deep & Deep Publications, New Delhi.

The Business Today - Various issues.

The Financial Express - Various issues.

Vehmaneu, P. (1994), Toimintolaskenta - *The Finish Journal of Business Economics.*

3

HEALTH CARE MANAGEMENT IN QUARRY INDUSTRY : A Case Study in Madurai District

— *M. Soundarapandian* and *C. Rajkumar*

Introduction

Quarry Industry occupies an important place in the industrial structure of the Indian Economy. It provides not only employment opportunities but also forms as a foundation for an infrastructural facilities. The process of quarry industry and safety measures of the quarry industry workers needs to be given importance.

Stone for building is generally are of five kinds — granites, stones, lime stones, slates and marbles. Many building stones are also used to make rollers for paper-making machines and for grinding-mills. Building stones are usually identified by the names of their type sometimes varying from one locality to another, and knowledge of where they come from is very useful to the builder or architect in judging the purposes for which they can best be used. Large regular lumps of stone are required for building preferably parallel faces. Rock in their natural form are divided by cracks of fissures, which are known in the trade as joints. These joints often enable quarry men to separate masses of stone with their faces roughly parallel to each other. Some types of stones, known as 'free stones', can easily be in any direction. Portland stones are of this type.

This ancient industry forms a branch of masonry and is one of the building trades. Now-a-days the hand dressing of stones by a branch or banker has been largely superseded by machinery. The machines are so large and costly that they adjoin the quarries or are found only in workshops belonging to building contractors.

Building in stone is one of the most cherished traditional crafts in Britain, cresting her greatest monuments of architecture cathedrals, abbeys, parish churches, colleges, and mansions, as well as some of her most beautiful old cottage. The greatly increased use of machinery for stone dressing has led to a saving in skilled manual labour, and so has the use of 'reconstructed stone' in place of natural stone.

Reconstructed stone is really concrete, usually mixed in the proportion of four parts grand to one part of portland cement and then faced with chips of stones or stone dust from the works at the quarry. Reconstructed stone, therefore, looks very much like the natural stone with which it is faced, and there is no need for dressing either by machinery or by hand.

The greatest difficulty experienced in quarrying is most of lifting and having the stones loosened and broken up from the bottom at a quarry. Hence it is started aside and as it goes deep, an inclined track is made for the haulage of material either by bullock carts at trucks running on a light railway. It is important to arrange a proper layout to ensure economic and safe working of a quarry.

Rocks of different types, which are strong and durable are used for highway construction. The curshed stones, used in concrete, depend largely upon the kind of structure to be constructed. The chipped stone aggregated in concrete serve as a filling material to be constructed. The course aggregates may vary in size from 10 to 21.5 cm for the ordinary building construction purpose. For the construction of highways and air strips the maximum size varies from 3.81 to 6.35 cm.

Any type of hard and tough rocks are used as rail road ballast and usually used as ballast but due to its cheap market value any type of rocks available locally are preferred. Sometimes dark coloured dicrite and hornblende sadists are also used as ballast for rail road. The angularity of broken stones determine a very high stability for the railway tracks.

Quartz is sometimes used in road metals as it can stand the effects of weathering and also due to its hardness. The behaviour of rocks under attrition and impact depends on the following considerations:

1. Freshness of the rocks.
2. Texture and structure.
3. Nature of the component minerals.

In stratified rocks, there are bed joints as well as vertical over. Even unstratified igneous rocks, the mass of the rocks is usually sub-divided into heavy natural joints in separating by one block from another. The first block has to be sacrificed by removing it into small pieces by wedges, chisel and hammer or by blasting, but subsequently, it is easier to get out contiguous blocks.

Sometimes heating is resorted to for splitting a rock, consisting of large exposed powders, particularly if large blocks are required. Bush wood is heaped on the surface of such a rock and is set fire to. This causes the upper layer to expand and separate from the lower mass. This is usually attended with a dull bursting sound.

The hardness and toughness are of primary importance, particularly during quarrying operation at the time of drilling and blasting at rock materials. The cost of rock production before crusting depends on the physical properties of rock. The investigation revealed that the industry can be classified in two classes. One class consists of the big contractors who can invest large amount and the work is carried out mostly by means of machines. These contractor can invest large amount on machinery etc., and can monopolize quarries by getting them leased to themselves.

The second class consists of artisans mostly belonging to

scheduled castes and backward classes. This study area consists of mainly small manufacturers and they have not installed much machine or preventive measures to protect the workers.

The crude rocks are explained from quarries and the primary crushing is being carried out by jaw crushers and also by gyratory crushers. The pulverised fine fractions are removed by screening, as during crushing a good amount of dust is accumulated in the crushers.

In dirty and dusty atmosphere a worker cannot breathe properly and it causes many diseases. Bysinosis, the respiratory complaint, resulting from the formation of stone dust, develop only after a number of years of exposure. Quarry silicosis is caused by breathing stone dust when rocks or raw stones broken out.

The chief effect of exposure to raise, in terms of both frequency and severity is known as noise deafness. Other effects of industrial noise may be expressed in terms of fatigue and inefficiency.

There are three ways of reducing noise :

1. Eliminating of noise out of its sources,
2. Reduction of noise by altering the surroundings, and
3. Personal protection against noise.

Objective

Following are the objectives of the present study :

1. To identify the location of quarry industry and the related diseases to quarry industry workers,
2. To assess the contribution of quarry owners towards, the treatment for occupational diseases, and
3. To study about the safety and welfare measures of the quarry industry.

Methodology

In this study we used primary as well as secondary data. Primary data directly collected from quarry owners and quarry nearest Hospital Doctors through questionnaire.

There are four quarries running in Usilampatti Taluk. The primary data collected from total four quarry Industry owners and four Doctors of Government Hospitals nearest to quarry Industry and the necessary information is collected from them.

Secondary data are collected from various books, magazines and Government Reports and publications of various associations connected with historical documentation and other sources of published information. The sources of unpublished data are many. They are collected from research works, trade associations, labour bureaus and other public, private, individuals and organisations.

Results and Discussions

In order to study the Health Care Management in Quarry Industry workers, opinion from the four owners of the quarry has been collected.

The name of the quarry places are :

1. Thottappanayakkanoor,
2. Thidiyan ,
3. T. Ariyapatti,
4. Uthappanayakkanoor,

and they are situated in Usilampatti Taluk. All the quarry owners are private and partnership. The number of employees per unit ranges from 15 to 25. An interesting point to note here is that there is no trade union in these industries and the workers are not giving any nuisance to the owners regarding their health care aspects. But following are the tables presenting the informations about the quarries, quarry related diseases to workers, opinion of the quarry owners and doctors.

Table 3.1 : Details about Quarry Owners in Usilampatty

Unit No.	Place of Industry	Starting Year	Private or partner	Total No. of workers M F C
1.	Thottappanayakkanoor	1991	Partner	14 / 9 / 2
2.	Thidiyan	1980	Private	4 / 10 / 1
3.	T. Ariyapatti	1984	Private	10 / 8 / 2
4.	Uthappanayakkanoor	1990	Private	12 / 6 / 2

Source : Survey Data 1998.

The above Table 3.1 are explains about the quarry places and number of workers are working in industry, managing system and year of establishment.

Table 3.2 : Nature of Diseases in a Quarry Industry

Sl. No.	Stone dust related Diseases
1.	Asthma
2.	Tuberculosis
3.	Lung cancer
4.	Whooping cough
5.	Anemia

Source : Computed from primary data.

Table 3.2 explains that the nature of diseases in a quarry industry in workers. The stone creates hard dust at the time of cutting the stone in quarry industry and crushing machines. The dust accumulates inside while breathing in which is dangerous to health. The dust creates many more diseases like, Asthma, Tuberculosis, Lung cancer, Whooping cough, Anemia. All the above diseases can attack and are injurious to the health of workers. The tuberculosis and particularly lung cancer if once attacked have no cure.

Health of workers is the primary responsibility of employer. Table 3.3 shows the future plans for the improvement of health of workers.

The three important future plans of the quarry owners are :

1. Giving more safety,
2. Organising the labour, and
3. Reformulating the compensation structure,

Table 3.3 : Health Care Measure

Unit Nos.	Place of Industry	Safety measure (in. Rs.)	Health care measure	Dust control
1.	Thottappanayakkanoor	200	Sanitary measures	Regular physical exam.
2.	Thidiyan	100	Nil	Regular physical exam.
3.	T. Ariyapatti	200	Nutrition	Substitution
4.	Uthappanayakkanoor	80	Nil	Complete measures

Source : Survey data 1998.

The industrialists are ready to bear Rs. 50 to 200 as safety measure costs. Regarding health care measures, these industrialists are providing sanitary and nutrition measures. Having realised the problem of dust the workers are substituted in alternative days and they are given regular physical medical checkup. In addition to these there are dust control measures that are also provided by these industrialists.

The present study is based upon the Health care measurement analysis. The information one may collect from the industrial owners. But in order to cross-check this, an attempt has been made to interview the doctors in the quarry industry study area. Four doctors had been interviewed and data on two patients for each doctor had been collected and presented in Table 3.4.

Table 3.4 : Doctor's Report of Nearest Places of Quarry Industry in Usilampatti

Doctor's Report	Patient	Age	Marital Status	Sex	Name of Diseases	Suggestion	Causes	Duration	Cost (in Rs.)	Cured/ Not
I.	Patient 1	44	Married	Male	Tuberc-ulosis	Rest and short hour work	Air Pollu-tion (stone dust)	2 years	75 (per month)	uncured
	Patient 2	48	Married	Female	Lung cancer	Continue treatment	Stone dust	5 years	60 "	"
II.	Patient 1	18	Unmarried	Male	Cough	facemasks and protec-ted eye glass	quarry dust pollution	6 months	50 "	cured
	Patient 2	52	Married	Male	Tuber-culosis	Change alternative	Silica dust	5 years	75 "	uncured
III.	Patient 1	17	Unmarried	Male	Cough	masks	Dusts/smoke	2 years	40 "	cured
	Patient 2	49	Married	Male	Lung cancer	Change alternative	Quarrystone dust	5 years		uncured
IV.	Patient 1	55	Married	Female	Tuber-culosis	Rest and short hour work	Stone dust	2 years	50 "	"
	Patient 2	43	Married	Male	Asthma	Facemask	Dust/smoke	6 months	50 "	"

Source : Survey Data, 1998.

Table 3.4 represents the first doctor had given data for one male and another female. The diseases diagnosed by the doctor are Tuberculosis and lung cancer and the duration of the diseases are two years or three years respectively. The doctor admitted the fact that the stone dust is the cause for these and the suggested rest and long time treatment. But the affected persons had been cured.

The second doctor had given data for two males and the diseases are cough and tuberculosis. For cough, the reason given by the doctor is quarry dust and for Tuberculosis silica dust. The doctor prescribed facemasks to protect the eye and for Tuberculosis affected persons were suggested for going to an alternative jobs. While the cough affected person has been cured, but not Tuberculosis affected person.

The third doctor had given information on cough affected male person and lung cancer affected. That is the cause for this and we advised to use mask and change of job like others. We also found stone dust as a cause for these diseases and we also prescribed change of job and provision of mask. The above information gives us the idea that the workers are after affected by cough, lung cancer, tuberculosis and asthma, and the duration of the diseases are ranging from 6 months to 5 years.

The doctors themselves admitted the fact that some diseases are curable and others not. The cost of medical treatment is also not provided to them upto the level of the seriousness of the diseases. Unless and until the cost is subsidised by either the owner or the Government, these diseases are the permanent factors of the quarry workers in this area.

Findings and Suggestions

These findings and few suggestions are given which can be implemented by the quarry owners as well as by the government :

1. The major diseases which are affecting the quarry workers are Asthma, Tuberculosis, lung cancer, whooping cough, Anemia.
2. Quarry working is a very difficult job and quarry wages are paid on the basis of the quantum of work done. The income

earned by these quarry workers is insufficient. So that the living conditions are very poor. The quarry workers are wearily indebted to the moneylenders and friends. The lenders play a major role in giving loans to the quarry workers.

3. The nature of work in the quarry industry is a hazardous work and it is prone to accidents at any time. In the absence of any strict regulations to be implemented in the quarry industry, the quarry owners are reluctant to adopt any safety measures to protect the workers from any accident. In this study area all the four quarry owners have not adopted any safety measure to protect the quarry workers.

Based upon the above analysis few suggestions are given which are having policy implications :

1. Since the quarry industry are lacking medical facilities provided by the quarry owners, in addition to this good sanitation and water facilities should be given in the working area by the quarry owners.
2. The agricultural workers are getting wages regularly. But quarry workers are paid weekly wages and low wages which are even irregular in nature. The government and quarry owners should improve the wage structure in the quarry industry.
3. The formation of Trade Union is necessary in order to save the workers from the exploitation of contractors and quarry owners.

Conclusions

The study is an effort to assess the Health Care measures for the quarry industry in Usilampatty area. On voluntary basis the quarry owners must come forward to rectify the problems of quarry industry site. The Government, must enact and implement proper rules and regulations in order to enhance the standard of living of the quarry workers, and free from any kind of the exploitations in future. Both the Government and Quarry Owners must look after the medical care facilities provisions.

References

Deb, S., *Rocks and Minerals for Construction Works,* Industrial Minerals and Rocks of India, 1976.

Deshpande, R.S., *Quarrying — Materials of Constructions*, Enlarged 7th Edition 1986 pp. 18-25.

Gallo, Michael A., "Hazardous to your Health", *Environmental Health Perspectives,* Vol. 105, No. 8, August 1997.

Hutchins, Woots, M.D., "Industrial Hygiene by Employers Organisation", *The American Journal of Public Health,* Vol. XV, 1925.

Jaitlal, Harish, "Sandstone mines — Eating into their lungs". *The Hindu Survey of Environment,* 1993.

The Sunday Observer, "Killer Diseases in Quarries", *Environmental Resources Abstract,* Vol. 6, No. 4, Oct-Dec. 1988.

4

INVENTORY MANAGEMENT THROUGH JUST IN TIME METHODOLOGIES IN RURAL INDUSTRIES

— *N. Kannan Nair* and *R. Seerengarajan*

Introduction

Agriculture and rural industries are the backbone of the Indian Economy. While the progress in the agricultural activities seems to be satisfactory, the achievement in Rural Industries have not made any mark. Therefore, attention is needed to increase the productivity and also maximise the returns in this sector. These can be achieved through adoption of scientific management techniques by rural industries. Among the areas that need attention are the stocks held in rural industries. Since the value of raw materials involves 50 per cent to 80 per cent of the total cost of the production, a slight reduction in this cost will certainly help to increase the profit considerably. Hence, the managers of Rural Industrial Units should give more attention in the management of inventories. In inventory management, just in time methodology have greater role to play in the years to come.

Just in time is the method of integrating manufacturing activities and inventories based on the actual demand rather than a production schedule. The prime objective to JIT is to reduce the manufacturing cost through inventory reduction and elimination of wastage arising from the following areas :

(i) Over production,
(ii) Waiting time,
(iii) Bottlenecks in material movement,
(iv) Excessive inventories of raw materials, WIP and finished goods,
(v) Increased through put time,
(vi) Low labour utilisations,
(vii) Generation of waste from rework.

The major advantages of JIT are :

(a) 35 per cent to 70 per cent reduction in raw materials stocks,
(b) 50 per cent reduction in cost of quality,
(c) 40 per cent to 80 per cent reduction in space requirements,
(d) 25 per cent reduction in indirect and direct labour,
(e) 10 per cent reduction in lead times,
(f) 80 per cent reduction in finished goods inventory,
(g) 30 per cent reduction in supervision and monitoring costs.

JIT can be operationalised through Kanbans. Kanban is the Japanese word for a tag attached to a bin of inventory. It is a visible card and authorises production activity in current and upstream stations. It triggers movement of the materials and help in minimising the work-in-progress and finished goods inventories.

One of the major issues in rural industries establishments is the huge stocks of inventories that affect the profitability. Inventories carry cost related items and major cost is the money invested in stocks which can be equated to normal bank lending rate of 15 per cent. If an idle stock carries 15 per cent charge, then it is a matter of concern for rural industrial units. Most of rural industrial units make meagre profits due to several external factors like competition, lack of economies of scale and high labour costs. Hence, just in time methods could be installed in rural enterprises that really help them to sustain their activities and maximise returns through inventory reductions. In order to assess the role of inventories on profitability and interest charges a study has been designed in four KVI institutions operating in Dindigul District, Tamil Nadu.

In Dindigul district there are four Khadi and Village Industrial units undertaking the KVI activities. They are :

1. Gandhigram KVIPC Trust, Gandhigram,
2. Madurai North Sarvodaya Sangam, Palani,
3. Gandhi Seva Sangh, Chatrapatty,
4. Grama Rajya Nirman Sangh, Batlagundu.

These are the only four sarvodaya institutions that are operating in Dindigul District apart from TNKVIB units. All the above independent units had been taken for the study.

Results and Discussions

To assess the impact of inventories in the profit and interest charges, correlation and regression analysis were undertaken. This analysis helps to bring a dependable conclusion on the inventory to be maintained in KVI units. Inventories include the stocks of raw materials, work in progress and finished goods held by the units. Profitability is the net profit shown by the respective units in their profit/loss account obtained from the sample units.

Interest charges are the charges paid by the institutions towards working capital loan to KVIC. When institutions maintain huge stocks, naturally interest charges on working capital will be high. 'Inventory' is an idle resource of any kind having an economic value. When the resource is kept unused it becomes idle resource that carries cost with it and affects the profitability. In spite of the cost association with stocks, still inventory is maintained for the following purposes.

1. Transaction purpose,
2. Precautionary purpose,
3. Speculative purpose,
4. Decoupling purpose.

In procuring materials, there is a time factor from the date of initiation of purchase to the arrival at unit's door steps. Stocks are maintained to cushion the lead time consumption. Due to introduction of telephone/FAX or e-business facilities, the lead times may be reduced thereby reducing the stocks. Developed communication and advanced transportation facilities have helped to reduce lead times and several organised industries have gone for inventory reductions.

Seasonal factor forces higher inventories during harvest period for agricultural raw materials. But the unit has to compute the cost difference in maintaining higher inventory purchased during season at lower price and the inventory carrying charges. Accordingly suitable decision may be made whether to adopt right time purchase or seasonal purchase. Such speculative purchases could be due to non-availability of items as demand exceeds supply or fear of increased price levels.

Decoupling factor builds inventories in between work stations so that the continuity in production operations could be maintained which otherwise result in increased set up costs. By proper scheduling of production operations, the inventories could be reduced to the barest minimum.

In order to analyse the impact of inventories in the profitability and other trade charges the following exercise has been attempted.

Tables 4.1 to 4.4 presents the position of inventory held by Gandhigram KVIPC Trust against the total value of production and profitability values for a period of 12 years from 1983-84 to 1994-95.

Table 4.1 : Gandhigram KVIPC Trust, Gandhigram

Sl. No.	Year	Value of production in Rs. lakhs	Value of Inventory in Rs. lakhs	Ratio of Inventory with the value of production	Net profit in lakhs (Rs.)	Interest charges Rs. in lakhs
1	2	3	4	5	6	7
1.	1983-84	142	82	0.57	1.01	2.20
2.	1984-85	162	85	0.81	2.11	2.40
3.	1985-86	189	107	0.86	4.04	2.80
4.	1986-87	198	136	0.69	2.37	3.10
5.	1987-88	214	151	0.70	4.73	3.57
6.	1988-89	204	146	0.71	3.85	3.23
7.	1989-90	243	162	0.66	2.44	4.11
8.	1990-91	266	191	0.71	2.37	2.71
9.	1991-92	244	224	0.91	2.87	2.80
10.	1992-93	263	241	0.91	2.87	2.80
11.	1993-94	375	220	0.59	(–)12.75	9.97
12.	1994-95	344	207	0.60	4.85	5.16
Average		236.8	162.6	0.68		

Source : Audited statement of Annual Accounts of Gandhigram, KVIPC Trust, Gandhigram.

Table 4.2 : Madurai North Sarvodaya Sangh, Palani

Sl. No.	Year	Value of production in lakhs of Rs.	Value of inventories in lakhs of Rs.	Ratio of inventories to production	Net profit in lakhs of Rs.	Interest charges Rs. in lacs
1.	1983-84	37.48	29.26	0.78	–0.28	0.25
2.	1984-85	38.49	30.00	0.77	0.82	0.30
3.	1985-86	44.30	22.9	0.51	0.60	0.32
4.	1986-87	41.34	33.0	0.80	0.50	0.47
5.	1987-88	49.60	33.74	0.68	0.10	0.37
6.	1988-89	59.41	34.10	0.57	0.37	0.35
7.	1989-90	68.13	54.45	0.80	1.03	0.74
8.	1990-91	73.25	58.92	0.80	1.41	0.67
9.	1991-92	88.65	70.84	0.80	1.74	0.68
10.	1992-93	87.07	88.79	1.02	1.74	0.47
11.	1993-94	113.14	82.50	0.72	–1.58	0.80
12.	1994-95	130.30	102.19	0.78	2.48	0.78
Average		69.29	53.40	0.74		

Source : Audited statement of Annual Accounts of Madurai North Sarvodaya Sangh, Palani.

Table 4.3 : Gandhi Seva Sangam, Chatrapatti

Sl. No.	Year	Value of production in lakhs of Rs.	Value of inventories in lakhs of Rs.	Ratio of inventories to production	Net profit in lakhs of Rs.	Interest charges Rs. in lacs
1.	1983-84	14.80	3.23	0.21	0.13	0.43
2.	1984-85	15.20	6.59	0.43	0.26	0.49
3.	1985-86	16.20	4.81	0.29	0.22	0.55
4.	1986-87	19.88	4.44	0.22	0.15	0.68
5.	1987-88	17.58	6.89	0.39	0.14	0.56
6.	1988-89	19.44	14.26	0.73	0.17	0.64
7.	1989-90	27.32	15.89	0.58	0.21	0.40
8.	1990-91	33.53	16.35	0.49	0.10	0.72
9.	1991-92	25.70	10.80	0.42	(-)0.41	0.85
10.	1992-93	29.94	11.24	0.38	(-)2.32	1.47
11.	1993-94	23.50	12.20	0.52	(-)2.00	0.83
12.	1994-95	43.57	15.18	0.35	0.14	0.23
Average		23.88	7.30	0.42		

Source : Audited statement of Annual Accounts of Gandhi Seva Sangam, Chatrapatti.

Table 4.4 : GRNS, Batlagundu

Sl. No.	Year	Value of production in lakhs of Rs.	Value of inventories in lakhs of Rs.	Ratio of inventories to production	Net profit in lakhs of Rs.	Interest charges Rs. in lakhs
1.	1983-84	17.06	10.76	0.61	(-) 1.54	0.11
2.	1984-85	21.91	19.72	0.90	(-) 2.21	0.40
3.	1985-86	20.51	18.18	0.88	(-) 3.06	0.33
4.	1986-87	19.75	27.31	1.38	(-) 3.59	0.25
5.	1987-88	25.65	29.86	1.16	(-) 5.14	0.15
6.	1988-89	19.53	35.15	1.79	(-) 4.94	0.16
7.	1989-90	22.74	39.92	1.77	(-) 6.64	0.48
8.	1990-91	23.34	39.92	1.69	(-) 1.97	0.37
9.	1991-92	26.59	39.42	1.58	(-) 1.85	0.77
10.	1992-93	27.59	38.97	1.44	(-) 1.48	0.07
11.	1993-94	34.54	37.65	1.08	(-) 0.13	0.71
12.	1994-95	40.30	47.18	1.09	(-) 2.90	0.30
Average		25.05	32.10	1.28		

Source : Audited Statement of Annual Accounts of Gramrajya Nirman Sangh, Batlagundu.

Column No.3 in each table presents the value of production in Rs. lakhs. Column No. 4 indicates value of inventories Rs. in lakhs. While column 5 represents the ratio of inventories held by the unit against the value of production. Column Nos. 6 and 7 represent the net profit (Rs. in lakhs) and interest charges in the corresponding years respectively.

For Gandhigram KVIPC Trust, Gandhigram, the production value recorded an average of Rs. 236.8 lakhs while the value of inventories also found at Rs. 162.6 lakhs. The percentage inventory ranged from 51 per cent to 91 per cent with an average of 68 per cent. This indicates that 68 per cent of goods was maintained as inventory in this unit.

In the case of Madurai North Sarvodaya Sangh, Palani, the value of productions was recorded an average of Rs. 69.29 lakhs and the value of inventories maintained at Rs. 53.40 lakhs average. The percentage inventory in this institution ranged from 51 per cent to 100 per cent with an average inventory of 74 per cent of the value of production.

For Gandhi Seva Sangam, Chattrapatti, the average value of production was at Rs. 23.88 lakhs at a value of inventory was maintained at an average of Rs. 7.30 lakhs per annum. The unit has maintained an inventory of 42 per cent to the value of production.

In respect of Gramarajya Nirman Sangh, Batlagundu, it has produced goods worth Rs. 25.05 lakhs per annum and it has maintained excess inventories exceeding average value of production at Rs. 32.10 lakhs per annum. It has maintained 128 per cent of inventories against the value of production. Among the four units under review, Gandhi Seva Sangam, Chatrapatty has maintained lower percentage of inventory at 42 per cent on the value of production and Gramarajya Nirman Sangh, Batlagundu has maintained highest inventory of 128 per cent on the value of production. The Gandhigram KVIPC Trust, Gandhigram and Madurai North Sarvodaya Sangh, Palani had performed moderately. The GRNS, Batlagundu which maintained inventories exceeding the production value has incurred loss in eleven years out of the total period of 12 years. This indicates that excess inventories will effect profitability of the units.

Hence, the correlations coefficient and regressions analysis were undertaken to measure the degree of associations between the percentage inventory to the net profit for all the institutions under review.

Table 4.5

	X	Y
X	1.000	(–)0.293
Y	(–)0.293	1.000

Significant at 0.05 level.

Between the ratio of inventory (X) and profitability values (Y) there exists negative correlation coefficient of 0.293 suggesting that inventories have negative influence on the profitability values. In order to predict the influence of inventory with profitability regression analysis were undertaken grouping all the values inventory against profitability. The results are :

R^2 = 0.086
Adj R^2 = 0.066
S.E. of the Estimate = 3.3722
F(1,46) = 4.313 significant at 0.05 level

The coefficients are presented in Table 4.6.

Table 4.6

Model	Unstandardised	SE	t	Significance
Constant	1.790	1.118	1.60	0.116
X	(–)2.682	1.292	–2.077	0.043

The regression equation will be, Y=1.790 – 0.0268X

This indicates that when inventory increase by 10 per cent on production value it results in reduction in profitability by Rs. 2680. Hence, the units under review can reduce inventory to improve profitability as confirmed by the regression model.

The performance of the individual Khadi and Village Industries units has been analysed through one way anova Table 4.7.

Table 4.7 : Anova — one way

Source of variation	Sum of squares	d.f.	Means of squares	F value	Level of siginificance
Between groups	99.703	3	33.234	3.095	0.036
Within groups	472.461	44	10.238		

The calculated value of F = 3.095 is greater than table value of F. 2.81. This signifies that there is significant difference between the performance of the units in respect of inventory and profitability. Hence, this indicate that the units under review have performed differently among themselves in respect of inventor and profitability.

Inventory and Interest Charges

Inventories contribute to the major part of working capital and working capital requirement is funded by KVIC, Mumbai to KVI institutions. These funds are extended to KVI institutions. These are in the form of working capital loan that carry an interest rate of 4 per cent per annum which is highly subsidised. Inventories which are stocks maintained to cushion the uncertainties in production process. Inventoris force institutions to incur carrying costs of which the interest cost is the major component. Henceforth, an attempt is made to estimate the nature of relationship between inventories and interest charges in the study units. Here value of inventories are taken as X_1-values and interest charges are taken as Y_1-values. The correlation coefficient was estimated for the four KVI institutions and overall values are given in Table 4.8.

Table 4.8 : Correlations estimate — Value of inventories with interest charges

	Interest Charges (Y_1)	Value of inventories (X_1)
Interest charges (Y_1)	1.00	0.843
Value of inventories (X_1)	0.843	1.00

There exists very high positive correlation between inventory and interest charges. The correlation coefficient was 0.843 at 1% significance level.

For Gandhigram KVIPC Trust, the correlation coefficient was 0.613 exhibiting a positive correlation and for Madurai North Sarvodaya Sangh, Palani the correlation coefficient was at 0.776 representing the same trend of overall grouped data. In case of Gandhi Seva Sangam, Chatrapatti and Grama Rajya Nirman Sangh, Batlagundu, the inventories and interest charges do not behave in the similar manner due to the fluctuating inventory positions and non-payment of interest charges as in the case of GRNS, Batlagundu.

To determine the impact of value of inventories to the interest charges, a regression model drawn and the equation is

$$X_1 = -0.156 + 0.0237\, X_1$$

X_1 is very predictor of Y_1 and significant at 1 per cent level.

As per the model, for the overall data, for an increase of inventory value by Rs. one lakh, the interest charges shoot up by Rs. 2370. This is the case with 4 per cent interest charged by KVIC.

On the basis of the above, the following conclusions can be drawn:

1. The units maintain very high percentages of inventories ranging from 42 per cent to 128 per cent on the value of production.

These units can reduce the inventories by applying just-in-time principle atleast in the area of raw materials and work-in-process.

2. For grouped data, the ratio of inventory has negative relationship with profitability and every 10% increase of inventory on production value will reduce profit by Rs. 2380 in these low profit-labour intensive KVI activities. To improve profitability of these KVI activities the units not only concentrate in improving the operational efficiencies but also reduce inventories that contributes to increase in profit and reduce interest charges.
3. Inventory planning has to be undertaken by these units rather than accumulating stocks of raw materials, work-in-process and finished goods. The plan should concentrate on various methodologies to meet the demand and other production requirements with minimum inventories or application of just-in-time principles. This process requires orientation to the staff of KVI institutions through some refresher courses and training programmes of KVI training institutions.

Considering all the units under review in respect of interest charges with inventory values, for an increase in inventory of Rs. one lakh, the interest charges will shoot up by Rs. 2370 per annum showing positive correlation. To withstand the emerging severe competitive situations, the Khadi and Village Industrial units may have to undertake several cost reduction strategies and one such strategy is to maintain Just in Time inventories. However, detailed plant level studies will throw more light on these areas which could be considered for further research.

References

Gopalakrishnan, P. and Sandilya, M.S., *Inventory Management Text and Cases,* Mecmullar India, New Delhi, 1984.

Gopalakrishnan, P., *Handbook of Materials Management,* Prentice Hall of India Pvt. Ltd., New Delhi, 1996.

Tai ICM Ohiv and Setswo Meto, *Just in Time, Production,* Press Inc., Cambridge, USA, 1988.

Walto E. Goddera, *Just in Time,* Oliver Right Publications, USA, 1986.

5

MANAGEMENT OF HANDICRAFT WOODEN TOYS IN AMBASAMUDRAM TALUK OF TIRUNELVELI DISTRICT

— *S. Hasan Banu*

Introduction

The Small Scale Industry, in today's world, holds the key to growth with equity. This sector needs particular attention as it can play a positive role in the development of entrepreneurs and managers. It is this sector that materialises Schumpeter's vision of entreprenueur who is an "ideas man" and a man of action who is dithered by the structures of environment. Therefore this sector is aptly called a "seed-bed" or "nursery" of entrepreneurship and managerial talent. Mahatma Gandhi made a heroic effort to revive rural industries. He felt that they were a means of providing gainful employment.

The Prime Minister Shri P.V. Narasimha Rao called upon small scale sector to produce quality goods to compete with the best in the world. The Prime Minister said that the small scale sector in India was one of the success stories and the fears of the prophets of doom that this sector would be swallowed by the policy of opening up had been proved wrong. He however cautioned that there should be no room for complacency. If fostered properly, the small scale sector could go up, he said and added that the export figures in this area were exceedingly encouraging.

Small Scale Industries (SSIs) play a vital role in Indian economy. This sector covers a wide range of manufacturing and service activities and consists of 26 lakh units. Its share in manufacturing is about 40 per cent of the total Industries output of Rs. 293.031 crore. According to the *Economic Survey* of 1995-96 the small scale industry recorded in real terms, a growth rate of 10.1 per cent in 1994-95 against a provisional estimate of 9.88 per cent and compared with 7.1 per cent in 1993-94 and 5.6 per cent in 1992-93.

The sector provides employment to as many as 160 lakh people spread over 28 lakh units all over the country. And the indirect employment created through forward and backward linkages is an additional contribution. The sector produces a wide range of products numbering more than 7500 items.

The definition of the SSI has undergone several changes on account of changes taken place in the economic and industrial environment in the country. In 1950 the Small Scale Industries Board defined the Small Industry as a unit employing less than 50 persons with the use of power, and less than 100 persons without the use of power and with capital assets not exceeding Rs. 5 lakhs. Just the definition of SSIs changed from 1959 to 1999-2000. Now at present the Union Minister for Finance while presenting the Union Budget for 1999-2000 had announced lowering down of Investment limit for SSI from Rs. 300 lakhs to Rs. 100 lakhs. Table 5.1 reveals the Investment limit for SSI from 1950 to 1997.

Implications of liberalisation for the small scale sector have been analysed, and directions suggested for strengthening the sector in two recent reports: (i) Report of the Expert Committee on Small Enterprises (Abid Hussain Committee) submitted to the Union Ministry of Industry in January 1997, and (ii) Report of the High Level Committee on Credit to Small Scale Industries (S.L. Kapur Committee) submitted to the Reserve Bank of India in June 1998. Subsequently, Planning Commission, Government of India has set up a Study Group on the Development of Small Enterprises in May

Table 5.1 : Evolution of Investment Limit for SSIs

Year	Investment limits	Additional conditions
1950	Upto Rs. 5 lakhs in fixed assets	Less than 50 persons with power or 100 without power
1960	Upto Rs. 5 lakh in fixed assets	No condition
1966	Upto Rs. 7.5 lakh in plant and machinery	No condition
1975	Upto Rs. 10 lakh in plant and machinery	No condition
1980	Upto Rs. 20 lakh in plant and machinery	No condition
1985	Upto Rs. 35 lakh in plant and machinery	No condition
1991	Upto Rs. 60 lakh in plant and machinery	No condition
1997	Upto Rs. 300 lakh in plant and machinery	No condition

Source : Dr. Suresh Mehta, SSI Policies in the Changing Economic Environment, *IBA Bulletin,* February 2000.

1999 under the chairmanship of Dr. S.P. Gupta, Member, Planning Commission.

Statement of the Problem

The small village and cottage industries have their own problems. Such problems should be located and rectified because those industries are highly labour intensive, and contribute heavily towards the growth of economy.

The development of village and cottage industries was generally affected due to the following reasons :

1. The problem related to power, fuel, transportation, which is the basis for their development.
2. The problem related to getting the raw materials in time.
3. Most of the units have to import the raw materials from outside districts or even other States.
4. Lack of control over quality, absence of products improvement are also some of the problems.
5. The problem relating to marketing of SSI products in market.
6. The idleness of the artisans indicates that the artisans remain

without work.

7. Generally, SSIs are being managed as ONE MAN SHOW and so obviously lacks specialisation simultaneously in all important areas, viz. Technical, Managerial, Organisational or Financial, which is usually seen in medium and large industries.

Scope and Objectives of the Study

The study has been undertaken from the point of view of the entrepreneurs engaged in Handicrafts Wooden Toys Industries in Ambasamudram region. The basic problems of any industry are production problem, financial problem, labour problem, raw materials problem, and marketing problem. These factors are interrelated. If these factors are effectively managed, the concern will be successful. Hence the scope of this study is production, labour, finance and marketing aspects of Handicraft Wooden Toys Industries in Ambasamudram Region.

The present study aims to analyse the problmes faced by Handicraft Wooden Toys on the basis of SWOT analysis (strength, weaknesses, opportunities, threats).

1. To analyse the various problems which are related to procurement of raw material in the case of production of wooden toys.
2. To identify and analyse the other causes of production problems.
3. To identify and analyse the various problems which are related in the case of marketing the wooden toys.
4. To identify and analyse the causes of financial problems.
5. To analyse the various threats faced by these units.
6. To give suitable suggestions to make remedy to these sick units.

Sampling Design

Handicrafts wooden toys of various types and designs are used as an entertainment by the children and also serve as an important item of gift on occasions of festivity. In Ambasamudram Taluk nearly 72 wooden carving companies are operating and 500 workers are working in these companies. But all the units are not registered. So for my study I take only few units from the total units.

The pilot study was conductd with 40 respondents in the Ambasamudram region and as per the findings some improvements were made in this study.

It is learned that there is a good number of Handicraft wooden toys running unregistered for some reasons or other. The researcher, covering a period of one month, conducted field work for this study. For collecting the primary data from the entrepreneurs an Interview Schedule was used.

As the study is related to comprehensive coverage of the practical problems of Handicraft wooden toys in Ambasamudram region. Secondary data was not used much. On the basis of primary data efforts were made to work out practical solutions. To substantiate the findings of the primary survey, secondary sources and articles in the periodicals and publications have also been used.

Profile of the Study Area

Tirunelveli District in Tamil Nadu is roughly triangular in shape and lies between 8°-05′ of the Nothern latitude and 77°-5′ and 78°-25′ of the Eastern latitude. The district was bifurcated into Tirunelveli Kattabomman and Chidambaram district in 1987. The present study area description is related to the bifurcated new Tirunelveli Kattabomman.

The district receives an average rainfall of Eight Hundred and Fourteen point Eight Millimetres.

Table 5.2 illustrates the average annual distribution of rainfall in the district.

The district has a minimum temperature of 20° C during January and a maximum of 37.6°C during May.

Ambasamudram Taluk is in Tirunelveli Kattabomman district of Tamil Nadu. Ambasamudram is the Taluk headquarters. The Taluk is famous for its agriculture. Paddy is the main crop cultivated throughout the Taluk.

Table 5.2 : Average Annual Distribution of Rainfall

Sl. No.	Months	Normal
1	January	50.2
2	February	30.2
3	March	41.3
4	April	59.8
5	May	38.0
6	June	29.6
7	July	26.4
8	August	23.3
9	September	30.2
10	October	166.0
11	November	208.2
12	December	111.6
	Total Rainfall	814.6

Source : Government of Tamil Nadu, Tirunelveli District Hand Book.

The north of Ambasamudram Taluk is Veerakeralamputhur Taluk. In the west is Tenkasi Taluk. The east is bound by Tirunelveli Taluk and to its south is the Nanguneri Taluk.

The success in agriculture of this Taluk is due to the river Tambrabarani. The birthplace of Tambrabarani is the Western Ghats in the Kerala border. It has 2 dams, one at Karayar and another at Servalar which is 1225 MCFt.

The water from these dams is canalised through the following canals :

(a) North Kodai Melalagian Kalvai,
(b) South Kodai Melalagian Kalvai,
(c) Nathiunni Kalvai, and
(d) Kannandian Kalvai.

The four canals mentioned above irrigate about 18,150 acres of land in the district of Tirunelveli Kattabomman.

In addition to Tambrabarani there are the Ramanathi and the Gatana Rivers. Ramanathi originates from a dam at Kadayam with a capacity of 150 MCFt and the Gatana River has a dam at Alwarkurichi with a capacity of 350 MCFt. The total 'Punjai' cultivable area in Ambasamudram is 14,140 hectares. The area of this Taluk is 798 square metres. Number of Panchayats -73, No of Unions - 4, No. of Villages -101 and No. of Townships - 1. Ambasamudram, Veeravananallur, Kallidaikurichi and Chermadevi were classified as class IV towns in 1901 itself. All the places in Ambasamudram are linked by rail and road.

The climate of Ambasamudram is said to be normal. The maximum temperature is nearly above 42.22°C and the minimum seldom below 26.66°C. Ambasamudram region thrives on the rain from the two monsoons, namely, the South-West monsoons from June to September and the North-East monsoon from October to December.

Problems

Production Problems

Production implies conversion of raw materials into finished products. One of the objectives of entrepreneurship is to achieve the mximum production in the best possible manner at the lowest cost. This can be ensured only through proper production planning and control. Planning of production involves the development of objectives, forecasts, policies, procedures, schedules and budgets.

Handicrafts wooden products are generally made from rubber wood. The wood is cut and shaped according to the size of the toys. It is carved through carving lathe machine. Workers carve it by hand through tools, with lac button, and with aloeveera. Handicrafts wooden toys products generally made are :

1. Children Cart.
2. Children cradle stick.
3. Children cooking sets.
4. Children Aeroplanes, Rail Engine, Balanced Toys.

5. Coconuts shell light.
6. Coconuts Jewel Box.
7. Pooja lights.
8. Mandap.
9. Pen stand.
10. Rotti Plagai & Roller.
11. Door curtains.
12. Sivalingam.
13. Dumbles.

Handicraft wooden toys are popular because of its :

1. Attractive fast colours.
2. Low cost.
3. House Decoration.
4. Useful at the time of Pooja periods (Navarathri Golu).

Requirement of Raw Materials in the Production of Wooden Toys

The following raw materials are necessary to produce the Handicraft wooden toys.

1. *Rubber Wood*

The workers receive the Rubber wood from Kulasekharam and Marthandam at Kanyakumari District.

2. *Lac Button*

This was manufactured at Gondiya, Madhya Pradesh State. This raw material is very important to make a colour of wooden toys.

3. *Abrasive Paper*

This is used to make the polish of the wood.

4. *Aloeveera*

This is also used to make the polish of the toys.

5. *Skilled Labourers*

This product can only be made through skilled labourers.

1. Carving Lathe (There are two types of lathe. It may be standing Lathe, Sitting Lather).
2. Electric Motor.
3. Belt (Main Belt, Small Belt).
4. Miscellaneous Tools.

Raw Material Problems

The necessity of raw materials hardly needs any emphasis for establishing any Industrial activity, and therefore, its influence in the emergence of entrepreneurship. In the absence of raw materials, neither any enterprise can be established nor an entrepreneur can emerge. The Japanese case, for sample, witnesses that lack of raw materials clearly does not prevent entrepreneurship from emerging but influenced the direction in which entrepreneurship took place.

1. It is very difficult to get the lac button at the time of rainy season period. Because the lac derived from some insects wastage. It cannot be able to construct the house at the time of rainy season period.
2. Because of forest intervention it is very difficult to procure the wood. The cost of the wood also is not uniform.
3. Rubber wood is perishable wood. Due to some insect problems it is very difficult to store the wood.

Table 5.3 : Problems in Procurement of Raw Material in the case of Handicrafts Wooden Toys

Sl. No.	Factor	No. of Respondents	Percentage
1.	High Cost	10	25
2.	Irregular Supply	10	25
3.	Monsoon Conditions	10	25
4.	Forest Restrictions	10	25
	Total	40	100

Source : Primary data.

Table 5.3 reveals the problems associated with procurement of raw materrial.

It is evident from Table 5.3 that all the factors equally affect the procurement of raw materials in the case of Handicrafts toys.

Problems Associated in Production Process

1. The factory fully depends upon the electricity. During the power cut season period it is very difficult to make production.
2. In sufficient supply of wood, lac, and labourers it cannot be done in large size manner.
3. During the rainy season period the production will be very low, because drying the wood is very difficult at wet season period.
4. The Rubber wood is also more in demand for match industries. So during the Deepawali season period the wood has not been received regularly.

Because of such problems the factory does not utilise the concern at full capacity. Table 5.4 reveals the capacity of factory utilisation.

Table 5.4 : Capacity Utilisation

Sl. No.	Factor	No. of Respondents	Percentage
1.	Working with full capacity	10	25
2.	Not working to optimum capacity	30	75

Source : Primary Data.

As shown above 75 per cent of the Handicraft entrepreneurs in the area does not use their factory with full capacity. Table 5.5 reveals the reasons for underutilisation of full capacity.

The study reveals that shortage of materials (wood, lac button shortage of labour, shortage of power are the major reasons for underutilisation of production capacity. About 8 per cent of the units suffer from lack of marketing and 2 per cent suffer due to shortage of finance. Finance is not a big problem, because the Bank, and some other financial institutions provide loans and subsidies to these units.

Table 5.5 : Reasons for underutilisation of production capacities

Sl. No.	Factor	No. of Respondents	Percentage
1.	Shortage of material, wood (perishable nature)	10	25
2.	Shortage of labour	10	25
3.	Shortage of power	10	25
4.	Shortage of finance	2	5
5.	Lack of marketing	8	20
	Total	40	100

Source : Primary Data.

Labour Problems

The quality and quantity of labour is another factor, which influences the emergence of entrepreneurship. It is noticed that cheap labour is often less mobile or even immobile. And, the deleterious effects of labour immobility negate the potential advantages of low-cost labour. Adam Smith also considered division of labour as an important element in economic development. According to him, divisions of labour which itself depends upon the size of the market leads to improvement in the productive capacities of labour due to an increase in the dexterity of labour. Notwithstanding it appears that the labour problem clearly does not prevent entrepreneurship from emerging. For example the problem of low cost immobile labour can be circumvented by plunging ahead with capital intensive technologies, as Germany did. It can be dealt by utilizing labour intensive methods like Japan, for example. By contrast, the disadvantages of high cost labour can be modified by the introduction of labour-saving innovations as was done in the USA.

Table 5.6 : Labour Problems at Present

Factor	No. of Respondents	Percentage
Having problems	30	80
Having no problems	10	20
Total	40	100

Source : Primary data.

Table 5.6 clearly shows that 80% of the Handicraft Wooden Toys Entrepreneurs have labour problems.

Reasons for Labour Problems

According to handicraft wooden toys entrepreneurs, absentees, negligence of work, demand for more wages, giving advances to workers switching from one entrepreneur to another entrepreneur are the main reasons for shortage of labour. Table 5.7 reveals the reasons for shortage of labour associated with handicraft wooden toys entrepreneurs.

Table 5.7 : Labour Problems of Handicraft Wooden Toys Entrepreneurs

Sl. No.	Factor	No. of Respondents	Percentage
1.	Absenteeism	5	20
2.	Demand for high wages	10	25
3.	Neligence of work	10	25
4.	Switchover to another entrepreneurs	15	30

Source : Primary data.

It is evident from Table 5.7 that around 25 per cent workers are crippled by demand for higher wages by the labour force. Absenteeism accounted for 20 per cent of the problem.

Again a common practice of giving advance on wages to workers is found. Unscrupulous entrepreneurs to retain the workers by giving advances to them often misuse this. On the other hand it is also found that after getting a considerable advance from the entrepreneurs, the labour force switched over to another entrepreneurs.

Financial Problems

Capital is one of the most important prerequisites to establish an enterprise. Availability of capital facilitates the entrepreneur to bring together the labour of one, machine of another and raw material yet another to combine them to produce goods. Capital is, therefore, regarded as lubricant to the process of production our accumulated experience suggest that with an increase in capital instalment, capital-output ratio tends to increase. This results in increase in profit, which ultimately goes to capital formation.

Generally SSI units face more problems in the case of getting finance from the outside that is they get finance at high rate of interest. If they get it from the bank, the bank does not realise the loan very quickly. The banks subsidies are also not enough to this unit.

Financial problems faced by Handicraft wooden toys Entrepreneurs. Finance is the lifeblood of any industrial units. Adequate finance should be available at the appropriate time. In the case of wooden toys entrepreneurs the capital requirement is not a big problem. Because the bank and government provide all incentives and subsidies to this industry. Not only that the entrepreneurs have enough capital to start this industry, because the requirement of capital of this unit is very meagre.

Marketing Problem

The American Marketing Association defines marketing as "The performance of business activities that direct the flow of goods and services from producers to consumer or user". Philip Kotler defines marketing as a "Human activity directed at satisfying needs and wants through exchange processes."

The fact remains that the potential of the market constitutes the major determinant of problems reward from entrepreneurial function. Frankly speaking if the proof of pudding lies in eating the proof of all production lies in consumption/marketing. The size and composition of market both influence entrepreneurship in their own ways. Some experts refer to Germany and Japan as prime examples where rapid improvement in market was followed by entrepreneurial appearance.

SSI units predominantly sell their products in the domestic market through wholesalers or retailers or directly to the end-users. Generally the SSI units are facing the following problems in the field of marketing as follows :

(a) Lack of wide enough market — small units are not able to penetrate deep even into the domestic market let alone the international one.
(b) Lack of adequate knowledge about the market both national and international knowledge about needs and quality specifications of consumers is almost negligible.
(c) Small units do not have the money and manpower to carry out the market users.

Problems associated in marketing the Handicraft Wooden articles :

1. These products are more demanded only in Tourist places. Even the demand for such products are more at the time of vacation because of power-cut the supply of goods are very low.
2. These goods are not exempted from tax. The tax rates structure also different in each State. The tax tariff systems suppress the marketing of these wooden toys.
3. Exportation of these articles is very difficult due to perishable nature of this wood.

Due to stiff competition, irregular supply of raw materials, labour problems, irregular supply of power, taxation problems these units are becoming sick units. Table 5.8 reveals the marketing problems associated with Handicraft Wooden toys entrepreneurs.

Table 5.8 : Marketing Problem associated with Handicraft Wooden Toys

Sl. No.	Factor	No. of Respondents	Percentage
1.	Stiff competition	5	12.5
2.	Irregular supply of raw material	10	25
3.	Tax Problems	10	25
4.	Irregular Supply of power	10	25
5.	Irregular Supply of Labour	5	12.5
	Total	40	100

Source : Primary Data.

It is evident from Table 5.8 that 75 per cent of the wooden toys entrepreneurs are affected mainly by the irregular supply of raw materials, tax problem, irregular supply of power. Another 25% are affected by the other reasons.

Role of Government

The Government by its actions or its failure to act does influence both economic and non-economic conditions for entrepreneurship. Any interested Government in economic development can help through its clearly expressed Industrial Policy, promote entrepreneurship in one way or other. By creating basic facilities, utilities, and services and by providing incentives and concessions, the Government can provide the prospective entrepreneurs to facilitate socio-economic setting. Such conducive settings minimize the risks, which the entrepreneur is to encounter. Thus the supportive actions of the Government appear as the most conducive to the entrepreneurial growth, scholars like Medora concludes that "the late inception in India was not due to non-commitment of the political structure."

From Table 5.9 it has been understood that around 37.5 per cent of the wooden toys factory workers receive training facilities from the Government. And also 37.5 per cent of the entrepreneurs also receive the facilities for marketing of their goods and 25 per cent of entrepreneurs receive subsidy facilities from the Government.

Table 5.9 : Government Role in respect of Hndicraft Wooden Toys Industry

Factor	No. of Respondent	Percentage
Training facilities	15	37.5
Arrangement for Marketing of goods	15	37.5
Subsidy facilities	10	25
Technical consultancy	Nil	—

Even though the Government provides all facilities to the entrepreneurs the tax charged by the Government suppress these articles for marketing of these goods.

Suggestions

Steps to improve wooden toys of Handicraft Industries :

1. The Government of Tamil Nadu should remove the tax tariff.
2. The Government of Tamil Nadu helps to procure the wood, raw materials at cheap rate.
3. During the power cut season period the Government should give concession to remove the power cut to these industries.

Comparison with Other Government

Finally the U.P. Government exempts these goods from tariff under notification No. ST. 911/X/Dated/w.e.f. 1-4-1956. The Government also provide seasoned wood and Rosewood through labour co-operative stores. These incentives motivate the Handicraft workers to take necessary steps for rehabilitation of these sick units and also exempt this tiny wood toys unit from tax, which will improve the performance of these units. And also the Government should provide the raw materials through labour Co-operative stores rationally.

References

Desai, Kolter, *A Student on Rural Economics,* Bombay, Himalaya Publishing House, 1985.

Desai, Vasant, *Dynamic of Entrepreneurial Development and Management,* New Delhi, Himalaya Publishing House, 1992.

Gupta, C.B., Srinivasan, N.P., *Entrepreneurship Development in India,* (Text and cases) New Delhi, Sultan Chand & Sons, 1992.

Khan, R.R., Management of Small Scale Industries, New Delhi, Sultan Chand & Co., 1979.

Saravanavel, P., *Entrepreneurial Development, Principles, Policies and Programmes,* Madras, Ess Pee Kay Publishing House, 1997.

Sekar, P.C., *Entrepreneurship and Management of Small Business,* Madurai, EnPee Publications, 1998.

Steinnetz and Kline, B., *Managing the Small Business,* Bombay Taraporevala and Sons (Pvt.) Limited, 1982.

6

MANAGEMENT OF ERODE WEAVERS CO-OPERATIVE PRODUCTION AND SALES SOCIETY LIMITED : A Study of Performance

— *N. Meenakshisundaram*

Introduction

The co-operative societies are playing a significant role in the economic empowerment of weaker sections of the society. It can be seen from the Five Years Plan that the Government has been taking number of measures to promote co-operative societies in India. One of the co-operative development sectors is Handloom activity. The Government is extending financial support as one of the promotional measures of co-operative societies. Therefore, it is essential that these societies are getting strengthened by their performance. Hence a study on the Performance of Erode Weavers Co-operative Production and Sale Society, Erode has been undertaken with the following objectives :

1. To analyse the progress in production and sale of Handloom products produced and sold by the society.
2. To study the financial position of the society.

3. To assess the profitability position of the society.

To study the Uses and Sources of Funds for a period of five years from 1994-95 to 1998-99. The data required includes both primary and secondary, which were collected from the society under the study in tone with the above objectives of the present study.

Production and Sales

The society produces variety of products which consists of Bed linen, jacquard fabrics, pillow covers, napkins, floor mats, kitchen made ups, table cloths, furnishing and other household varieties, of which bed spreads occupy a major share.

It is found that the progress in production has been decreasing considerably with an average decline of 14.47 per cent during the study period. The production in constant prices ranged from Rs. 384.04 lakhs in 1994-95 to Rs. 269.01 lakhs in the year 1998-99 as can be seen in Table 6.1.

Table 6.1 : Production of Handloom Products of the Society

(Rs. in lakhs)

Year	Value of Production at current prices	Wholesale price index	Value of Production at price level 1994-95	Rate of growth in %
1994-95	384.04	262.90	384.04	—
1995-96	395.40	295.80	351.42	- 8.49
1996-97	438.92	314.60	366.79	- 4.49
1997-98	375.90	329.80	299.65	- 21.97
1998-99	396.78	352.40	296.01	- 22.92
Average growth rate				- 14.17

Source : Records of the Society.

The production growth rate decline is due to competition for the handloom products from organised mill sector and reduction due to migration of weavers from handloom to powerlooms.

The society has the practice of selling its products through direct sales and through intermediaries like Co-optex and All India Handloom Fabrics Marketing Co-operative Society Ltd.

Table 6.2 : Sales Analysis of Handloom Products

(Rs. in lakhs)

Year	Value of Sales at current prices	Wholesale price index	Value of Sales at price level 1994-95	Rate of growth in %
1994-95	432.13	262.90	432.13	—
1995-96	400.77	295.80	356.19	- 17.57
1996-97	491.25	314.60	410.52	- 5.00
1997-98	451.42	329.80	359.85	- 16.73
1998-99	612.55	352.40	456.98	- 5.75
Average sales				- 8.39

Source : Records of the Society.

In actual or current prices, the value of sales has increased from Rs. 432.13 lakhs to Rs. 612.55 lakhs during the period of 1994-95 to 1998-99. But in constant prices, the value of sales shows a fluctuating trend with an average negative growth rate of - 8.39 per cent as shown in Table 6.2.

Financial Position

The Current Ratio of the society for the study period is more than the standard norm, which shows that the society is able to meet its current obligations. The average Current Ratio of the society is 2.78:1. The high current ratio during 1996-97 and 1997-98 indicates that the society has maintained a huge stocks as shown in Table 6.3.

Table 6.3 : Current Ratio of Erotex

Year	Current Assets (Rs. in lakhs)	Current Liabilities (Rs. in lakhs)	Current Ratio
1994-95	279.21	123.67	2.25
1995-96	340.91	125.10	2.72
1996-97	431.13	134.56	3.20
1997-98	411.89	127.36	3.26
1998-99	457.75	182.44	2.51
Average Current Ratio			2.78

Source : Records of the Society.

Table 6.4 : Quick Ratio of Erotex Society

Year	Quick Assets (Rs.in lakhs)	Quick Liabilities (Rs. in lakhs)	Quick Ratio
1994-95	165.49	123.67	1.34
1995-96	158.14	125.10	1.26
1996-97	228.93	134.56	1.70
1997-98	167.51	127.36	1.31
1998-99	242.41	182.44	1.33
Average Quick Ratio			1.39

Source : Records of the Society.

The society maintains the quick ratio at the standard norm, which shows that the society is able to meet its short-term debts out of short-terms assets with an average quick ratio of 1.39:1. However the society has to take measures to reduce stock of finished goods as can be seen in Table 6.4.

Table 6.5 : Debt Equity Ratio

Year	External Fund (Rs. in lakhs)	Internal Fund (Rs. in lakhs)	Debt Equity Ratio
1994-95	211.85	125.53	1.69
1995-96	246.67	139.06	1.77
1996-97	326.53	153.03	2.13
1997-98	313.13	154.99	2.02
1998-99	339.81	167.76	2.02

Debt Equity Ratio = External Fund/Internal Fund
Source : Records of the Society.

Table 6.6 : Profitability Ratio

Year	Opening Balance of Capital (Rs.)	Addition on capital (Rs.)	Total (Rs.)	Profit (Rs.)	Profitability Ratio
1994-95	149.65	—	149.65	26.17	0.17
1995-96	149.65	13.07	162.72	27.57	0.17
1996-97	162.72	13.66	176.38	30.74	0.19
1997-98	176.38	0.92	177.30	37.32	0.21
1998-99	177.30	11.33	188.63	46.54	0.25

Source : Computed from Office records of the Society.

Profitability Position

The Gross Profiit shows a fluctuating trend, with an Average Gross Profit Ratio of 17.55. In the year 1998-99 Gross Profit Ratio decreased to17.37 per cent from 20.49 per cent in the year 1997-98. This was due to the high cost of production. Efforts to decrease the cost of production should be adopted by the society as shown in Table 6.7.

Table 6.7 : Gross Profit to Sales

Year	Sales (Rs. in lakhs)	Gross Profit (Rs. in lakhs)	Gross Profit Ratio (in %)
1994-95	432.13	62.77	14.52
1995-96	400.77	68.35	17.05
1996-97	491.25	98.92	18.30
1997-98	451.42	92.52	20.49
1998-99	612.55	108.16	17.37
Average Gross Profit Ratio			17.55

Source : Computed from office records of the Society.

The net profit ratio shows that an average of 7.01 per cent if sales amount is left to the owners after meeting all costs. The Net Profit has been increasing slightly year after year, except in the year 1998-99 (7.60%), where it shows a decrease, when compared to the Net Profit Ratio of 1997-98 (8.27%) as shown in Table 6.8.

Table 6.8 : Net Profit to Sales Ratio

Year	Net Sales (Rs. in lakhs)	Net profit (Rs. in lakhs)	Net Profit to Sales Ratio (in %)
1994-95	432.13	26.17	6.06
1995-96	400.77	27.57	6.88
1996-97	491.25	30.74	6.26
1997-98	451.42	37.32	8.27
1998-99	612.55	46.54	7.60
Average Net Profit			7.01

Source : Computed from office records of the Society.

The aveage profitability per rupee of investment is 4.88. The return on investment for most of the years is almost the same though there is considerable improvement in sales, which is due to increase in overhead expenses as can be found in Table 6.9.

Table 6.9 : Return on Investment

Year	Net Profit (Rs. in lakhs)	Total Investment (Rs. in lakhs)	Return on Investment (in %)
1994-95	26.17	563.65	4.64
1995-96	27.87	623.35	4.62
1996-97	30.74	716.14	4.29
1997-98	37.32	724.05	5.15
1998-99	46.54	787.86	5.91
Average Return on Investment			4.88

Source : Computed from office records of the society.

The Total Assets Turnover Ratio shows that the fixed assets are not employed efficiently by the society. The total assets turnover ratio ranges from 0.62 to 0.78 times during the study period. Hence the society needs to take steps to utilize its assets better.

Profitability Ratio ranged from 0.17 to 0.25 with an increasing trend. The Profitability Ratios are quite moderate and the society has performed well.

Sources and Uses of Funds

The Erode Weavers Co-operative Society under study had raised funds from different sources ranging between Rs. 61.70 lakhs to 34.53 lakhs.

During the year 1997-98 the society had disposed of some of its fixed assets to the extent of Rs. 19.14 lakhs.

The Society had used a major share of funds on the creation of Current assets such as raw materials, finished goods, creation of sundry debtors etc.

The long-term funds are used for short-term purpose and hence the society is unable to create more fixed assets that should result in the expansion of Handloom activities.

For long term funds the society heavily depends upon banks. Reserve and surplus have contributed very meagrely to sources of funds.

Suggestions

1. Diversification of existing product range and imparting new designs in the product.
2. Improving the quality of the product by the use of quality dyes and enhancing the fabric functional values through finishing operations.
3. Opening of private sales through more agencies apart from direct sales and selling through co-optex.
4. Efforts should be made in stabilisation of the sale and production with target and meeting the demands promptly.
5. Effective capacity utilisation of existing looms is required.
6. The method of fixing target for each registered weaver, for a year and motivation of those target achievers through appropriate incentive measures should be adopted by the

society.

7. Appropriate inventory planning should be followed in order to avoid stock outs of finished goods.
8. The dye house should be operated efficiently to minimize lead time in dyeing yarns for timely supply of raw materials to the weavers.
9. The society should take steps to reduce the overhead expenses so as to increase the Net Profit of the firm and also to increase the Return on investment.
10. Attention must be paid by the society for the use of long term sources of funds for creation of long-terms assets that would result in the expansion of Handloom activities.
11. Efforts should be made to decrease the cost of production by adopting effective inventory management practices such as purchase of yarn that would be favourable to the society.

Conclusion

The performance of the society on the whole seems to be sound, but concentration of efforts in areas of production and sales should be undertaken by the society. The society must try for diversification of the products and also to tap the export potential for handloom furnishing and other bed spreads, by improving the quality of the products. Reduction in the overhead expenses and cost of production will help the society to enhance its profit.

References

Bhalla, V.K., *Financial Management and Policy*, New Delhi, Anmol Publication Pvt. Ltd., 1997.

Goel, B.S., *Production Operation Management*, Meerut, Pragati Prakashan, 1996.

Kuchhal, S.C., *Financial Management — An Analytical and Conceptual Approach*, Allahabad, Chaitanya Publishing House, 1995.

Kulkarni, P.V., *Financial Management — A Conceptual Approach*, Bombay, Himalaya Publishing House, 1983.

Manmohan and Goyal, S.N., *Principles of Management Accounting*, Agra, Sahitya Bhawan Publication, 1998.

Mathur, B.S., *Co-operation in India*, Agra, Sahitya Bhawan Publications, 1980.

Pandey, I.M., *Financial Management*, New Delhi, Vikas Publishing House Pvt., Ltd., 1993.

Phophalia, A.K., Sarita Sharma and Basotia, G.R., *Financial Management Function, Planning and Policy*, New Delhi, Kanishka Publishers, 1997.

Pillai, R.S.N. and Bagavathi, V., *Management Accounting*, New Delhi, Sultan Chand & Co., Ltd., 1999.

Prasanna Chandra., *Financial Management Theory and Practice*, New Delhi Tata McGrawhill Publications Ltd., 1997.

7

MANAGEMENT OF FINANCE IN KHADI AND VILLAGE INDUSTRIES INSTITUTIONS : A Study

— R. Radhakrishnan

Balance sheet gives a static picture of the state of finance of a business at a given point of time, showing how funds have been acquired by the business and used therein. But when balance sheets of a business at two or more points of time are compared it will be possible to perceive the changes in both value and pattern of acquisition and deployment of funds in the business. Analysis of such changes will throw light on shift in objectives and strategy of the business as well as exogenous factors influencing the business policies.

Thus analysis of the sources and use of fund will enable us to understand the business policy and assess impact of business transactions on its financial conditions. Instrument of such analysis is called fund flow statement. It is presented in two equated sections, namely source and uses. It has other names like fund statement, statement of sources and applications of funds etc. In view of the importance of fund flow statement Accounting Principles Board of the American Institute of Certified Public Accountants in its

Opinion No. 19 (1971) has prescribed that a statement summarizing changes in financial position should be presented as a basic financial statement.

There are three forms of fund flow statement, namely (a) cash flow, (b) statement of changes in working capital, and (c) statement of changes in total financial resources. Cash flow statement covers changes in the flow of cash only in the business transaction. The statement of changes in working capital embodies sources and uses of working capital statement of changes in total financial resources alone covers total financial conditions comprising cash and non-cash transactions, working capital and fixed capital. In fact the Accounting Principles Board, has also recommended, the third form of the statement covering total financial resources as evident from the comprehensive title. Statement of changes in financial position in preference to titles retaining to cash or working capital. Therefore fund flow in the present study will cover all long-term and short-term financial resources employed by the institution.

Liabilities like capital fund, retained profit, loans and sundry creditors are sources of additional funds or resources, whereas assets resulting from the deployment of funds are uses of funds. Again assets like stocks, cash, and debtors can be used in order to reduce liabilities like sundry creditor or loan. Thus increase in liabilities and decrease in liabilities are the uses of financial resources. Changes in the value of assets and liabilities in the balance sheets over the ten-year period have been calculated and classified as sources and uses. Changes in the net value of fixed assets will not correctly convey variations in the value by fixed assets since net value excludes depreciation. Thus data on gross value of fixed assets and changes therein have been taken into account. Also depreciation reserve will be included among liabilities. Depreciation is a source of fund. But it will not be a source of fund if there is no revenue.

Four sources of funds and four groups of uses of funds can be identified in the balance sheet. Increase in long-term and short-term liabilities and decrease in long-term and short-term liabilities and increase in long-term and short-term assets are the four uses of funds.

Sources

Long-term funds can be derived from increased capital. Capital expenditure loan and retention of profit, besides provision for depreciation, among the long-term sources retained earning and depreciation reserve are internal funds and the other two capital and loans are external funds. A sound business should be in a position to accumulate retained earning regularly besides depreciation-provision. However, opportunities of additional internal funds for khadi and village industries are very limited because of relatively lower productivity of their technology and ban on building of general reserve. Similarly, provision for depreciation will also be very small in view of the relatively inexpensive machinery and equipment used in these activities. Yet, a well managed institution should be able to get regularly at least a modest amount of retained profit and depreciation provision every year. However, main source of long-term funds will necessarily be the external funds like addition to capital fund and capital expenditure loan.

In respect of short-term funds, working capital loan and sundry creditors should be used for short-term funds without impairing its liquidity. Disposal of unused and obsolete assets will yield liquid resources to decrease in long-term assets. Similarly, timely utilisation of stocks and collection of debtors will contribute in the form of decrease in short-term assets.

Uses

Discharging of long-term and short-term liabilities in due date is an important use of funds ensuring credit worthiness and liquidity of the business.

Acquisition of short-term and long-term assets is another use of funds which is essential for expanding the business operations. With regard to the use of funds for increasing assets care must be taken to ensure that

(a) all short-term funds are used for financing short-term assets and none is used on long-term assets, and

(b) long-term funds are used on both long-term and short-term assets and at least a part of it is necessarily on short-term assets as net working capital.

Performance of the four institutions under review can be evaluated on the basis of norms suggested below, namely :

1. Generation of internal funds,
2. Disposal of unused and obsolete fixed assets,
3. Liquidation of current assets,
4. Deployment of short-term funds for short-term uses, and
5. Use of long-term funds on long-term assets and as net working capital.

INSTITUTION - 'A'

Sources

A registered society, which engages in production and sale of KVI products, is selected for this study. This institution is directly aided by KVIC. Audited balance sheets of the institution for Ten years are collected and used for this study. Particulars of fund flow statement of the above Institution can be found in Table 7.1. Generation of additional resources fluctuated between Rs. 15.59 lakhs and Rs. 30.65 lakhs during the ten-year period with sharp upward fluctuation occurring during 1988-89 and downward fluctuation in 1989-90. The spurt in 1988-89 was largely due to increase in liabilities caused by rise in other reserves (other than depreciation reserves) and working capital loan. It may be recalled that the other reserves are meant for specific purposes like price fluctuation, artisan welfare etc., and they should not be equated with free reserve. The other large contributor of funds are working capital loan and depreciation reserve.

Thus major increase in the resources was not due to additional

Table 7.1 : Fund Flow Analysis

INSTITUTION - 'A'

(Rupees in lakhs)

Particulars	1984-85	1985-86	1986-87	1987-88	1988-89	1989-90	1990-91	1991-92	1992-93
1	2	3	4	5	6	7	8	9	10
A. Sources									
I. Net increase in fixed liabilities	3.99	2.24	6.41	4.24	12.63	7.59	4.71	19.32	9.89
Net decrease in fixed liabilities	17.17	19.09	15.12	10.82	18.02	4.73	2.54	0.72	2.47
II. Net decrease in fixed assets	0.00	0.00	0.00	0.00	0.00	0.00	3.49	1.39	0.00
Net decrease in fixed assets									
Total (A)	21.16	23.06	24.43	15.59	30.65	15.61	19.51	27.04	23.25
B. USES									
I. Net decrease in fixed assets	5.62	3.19	3.67	2.30	2.18	4.00	0.00	0.00	2.49
Net decrease in fixed assets	15.54	18.687	12.38	13.19	27.11	8.43	17.51	26.83	19.54
II. Net increase in fixed liabilities	0.00	1.18	0.00	0.10	0.21	0.00	0.00	0.00	0.00
Net decrease in fixed liabilities	0.00	0.01	8.38	0.00	1.15	3.18	2.00	0.21	1.21
TOTAL (B)	21.16	23.06	24.43	15.59	30.65	15.61	19.51	27.04	23.24

Source : The final statement of accounts of the above statement.

Table 7.2 : Balance Sheet

INSTITUTION - 'A'

Sl. No.	Particulars	1983-84	1984-85	1985-86	1986-87	1987-88	1988-89	1989-90	1990-91	1991-92	1992-93
1	2	3	4	5	6	7	8	9	10	11	12
I.	**LIABILITIES**										
a.	Capital fund & accumulated profit	8.51	9.21	10.02	10.98	11.70	12.46	12.92	12.43	14.04	14.61
b.	Capital expenditure loan	7.72	9.02	9.02	10.07	9.97	9.76	9.76	9.76	9.76	9.76
c.	Depreciation reserve	3.76	4.71	6.14	8.50	11.08	13.96	16.79	19.56	22.19	25.02
d.	Other reserve	16.96	18.00	16.82	18.85	19.79	28.78	33.08	34.51	50.59	57.10
e.	Total	36.95	40.94	42.00	48.40	52.54	64.96	72.55	77.26	96.58	106.47
II.	**CURRENT LIABILITIES**										
a.	Working Capital loan	49.08	52.02	60.28	72.85	78.58	89.21	89.99	91.73	91.73	91.73
b.	Sundry creditors	11.53	15.65	23.47	15.50	19.45	23.79	23.14	23.94	28.06	26.85
c.	Deposits & advances	13.74	23.58	26.59	29.15	29.15	32.23	29.70	28.43	28.22	30.34
d.	Other current liabilities	0.37	0.64	0.63	0.22	1.36	0.18	4.13	3.40	—	0.35
e.	Total	74.72	91.89	110.97	117.72	128.54	145.41	146.96	147.50	148.01	149.27
	Total (I + II)	111.67	132.83	152.97	166.12	181.08	210.37	219.51	224.76	244.59	255.74

Contd. ...

Table 7.2 : *(Continued)*

Sl. No.	Particulars	1983-84	1984-85	1985-86	1986-87	1987-88	1988-89	1989-90	1990-91	1991-92	1992-93
1	2	3	4	5	6	7	8	9	10	11	12
I.	**Assets**										
	Fixed asets (gross)	29.34	34.96	38.15	41.82	44.12	46.30	47.01	46.81	45.42	47.91
II.	**Current Assets**										
a.	Stock on hand	55.41	61.06	68.31	75.24	85.20	98.22	101.49	110.67	106.18	119.58
b.	Sundry debtors	17.36	23.05	26.99	26.11	27.68	32.97	38.11	29.34	42.52	33.63
c.	Advance, loan and investments	4.68	6.58	11.03	15.98	15.60	19.82	19.13	19.29	19.18	21.19
d.	Cash	1.00	2.73	01.00	1.50	1.35	2.21	0.63	5.51	4.50	2.51
	Accumulated Loss	0.00	0.00	0.00	0.00	0.00	0.00	0.00	0.00	0.00	0.00
	Other Current assets	3.88	4.45	7.49	5.47	7.13	9.85	13.13	13.14	26.79	30.92
	Total	82.33	97.87	114.82	124.30	136.96	164.07	172.50	177.95	199.17	207.83
	Total (I + II)	111.67	132.83	152.97	166.12	181.08	210.37	219.51	224.76	244.59	255.74

Source : KVIC records

capital fund or accumulated profit which contributed less than one lakh in each year. Reference to balance sheet shows that institution earned net profit varying between Rs. 0.60 lakh and Rs. 0.96 lakh on annual sales ranging from Rs. 75 lakhs and Rs. 162 lakhs employing capital from Rs. 20 lakhs to Rs. 30 lakhs. Such low profitability is common to all khadi institutions as they employ labour intensive technology of meagre productivity.

Since these activities are labour-intensive, capital expenditure loan has played the least role in yielding additional resources. Except in 1990-91 and 1992-93 reduction of current assets also made very small contribution as source of fund. It means that in other years, there was no significant improvement in the management of stocks and debtors.

Uses

Perusal of balance sheet of the institution under study reveals an unhealthy aspect in the deployment of funds. For most of the years, value of fixed assets exceeded the sum of capital fund accumulated profit, capital expenditure loan and depreciation reserve by Rs. 10 to 12 lakhs. It means that other reserves amounting to Rs. 10 to 12 lakhs were used for financing fixed assets, even though these other reserves were meant for specific purposes like artisan welfare and equalisation of price fluctuation. Additional long-term funds were gradually used to replace other reserves as source of funds for fixed assets and thus in 1992-93 value of fixed assets was nearly equal to sum of capital fund, retained profit capital expenditure loan and depreciation reserve. The remaining part of the additional long-term funds and short-term funds were used for financing current assets.

Reference to balance sheet of the institution reveals that increase in stocks on hand claimed largest part of the additional resources followed by loans and advances etc., and sundry debtors. Already analysis of the sources suggested slackness in the management of current assets and now the analysis of uses confirm it by highlighting the large fund absorbed by stocks, debtors etc.

In capital saving activity, it is natural for large funds to be employed as net working capital especially when the institution undertakes complete marketing without the aid of stockist and distributors. However, continuous increase in stocks and debtors without matching increase in production and sales cannot be justified from the point of view of managerial efficiency and this is found to lengthen the span of operating cycle of the working capital.

INSTITUTION - 'B'

Source

Particulars of fund flow can be found in Table 7.3 Institution 'B' is the only institution which incurred losses in five out of ten years under study. Though its performance in production and sales was not behind the other institutions under study, it failed to maintain sufficient cost control and this lapse reduced gross margin eventually leading to net loss. Subsequently the institution revamped its operation making a meagre amount of profit.

Significant increase in generation of additional resources can be found in 1986-87, 1988-89, 1989-90 and 1991-92. Since the institution started making profit from 1989-90 onwards, the long-term sources could not contribute much in the earlier years. In three years — 1986-87, 1989-90 and 1991-92 — it was increase in current liabilities-working capital loan yielded major additional resources. In 1992-93 only increase in fixed liabilities rose in other reserves yielding substantial additional resources. In 1988-89 decrease in current assets, i.e. stock on hand produced significant part of additional fund, thus important sources like capital fund, retained profit, capital expenditure, loan and depreciation reserve yielded very little in most of the years under review. Having been sick for long time the institution started recovering during the last four years making modest profit. In the last year under analysis (1992-93), it earned a net surplus of Rs. 0.7 lakh on sale of Rs.163 lakhs using capital of Rs. 20 lakhs. Hence, the preponderance of short-term funds.

Table 7.3 : Fund Flow Analysis

INSTITUTION - 'B'

(Rupees in lakhs)

Sl. No.	Particulars	1984-85	1985-86	1986-87	1987-88	1988-89	1989-90	1990-91	1991-92	1992-93
1	2	3	4	5	6	7	8	9	10	11
A.	**Sources**									
I.	Net increase in fixed liabilities	0.69	3.48	0.02	3.90	0.03	9.36	2.31	9.50	24.19
	Net decrease in fixed liabilities	3.17	6.18	22.85	0.70	11.71	31.68	9.74	27.16	2.59
II.	Net decrease in fixed assets	0.00	0.34	0.00	0.00	0.05	0.00	0.00	5.90	0.00
	Net decrease in fixed assets	2.88	3.37	0.00	12.34	20.61	17.09	3.79	0.35	0.00
	Total (A)	6.74	13.37	22.87	16.94	32.40	58.13	15.84	42.91	26.78
B.	**USES**									
I.	Net decrease in fixed assets	0.74	0.00	6.90	7.78	0.00	1.55	0.98	0.00	2.56
	Net decrease in fixed assets	3.84	4.19	10.43	5.46	21.12	35.92	13.39	30.75	20.37
II.	Net increase in fixed liabilities	2.14	6.78	4.56	0.00	4.58	6.73	0.00	0.00	0.00
	Net decrease in fixed liabilities	0.02	2.40	0.98	3.70	6.70	13.93	1.47	12.16	3.85
	TOTAL (B)	6.74	13.37	22.87	16.94	32.4	58.13	15.84	42.91	26.78

Source : The final statement of accounts of the above statement.

Table 7.4 : Balance Sheet

INSTITUTION - 'B'

(Rs. in lakhs)

Sl. No.	Particulars	1983-84	1984-85	1985-86	1986-87	1987-88	1988-89	1989-90	1990-91	1991-92	1992-93
1	2	3	4	5	6	7	8	9	10	11	12
I.	**Liabilities**										
a.	Capital fund & accumulated profit	9.22	7.31	0.63	0.65	0.66	0.66	0.86	0.86	1.13	1.74
b.	Capital expenditure loan	9.77	9.77	12.18	9.09	9.09	9.09	3.34	3.34	3.34	10.48
c.	Depreciation reserve	3.54	4.23	4.13	3.83	4.78	4.81	3.83	4.21	5.69	7.10
d.	Other reserve	9.84	9.23	10.68	9.51	12.45	7.87	17.03	19.23	26.32	42.45
e.	Total	32.37	30.94	27.62	23.08	26.98	22.43	25.06	27.64	36.48	61.77
II.	**Current Liabilities**										
a.	Working capital loan	34.14	35.72	37.72	51.86	50.30	54.70	68.85	70.18	97.27	92.99
b.	Sundry creditors	22.20	22.23	26.37	25.40	25.96	19.31	36.78	44.92	32.76	34.41
c.	Deposits & advances	6.30	7.86	5.46	14.17	12.03	19.34	5.41	4.04	4.73	4.06
d.	Other current liabilities	0.08	0.06	0.10	0.09	0.23	0.18	0.24	0.14	0.18	1.12
e.	Total	62.72	65.87	69.65	91.52	88.52	93.53	111.28	119.28	134.34	132.58
	Total (I + II)	95.09	96.41	97.27	114.60	115.50	115.96	136.34	146.92	171.42	194.35

Table 7.4 : *(Continued)*

Sl. No.	Particulars	1983-84	1984-85	1985-86	1986-87	1987-88	1988-89	1989-90	1990-91	1991-92	1992-93
1	2	3	4	5	6	7	8	9	10	11	12
I.	**Assets**										
	Fixed asets (gross)	12.22	12.96	12.62	19.52	27.25	27.25	28.80	29.78	23.88	26.44
II.	**Current Assets**										
	a. Stock on hand	60.59	60.29	57.77	59.57	60.90	49.39	78.19	83.51	93.95	101.45
	b. Sundry debtors	9.11	8.62	9.51	12.22	5.91	9.95	10.26	6.47	11.06	13.64
	c. Advance, loan and investments	9.11	7.02	9.28	12.07	8.88	11.20	9.25	13.14	18.35	25.73
	d. Cash	0.79	0.84	2.26	4.14	1.35	8.07	0.92	1.91	1.56	2.14
	Accumulated Loss										
	Other Current assets	3.27	6.68	5.83	7.08	11.21	5.11	8.92	12.11	22.62	24.95
	Total	82.87	83.45	84.63	95.08	88.20	88.71	107.54	117.14	147.54	167.91
	Total (I + II)	95.09	96.41	97.27	114.60	115.50	115.96	136.34	146.92	171.42	194.35

Source : KVIC records.

Uses

With regard to use of the fund, the institution failed to observe certain basic norms. Perusal of balance sheet reveals that the value of fixed assets exceeded the sum of capital fund accumulated profit, capital expenditure loan and depreciation reserve from 1986-87 onwards. During this period value of fixed assets exceeded the sum of long-term funds (including other reserves) from 1987-88 to 1990-91. Therefore, during the four years (1987-88 to 1990-91) short-term funds also were used for long-term purpose. In spite of the difficult financial situation, the institution acquired fixed assets worth Rs. 7.08 lakhs during 1987-88 without achieving any signified improvement in production, sales or profit in 1989-90.

The 1988-89 decrease in current assets, i.e. stock on hand produced significant part of additional fund. Thus important sources like capital fund, retained profit, capital expenditure loan, and depreciation reserve yielded very little in most of the years under review. With regard to use of remaining funds it will be found that net increase in current assets claimed most of the additional resources especially from 1988-89 onwards for raising the stock on hand with debtors following as a distant second item impact of use of fund in raw material cycle, storage cycle and collection cycle can be found in the anlysis of operating cycle. Thus management of finance during this period did not observe necessary caution or norms.

INSTITUTION - C

Sources

Statement of fund flow for Institution 'C' can be found in Table 7.5. The institution achieved significant improvement in flow of resources during 1985-86 and 1990-91 due to increase in current liabilities that is working capital loan. In 1986-87 increase in other reserve caused increase in resources.

Table 7.5 : Fund Flow Analysis

INSTITUTION - 'C'

(Rupees in lakhs)

Sl. No.	Particulars	1984-85	1985-86	1986-87	1987-88	1988-89	1989-90	1990-91	1991-92	1992-93
1	2	3	4	5	6	7	8	9	10	11
A.	**Sources**									
I.	Net increase in fixed liabilities	8.16	1.91	12.13	1.44	4.79	6.30	8.01	15.40	14.36
	Net decrease in fixed liabilities	2.43	17.92	7.34	11.38	17.98	9.19	16.16	0.02	5.83
II.	Net decrease in fixed assets	0.00	0.00	0.00	0.00	0.00	0.00	0.00	0.00	0.05
	Net decrease in fixed assets	1.51	0.57	0.50	4.26	0.00	5.01	12.45	13.49	9.80
	Total (A)	12.10	20.40	24.97	17.08	22.77	20.50	36.12	28.91	30.04
B.	**USES**									
I.	Net decrease in fixed assets	0.86	1.48	4.19	8.67	1.40	0.17	1.60	1.75	0.00
	Net decrease in fixed assets	7.34	16.89	5.05	6.85	21.37	20.33	35.02	21.42	30.04
II.	Net increase in fixed liabilities	0.00	2.03	0.00	1.27	0.00	0.00	0.00	0.00	0.00
	Net decrease in fixed liabilities	3.90	0.00	15.73	0.29	0.00	0.00	0.00	5.74	0.00
	TOTAL (B)	12.10	20.10	24.97	17.08	22.77	20.5	36.62	28.91	30.04

Source : The final statement of accounts of the above statement.

Table 7.6 : Balance Sheet

INSTITUTION - 'C'

(Rupees in lakhs)

Sl. No.	Particulars	1983-84	1984-85	1985-86	1986-87	1987-88	1988-89	1989-90	1990-91	1991-92	1992-93
1	2	3	4	5	6	7	8	9	10	11	12
I.	**Liabilities**										
	a. Capital fund & accumulated profit	10.93	12.56	13.66	14.11	14.38	14.89	16.45	17.28	18.02	18.73
	b. Capital expenditure loan	2.38	2.38	2.65	3.18	3.42	3.58	3.58	3.68	5.58	5.58
	c. Depreciation reserve	2.11	2.62	3.16	3.75	4.68	5.39	6.23	7.35	7.83	8.84
	d. Other reserves	14.68	20.70	18.67	29.23	27.96	31.37	35.27	41.23	53.51	66.15
	e. Total	30.10	38.26	38.14	50.27	50.44	55.23	61.53	69.54	84.94	99.30
II.	**Current Liabilities**										
	a. Working capital loan	29.05	29.05	39.88	47.22	50.06	58.22	62.00	67.01	67.03	70.16
	b. Sundry creditors	3.17	5.33	6.76	1.79	5.03	10.31	12.68	15.86	11.26	13.65
	c. Deposits & advances	19.51	15.61	21.17	10.46	15.76	20.34	22.87	30.63	30.21	30.52
	d. Other current liabilities	0.01	0.28	0.38	0.33	0.04	0.00	0.51	0.72	0.00	0.00
	e. Total	51.74	50.27	68.19	59.80	70.89	88.87	98.06	114.22	108.50	114.33
	Total (I + II)	81.84	88.53	106.33	110.07	121.33	144.10	159.59	183.76	193.44	213.63

Contd. ...

Table 7.6 : *(Continued)*

INSTITUTION - 'C'

Sl. No.	Particulars	1983-84	1984-85	1985-86	1986-87	1987-88	1988-89	1989-90	1990-91	1991-92	1992-93
1	2	3	4	5	6	7	8	9	10	11	12
I.	**Assets**										
	Fixed asets (gross)	18.88	19.74	21.22	25.41	34.08	35.48	35.65	37.25	39.00	38.95
II.	**Current Assets**										
	a. Stock on hand	35.00	37.27	40.80	45.85	49.36	55.60	64.61	74.59	83.62	89.37
	b. Sundry debtors	16.32	20.16	19.59	17.22	17.44	20.09	15.59	28.42	31.87	34.63
	c. Advance, loan and investments	4.06	5.29	6.66	6.52	8.65	11.38	18.09	5.64	14.58	4.78
	d. Cash	4.34	2.85	11.14	9.90	5.64	12.82	12.31	22.86	12.77	16.47
	Accumulated Loss	0.00	0.00	0.00	0.00	0.00	0.00	0.00	0.00	0.00	0.00
	Other Current assets	3.24	3.22	6.92	5.17	6.16	8.73	13.34	15.00	11.60	29.43
	Total	62.96	68.79	85.11	84.66	87.25	108.62	123.94	146.51	154.44	174.68
	Total I & II	81.84	88.53	106.33	110.07	121.33	144.10	159.59	183.76	193.44	213.63

The institution recorded substantial increase in fixed liabilities in 1986-87, 1991-92 and 1992-93 all due to increase in other reserves. Net surplus earned by the institution varied between Rs. 0.27 lakh and Rs. 1.36 lakhs on sales between Rs. 67 lakhs and Rs. 316 lakhs employing capital from Rs.15 lakhs and Rs. 33 lakhs. Therefore, retained earning could not make significant contribution to the inflow of resources. With regard to use of funds in this institution also value of fixed assets exceeded the sum of capital fund accumulated profit and years depreciation reserve in all as is evident in the balance. It means that a part of other reserves has been diverted for financing fixed assets whereas the other reserves (meant for specific purpose) should have been kept in fixed deposits.

Uses

With regard to other uses net increase in curent assets got the major share of the additional resources. This is reflected in 1985-86 as cash and stock, in 1989-90 as stocks and advances, in 1990-91 as debtors, cash and stock and in 1992-93 as stocks. In 1986-87 a significant part of the additional resources were used for reducing current liabilities (deposits, advances and sundry creditors). It would be seen that deployment of short-term funds was more balanced in this institution than the preceding two institutions which used additional funds largely for financing stocks and debtors.

INSTITUTION - 'D'

Source

Particulars of fund flow can be found in Table 7.7. The institution realised substantial increase in resources in 1986-87 (due to increase in current liability sundry creditors deposits and advances) and in 1989-90 (thanks to decrease in current assets — cash and advances).

Table 7.7 : Fund Flow Analysis

INSTITUTION - 'D'

(Rupees in lakhs)

Sl. No.	Particulars	1984-85	1985-86	1986-87	1987-88	1988-89	1989-90	1990-91	1991-92	1992-93
1	2	3	4	5	6	7	8	9	10	11
A.	**Sources**									
	I. Net increase in fixed liabilities	10.47	5.58	5.98	6.09	14.40	10.01	12.53	24.69	18.18
	Net decrease in fixed liabilities	3.85	2.09	9.37	9.77	10.44	4.92	8.03	1.49	14.81
	II. Net decrease in fixed assets	0.00	0.00	0.00	0.00	0.00	0.00	0.00	0.00	0.00
	Net decrease in fixed assets	0.96	2.35	7.56	0.00	1.05	18.65	6.48	2.48	3.53
	Total (A)	15.28	10.91	22.91	15.86	25.85	33.58	27.04	28.66	36.52
B.	**Uses**									
	I. Net decrease in fixed assets	1.97	0.00	7.09	2.65	3.99	2.64	1.15	0.67	0.58
	Net decrease in fixed assets	7.18	6.77	15.82	12.83	20.97	30.27	21.43	24.48	35.35
	II. Net increase in fixed liabilities	0.00	0.00	0.00	0.00	0.00	0.00	0.00	0.00	0.00
	Net decrease in fixed liabilities	6.13	3.42	0.00	0.38	0.19	0.67	1.82	3.25	0.00
	TOTAL (B)	15.28	10.19	22.91	15.86	25.85	33.58	27.04	28.66	36.52

Table 7.8 : Balance Sheet

INSTITUTION - 'D'

(Rupees in lakhs)

Sl. No.	Particulars	1983-84	1984-85	1985-86	1986-87	1987-88	1988-89	1989-90	1990-91	1991-92	1992-93
1	2	3	4	5	6	7	8	9	10	11	12
I.	**Liabilities**										
	a. Capital fund & accumulated profit	17.11	18.14	20.66	22.03	23.52	24.75	26.28	28.33	30.69	33.35
	b. Capital expenditure loan	10.39	10.56	11.76	11.19	9.34	8.64	11.64	9.00	8.74	8.15
	c. Depreciation reserve	1.62	2.14	2.63	3.52	3.89	4.58	5.58	6.59	7.51	8.46
	d. Other reserve	9.55	18.30	19.67	23.96	30.04	42.52	47.00	56.47	77.88	92.45
	e. Total	38.67	49.14	54.72	60.70	66.79	80.49	90.50	100.39	124.82	142.41
II.	**Current Liabilities**										
	a. Working capital loan	29.53	30.14	30.87	34.92	44.21	52.07	51.40	57.50	58.99	59.99
	b. Sundry creditors	1.88	1.20	2.56	6.99	7.17	5.95	6.42	8.35	7.21	12.49
	c. Deposits & advances	2.54	5.78	4.29	4.46	4.76	8.56	8.67	7.79	6.41	15.79
	d. Other current liabilities	8.25	2.80	0.87	1.59	1.21	1.02	5.36	4.42	3.69	3.84
	e. Total	42.20	39.92	38.59	47.96	57.35	67.60	71.35	78.06	76.30	91.11
	Total (I + II)	80.87	89.06	93.31	108.68	124.14	148.09	162.35	178.45	201.12	233.52

Table 7.8 : (Continued)

INSTITUTION - 'D'

(Rupees in lakhs)

Sl. No.	Particulars	1983-84	1984-85	1985-86	1986-87	1987-88	1988-89	1989-90	1990-91	1991-92	1992-93
1	2	3	4	5	6	7	8	9	10	11	12
I.	**Assets**										
	Fixed asets (gross)	18.59	20.56	20.39	27.48	30.13	34.12	36.76	37.91	38.58	39.16
II.	**Current Assets**										
	a. Stock on hand	32.90	34.11	31.76	43.87	49.26	61.09	75.14	78.99	80.02	102.94
	b. Sundry debtors	19.37	23.15	23.39	17.27	19.37	18.74	24.97	25.73	35.20	31.81
	c. Advance, loan and investments	4.61	3.65	4.37	3.67	4.38	10.99	4.10	4.69	7.01	9.29
	d. Cash										
	Accumulated Loss	—	—	—	—	—	—	—	—	—	—
	Other Current assets	1.80	2.55	4.85	4.11	5.16	7.73	17.72	11.24	22.90	33.06
	Total	62.28	68.50	72.92	81.18	92.01	113.97	125.59	140.54	162.54	194.36
	Total (I + II)	80.87	89.06	93.31	108.66	124.14	148.09	162.35	178.45	201.12	233.52

Source : KVIC records.

Again the institution acquired substantial increase in long-term funds in 1988-89 and 1991-92 (other reserves).

In this institution also share capital and accumulated profit recorded a slow growth, especially till 1989-90 (*vide* Appendix No. III.D.5). Like other three institutions this centre also derived major part of its resources in the form of short-term funds. It is true that this institution registered more consistent performance in respect of net profit even though relatively profitability was almost as meagre as in other three institutions. During the ten-year period its annual profit varied between Rs. 1.12 lakhs and Rs. 2.65 lakhs on sales from Rs. 91 lakhs to 168 lakhs employing capital between Rs. 29 lakhs and Rs. 50 lakhs (Appendix III). Therefore, with such modest profitability retained earning was not a major source of funds.

Uses

This is the only institution among the four under review which financed fixed assets from capital fund, accumulated profit, capital expenditure loan and depreciation reserve. In most of the years a part of the long-term funds were made available as net working capital. Like other institutions, increase in current assets absorbed, major part of the current assets especially after 1986-87 and in 1992-93 increase in current assets was nearly equal to the total inflow of resources. Among the current assets stocks on hand absorbed major part of additional resources in 1986-87 and 1989-90 in other years the pattern of utilisation was balanced.

As already noted these institutions adopt simple technology and consequently their products are not very competitive in the market donimated by factory sector. Therefore, retained profit cannot be expected to be asignificant source of additional funds. Moreover, these institutions are not allowed to build free reserves out of their profit. Many of the founders of these institutions were not wealthy enough to contribute sizable capital fund. Naturally most of the additional funds of these institutions were derived from short-term sources like working capital loan and sundry creditors.

Long-term additional funds consisted of capital expenditure loan sanctioned by Khadi and Village Industries Commission are other reserves like artisan welfare fund, P.F., or gratuity reserve. Thus the capital base of these institutions has been very weak. In veiw of the modest contribution from capital fund and retained earning any cost-hike of newly bought fixed assets beyond the amount of capital expenditure loan would involve diversion of other funds like other reserves, or at times short-time funds. Thus value and fixed assets at times exceeded the sum of capital fund, retained profit, capital expenditure loan and depreciation reserve. With regard to users sundry debtors and stocks have claimed lion's share of the resources because of the responsibility of the institutions for retail sales. This was one of the factors responsible for long operating cycle of the institutions.

The above analysis on flow of funds proves the hypothesis that short-term funds would occupy main place in the flow of funds, profit and retained earning would be negligible in the resources of the institution.

References

A.I.C.P.A., Accounting Principles Board, Opinion No.1, Reporting Changes in Financial Postition, American Institute of Certified Public Accountants, 1971, Para 7.

A.I.C.P.A., *ibid.* para 8.

Daniel, M.B., in his Financial Statements (American Accountancy Association. Chicago — 1939, p. 73) suggests a running form like income statement in which certain related source and uses are to be considered together. However, this format has not found favour with many.

Gitman, L.J., *Principles of Managerial Finance,* Harper & Row, New York, 1976.

Hampton, J.J., *Financial Decision Making : Concepts Programmes and Cases,* Prentice Hall of India, New Delhi, 1983.

Horne, A.J.C.V., *Financial Management and Policy,* Prentice Hall of India, VI Edition, 1983.

Kohle, Burton, A., *Principles of Financial Management,* Texas: Business Publications, 1983.

Weston, J.F. and Brigharn, E.F. *Essentials of Managerial Finance,* V. Ed. The Dryden Press, III Chap., V.P 120.

8

A STUDY ON TOTAL QUALITY MANAGEMENT IN SMALL SCALE INDUSTRIES IN CUDDALORE DISTRICT

— *D. Aravazhi* and *S. M. Chockalingam*

The Globalisation and Liberalisation of Indian economy, growing interpretation of economics, and increased interdependence of economic agents are reshaping the international and national competitive environment. These changes are prompting the far-sighted organisations to re-examine and modify their competitive strategies. Small and Medium enterprises are not exempt from these pressures. To survive and prosper in 2000 and beyond all businesses need to establish mechanisms enabling them to exert conscious and sustained effort to continuously improve all facets of their operations. The continuous improvement effort needs to be coupled with an acute awareness of changes in customers requirements: Competitive factors and broader variations in the business environment. In an increasingly competitive market place business with a strong continuous improvement culture and external focus are more likely to survive and prosper. Total Quality Management (TQM) is considered an important catalyst is this context.

Total Quality Management has been the focus of many organisations due to its contribution to success. With today's ever-increasing pressure from the consumers/customers in relation to demand for quality goods and services, firms are facing tough time especially in providing the quality goods and services than their competitors. It has now become increasingly important for firms to introduce and implement the concept of Total Quality Management (TQM) in their operations. The increased use of this concept in Japan. USA and other developed countries prompted and induced the developing countries like India also to follow this concept to reap the advantages of the same. Hence, it is hoped that this study would provide general insight into whether or not the concept of TQM is effective in small scale industries in India.

Many Indian firms and MNC's are investing much time and effort in the management of quality. Quality management has become an integral part of their strategy. TQM is the integration of all functions and process within an organisation in order to achieve continuous improvement of the quality of goods and services. The TQM is the concept that requires total commitment from top management to labour competence, communication and continuous improvements. TQM requires a complete turn around in corporate culture and management approaches from where top management gave orders and employees merely obeyed. It is considered as a vital element in any business that is hoping to survive in the market. Though its importance is not yet seen in the small scale industries, its effect is beginning to be felt as we began to import goods and services from overseas. The goods and services imported are of high quality and priced below our domestic goods and services, thus, putting pressure on local firms to improve the quality.

Small, medium and cottage industries are the life blood of modern economy. Hence, they should remain competitive and produce high quality outputs, which is of paramount importance not only at macro level but also at micro level. As small, medium and cottage industries are often the suppliers of goods and services required by large scale industries, and if they lack quality in their goods and services, it will have adverse effect on the competitive ability of the large scale industrial units. Total quality management is considered to be an important quality improvement tool, which is already followed by many large scale industries. However, the awareness and adoption of TQM technique by small scale industrial units are gaining its momentum in the present competitive scenario. Hence, the present study entitled, "A Study on Total Quality Management in Small Scale Industries in Cuddalore District" has been undertaken.

Following are the main objectives of the present study :

1. To study the concept and principles of Total Quality Management in general and its relevance to small scale industries.
2. To study the awareness of TQM concept and practice among the small scale industries in Cuddalore district.
3. To identify the problems in implementation, if any, and to offer suggestions to overcome the same.

Both primary and secondary data were used in this study. As regards the primary data, discussion with SIPCOT and personal interviews with small scale industrial units owners were held. The present study embraces the small scale industrial units functioning in Cuddalore town. Convenient sampling method is adopted to select 12 small scale industrial units. Because of the duration of the project, I was not able to do a more reliable study on other SSIs operating in Cuddalore district. The data was collected through a questionnaire and face to face interviews, lasting approximately 5 to 10 minutes. This was because questions has to be discussed and clarified before the interview can respond on certain incidence, questionnaire was left with people concerned and I was asked to collect them after few days. A sample size of 12 firms within Cuddalore town was chosen as convenient from those 12 firms, I only manage to collect back 10 responses, this represents an 85 per cent response rate.

Regarding to secondary data, reference to the official records maintained by the small scale industrial units, books, journals, magazines, government reports were also made. The collected data were compiled and analysed.

The Concept of Quality

Definitions of quality include 'fitness for use', 'confirm to requirements,' 'meeting the customer requirements', 'satisfying agreed customer requirements continually,' and 'meeting the requirements of the customer now and in the future'. Other often cited definitions are perhaps unnecessarily complicated.

Quality to a manufacturing engineering means putting the customer first and ensuring that any future, more stringent, requirements will be met. Quality is satisfying customer's requirement continually, now and in the future.

The Concept of Total Quality Management

Definition of TQM include 'continuously meeting agreed customer requirements at the lowest cost by releasing the potential of all employees', and 'the development of a total organisational way of life, which puts quality first in order to satisfy customer needs and expectations'. All the three words, total quality and management are important in understanding TQM. It involves everyone and everything in the organisation (total), provides customers with what they expect (quality) and quality is managed in (management) rather than inspected in, built in or even organised in. TQM is the development of a total organisational way of life, involving everyone in an organisation putting quality first to continually meet agreed customer requirements now and in the future.

According to International Organisation for Standardisation (ISO), "Quality means the totality of features and characteristics of a product or service that bear on its ability to satisfy stated or implied needs". In simple words, quality means meeting the customer or client needs every time.

According to Sashkin and Kiser, "Total Quality Management may be defined as creating an organisational culture committed to the continuous improvement of skills, team work, processes, product and service quality, and customer satisfaction. Total Quality Management refers to meeting the requirements of customers consistently by continuous improvement in the quality of work of all employees. For achieving total quality, three things are essential:

1. Meeting customers requirements;
2. Continuous improvement through Management process;
3. Involvement of all employees.

The following chart and tables shows total quality management model and the approaches to TQM implementation. The table and charts are self-explanatory.

How is a Successful TQM Implementation Maintained

TQM will not succeed by itself; it must be managed. TQM is not an instant answer to a specific problem; it requires an ongoing never ending commitment to obtain lasting benefits. It is a new operational philosophy, which is vital to ensure the viability and continuation of most of the world's organisations. TQM must become a way of life, so that the words total quality management are no longer spoken about, but are the natural way the organisation and its employees do things.

TQM is hard work and nearly always takes longer to establish than was first thought; top and middle management commitment is vital and must never diminish, and TQM must always be driven though the whole organisation, including customers and suppliers.

TQM in India

India awakened to the adoption of the concept of TQM in the late 1980s through 'Quality Control'. The quality control efforts did not prove to be adequate to raise the quality of Indian products and to increase their exports. But this scenario changed with the announcement of Industrial Policy 1991, which talked of integration of Indian economy with the world economy. The introduction of

Chart 8.1 : Total Quality Management Model

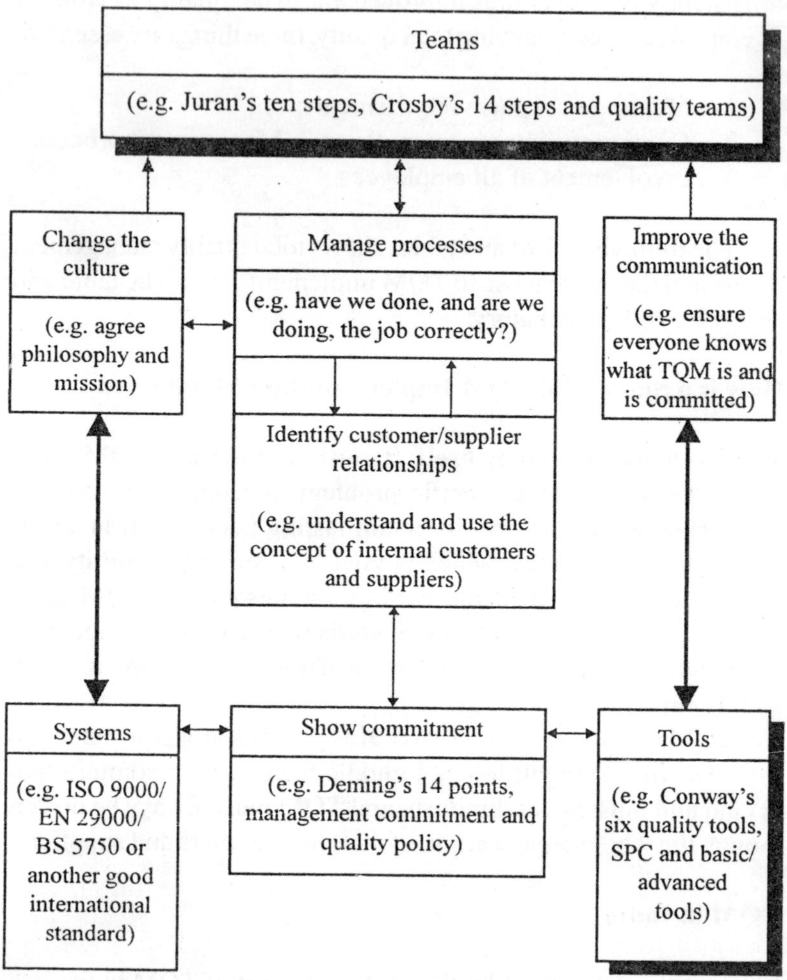

Table 8.1 : Five Approaches to TQN Implementation

Chase	Cullen and Hollingum	Kanji and Asher	Oakland	Robson
Prepare a business implementation plan. Management commitment, new business strategy, concrete policy guidelines, outline plan of action	Understanding Comparison of quality system with ISO9000, effectiveness of the use of statistics, employee attitude survey, identification of quality cost structure	Identification and preparation. Collect information about prime areas where improvement will have most impact on performance, prepare detailed basic work for improvement of all activities	Foundations-a model for TQM Understanding quality, commitment and leadership, design for quality	Establish a steering group
Implementation top-down. Main steering committee, Co-ordinators, quality improvement teams, departmental steering committees, departmental improvement teams	Top-management commitment Establish steering committee	Management understanding and commitment. Ensure that management understands the objective and methodology of TQM and will adopt them all the time	Role of the quality system. Planning for quality, systems design and content, system documentation, implementation and assessment	Select and train internal resources Facilitator, trainers
Develop a detailed implementation plan. TQM launch in about one year	Company-wide awareness Followed by repeating the attitude survey	Scheme for improvement Training and communication, management-led improvement activities	Tools and the improvement cycle Measurement of quality, costs of quality, tools and techniques for improvement, additional techniques for process improvement	Plan first steps with steering group Agree Phisosophy, mission
Implementation Education and training are essential	Planning. A systematic basic requirement	New initiative with new targets and critical examination New initiative taking the complete improvement process to everybody, obtain information about progress and consolidate success	Communication, organisational and teamwork requirements Organisation for quality, culture change through teamwork for quality	Communicate TQM concept to all employees Re-education process
Communication. A vital role, horizontal and vertical	Implementation. Agree objectives, plan to meet them, identify resources, decide priorities, allocate resources, execute plans, review results		Implementation Communications for quality, training for quality, implementation of TQM and management of change	Establish internal marketing process Devise recognition programme Set up internal audit teams. To cover organisation structure, management, communication, customer orientation, ownership, implement agreed findings
Continuous quality improvement Objectives, plan, resources needed, priorities, allocate resources, execute plans, review results	Review Goal is improved operating performance through cost reduction and elimination of waste			Steering group selects tools Introduced as appropriate
				Progressively develop internal resources to self-sufficiency

liberalisation increases such as relicensing of industries and removal of restrictions on the entry of foreign capital and technology into the country had the immediate effect of opening up Indian industry to international competition as also increased competition from within. In an extremely competitive environment, only the fittest can survive and for survival, every organisation has to embark upon a workable quality improvement process. This illustrates the significance of continuous quality improvement by the Indian Industry.

Table 8.2 : Awareness of TQM among Entrepreneurs

	No.
Aware	8
Unaware	2
Total	10

Source : Primary data.

Role of Small Scale and Medium Enterprises in Indian Economy

Historically, Indian SSIs have been started, operated and managed by the artisans and the skills have been passed on from generation to generation. Benefiting from the opportunities, the trading community also started setting up small industries in 60s and 70s backed by families and social support system. In recent years, young educated professionals as well as technologies have also come forward to set up SSIs.

Right from the beginning of the planning era in 1951, the Government of India accorded top priority, next only to agriculture, to the promotion and development of small enterprises in India as an integral part of the industrial policy announced in 1948 and subsequently elaborated in 1956. Despite compulsions of the subsequent developments and vast changes in the country's economic scene, the importance to this sector has been repeated in successive industrial policy pronouncements under which Government continued to accord high priority to small enterprises. As the small industries sector in India covers a broad spectrum, in addition to the promotion of rural industries, the Indian planners also gave conscious and well-articulated policy thrust to the promotion of modern small scale units using latest state of the art technologies.

Like the rest of the world, as medium size enterprises are wholly in the private sector, Government assistance is provided mainly through promotional scheme relating to finance, technology, marketing and human resource development such as training programmes for entrepreneurship development and skill improvement for managerial technical staff workers/artisans and provisions of Industrial estates/areas/parks complete with power, roads, telecommunications and technical assistance support. These policies have paid the country rich dividend in terms of growth of this sector during the last four decades.

Today, Indian SSIs occupy a place of pride in India's overall industrial structure. There are over three million small enterprises in India, manufacturing nearly 8000 different kinds of products in diversified industries and contributing overwhelmingly to the industrial production, exports and employment creation. Indian SSIs account for 40 per cent of gross value of Industrial output and contribute almost 45 per cent to India's exports, both direct and indirect of manufactured goods. Indian SSIs lead dignity of labour in terms of employment to roughly 16.7 million persons, accounting for 80 per cent of total industrial employment in India. The total number of small-scale units in the country in 1998-99 was 31.21 lakhs, compared to 30.14 lakhs in 1997-98. The value of production of small-scale units in 1998-99 aggregated Rs. 5,27,515 crores. The volume of employment in this sector stood at 171.6 lakhs as at the end of March 1999. Exports accounted for about 35 per cent of country's total exports. In 1998-99, SSIs exports valued at 49,481 crores increased by 11.4 per cent over 1997-98, reflecting Indian SSIs resilience, quality and price advantages not only in domestic but also in the global markets. These are positive achievements of the overall development scene of SSIs during the preceding decades. There have been unwelcome developments also. It is necessary to refer to these aspects in order to appreciate the challenge of the emerging scenario, particularly with reference to the majority of SSIs paid scant attention to technological upgradation, quality improvement and cost reduction — all inter-related during the last two-three decades. Because of the regime of quotas, controls and licensing, this policy gave rise to setting up of units by many people not having an industrial culture whose only aim is to make windfall gains. This mushroom growth led to competition among SSIs themselves. Another disquieting features of SSI development in the private sector and public sector in India has been resulted in a large number of SSI units being sick today with little scope for any improvement in the near future. According to data compiled by the Reserve Bank of India, as at the end March 1997, there are 2.35 lakh sick units with locked up bank credit of over Rs. 3600 crores. Causes of sickness in SSI units are both internal and external factors.

The external factors are increased competition, technological obsolescence, labour problems, power cuts, etc. The internal factors, which are inherent financial weakness, diversion of funds, inadequate management competence and marketing strategies. Many reasons for sickness of SSIs among this 21 per cent due to poor quality of product. In other words, 85 per cent of sick units are sick due to many internal factors which could be described as poor quality of product. These facts should make Indian SSIs, management start thinking and highlights the urgency and the importance to be given in implementation of total quality of product and services; otherwise many more SSIs may just vanish, not being able to face the onslaught of the ever-increasing global competitiveness.

Indian industry paid scant attention to technological upgradation all these years. Now that the grim realities of the global economy are starting us in the face, there is a general recognition that change is essential to cope with forces that are changing business environment across the globe. SSIs constitute a significant segment of Indian industrial sector, the time has come for the SSIs to introspect and focus on its contribution to the Indian economy and society in the new millennium.

The challenges to be faced by Industry in the emerging scenario are four-fold, viz.

1. Worldwide deregulation and privatisation;
2. Consumer preferences in regard to price and global quality standards.
3. The information boom; and
4. Growing demand for transparency and accountability.

Indian industry in general and Indian SSIs in particular, the subject that should require top most attention from management in the new environment in achieving management excellence through:

(i) enhancing access to information technology, and
(ii) modernisation and technology.

Upgradation for raising productivity, reducing costs and improving quality standards solely targeted at retaining a competitive edge both in the national and international markets. These are issues closely interrelated and by and large, cover a broad spectrum of the challenges which Indian industry must address if it has to survive in the emerging global economic scene of the 21st century.

The drive towards adopting ISI standards and conforming to ISO 9000 requirements add other dimensions to the imperatives of technology change in the coming decades. Rapid changes in consumer tastes, competitor's quality and cost factors will pose serious challenges for manager's skill in surviving in the new environment. The thrust of the management skill will have to focus on "Total Quality Management" (TQM) so as to enable this sector to be able to compete globally and to retain a competitive edge through cost reduction.

TQM and SSI

Total quality management refers to a management process and set of disciplines that are coordinated to ensure that the organisation consistently meets and exceeds customer requirements. TQM engages all divisions, departments and levels of the organisation. Top management organise all of its strategy and operation around customer needs and develops a culture with high employees participation. TQM companies are focused on the systematic management of data in all processes and practices to eliminate waste and pursue continuous improvements.

The goal is to deliver the highest value for the customer at the lowest cost while achieving sustained profit and economic stability for the company. Top management must commit to a vision and align to train its employees toward a common mission. To do this, cross-functional teams work on improvements that respond to customer requirements. Long term relationships with customers, suppliers and employees focus on quality beyond short-term profit.

Table 8.3 : Background of the Respondents

Industry	No.
Chemical	6
Packaging Materials	1
Engineering	1
Granites	1
Aluminium	1
Total	10

Source : Primary data.

TQM alters the way a company thinks about work and all of its relationships as it impacts every function, system and person connected with the company. TQM is a continuous journey towards excellence.

TQM is the way to succeed in the 1990s, but it is not to be practiced in isolation. It must be a central theme in strategic plans.

Many organisations have pursued TQM, but only a few have discovered its full ramifications and achieve success. The business field is littered with those that made a half-hearted, half-intentional, partially understood effort.

Table 8.4 : Implementation level of TQM

Stage	No.
Planning	7
Processing stage	2
Just implemented	1
Successfully implemented	0
Total	10

Source : Primary data.

Table 8.5 : Barriers of TQM — Implementation

Barriers	No.
Cost	4
Lack of support	4
Lack of knowledge	2
Total	10

Source : Primary data

A study has been conducted among the entrepreneurs in Cuddalore SIPCOT to test their awareness and implementation level of TQM in their operation. A well structured questionnaire with open ended and close ended questions were administered among the entrepreneurs. The study reviews about the awareness level, the implementation level and barriers of implementation. Most of the enterprises are aware of the concept of TQM, but the level of awareness is very low. They knew that the TQM concept as quality concept but technically, their requirements, the stages, procedures of TQM are not known to them. However the interviews and personal discussion held with the entrepreneurs indicate that they are mentally prepared to welcome the concept. Majority of the respondents said that they are in planning, processing stage of implementation. However such planning and processing are not complete and organised. Their approach towards the concept is not in the right direction. The opinion of entrepreneurs about the barriers of TQM implementation is about cost, support and lack of knowledge. The cost of consultancy and reorganising the work environment is beyond the reach of SSI. The support level from management, employees and suppliers are inadequate. The concerned people feels of the product and may result in losing market share. They are yet to realise the long term benefits of TQM. The knowledge about TQM among the management, employees is also very poor.

Conclusion

The positive aspect is that most of the entrpreneurs are mentally prepared to accept and welcome the concept of TQM. They are afraid about the cost of implementation and effect on selling price and the overall viability.

The SSI should organise workshops and seminars to discuss the concept of TQM, its merits, and necessity. The entrepreneurs should be made to realise the long term benefits of TQM. Instead of targeting individual units such programme should be comprehensive by including the manufactures suppliers and dealers and distributors so that successful implementation is possible within a short period.

References

Asokan, R., Quality circles — The magic lamp of Japanese success comes to India. *Business India,* 143, August 22, September 11, 1983.

Atkinson, P., 1991, *Leadership, Total Quality and Cultural Change, Management Service.*

Business Today 1995, *The TQM Implementation Interactive*, January 7-21.

Cole, R.E., 1980, Learning from the *Japanese Management Review.*

Crosby, Philip B., *Let's talk - 96 questions you always wanted to ask Philp B. Crosby.* New York, McGraw Hill, 1989.

Drucker, Peter F., *What we can learn from Japanese Management.*

Garvin, D.A., 1988, *Managing Quality,* New York Free Press.

Scott, Sink D., 1991, " TQM the Next Frontier or Just Another Bandwagon?" *Productivity Journal,* Vol. 32, (3) Oct. - Dec.

Udpa, S.R., 1993, *Quality Circles — Progress Through Participation,* Tata McGraw Hill Publishing Co. Ltd., New Delhi.

9

ROLE OF KVIC IN TRAINING THE EXECUTIVES IN SMALL SCALE INDUSTRIES

— *G. Chellathurai*

The main object of training is to equip and upgrade the persons in the skills necessary for the job and also to meet the requisites technical knowhow along with the development of proper aptitude among various functionaries. Training is one of the means for transfer of knowledge, skill and technology from the trainers to the trainees. Training is considered as one of the most vital and essential part of development and expansion of any industry. It is the process of assisting a person for enhancing his efficiency and effectiveness at work by improving and updating his professional knowledge. Training occupies a prominent place in the efficient management of any industry. It provides required skill and derived changes in the attitudes of the executives. It is an established fact that training for the executives in the rural industries is an important prerequisites of Rural Industrial Development. The executives in the rural industries are the entrepreneurs, artisans and other persons who are involved in the development of Rural Industries.

Training to the executives contained micro lab talks and exercise in inter-personal needs in all human interactions, FIROB (Fundamental, Inter-personal, Relationship, Orientation and

Behaviours), building and motivating team spirit, developing motivational skills and co-operative skills future strategies, appropriate technology and optimum utilisation of resources.

It is difficult to define rural Industry. Easier way can be a negative definition as 'Rural-Non-farm-Sector' (RNFS). KVIC has made it location specific as the industry situated in rural areas as per the revenue records. It has also added ceiling on capital to labour ratio as Rs. 50,000 per labour. The rural industries are unorganised sector. Rural Industries have played an important role in our national economy for a long time. Promotion of rural industries has been the central objective of many strategies adopted to bring about equitable distribution, raising the productive capacity of the rural people and increasing their participation in the process of development. The Rural Industries would continue to be supplementary source of income as well as part/full time employment activity to the rural artisans, landless labourers, women and the educated unemployed and underemployment mass in rural area.

Rural Industry consists of different kinds of Village and Small Scale Industries. The cottage industries are the most important components of rural industries. Rural industry means an industry appropriate for rural area. The rural industry serves the requirement of rural people as well as other markets. The financial needs of rural industries are small. It is more important that they function in the absence of infrastructural facilities and they provide a friendly environment.

Rural industries are inter-linked with agricultural activities, rural development and service sectors. They may also be grouped into Small Scale Industry, Tiny Industries and Rural Artisans (Self-employed). The main characteristics of these industries are to develop local initiative, co-operation and spirit of self-reliance in the economy and at the same time, help in utilization, of the available manpower for processing locally available raw materials by adopting simple techniques. They are capable of generating employment opportunities at the place of residence to a large section of population. Rural Industries will strive to build up village republics and human resources development. Rural Industrialisation provides ample scope for the promotion of artistic achievement and creation that have been suppressed in rural areas.

It has been observed that the large number of failures in decentralised industrial sector are mainly due to managerial inadequacies. There is a need to equip the artisans and their institutions with new concepts of entrepreneurship and managerial training. The programme for rapid growth of rural industries should be launched like a mass-movement, with the emphasis on rural brand. Efforts should be made to carry the message of rural development through rural industries to the rural mass. The traditional Village Industries and Crafts continue to play a significant role in improving new markets, particularly in case of handicrafts, handlooms and other varied crafts. These industrial activities were pursued mostly by self-employed workers and members of their households in and around their places of residence, on a full-time or part-time basis. The training of persons in rural industry may be for 'Wage employment and 'self-employment'. However, till to-day, the rural potentials have not been effectively utilised.

Even now 60 per cent of the artisans or village industries workers are carrying out their productive activities in a traditional way. The modernisation of rural industries as well as their diversification and promotion of small and micro enterprises by developing human resources have become very essential for rural industrialisation. Development of rural industries by way of technological upgradation, product diversification, design development and continuous flow of market intelligence have become very essential.

The specific objectives of the study are :

1. To study the various institutions providing Training for the Executives in the Rural Industries.
2. To assess the number of Training Institutions offering training with special reference to KVIC in India and Tamil Nadu.

3. To analyse the various types of training courses offered by the institutions.
4. To assess the number of persons trained through these institutions.
5. To suggest some future approach to the Training Institutions.

The present study is of descriptive nature. It is concerned with the number of institutions providing training for the executives in the Rural Industries and the various courses offered by the institution for the development of Rural Industries. The present study is based on secondary data. The secondary data regarding the various programmes under the KVIC were collected from KVIC Annual Reports, State Khadi and Village industries office, Madras, Tamil Nadu Sarvodaya Sangh at Tiruppur and other journals like *Khadi Gramodyog, Jagriti* published by KVIC.

Role of KVIC in Training Programmes

In order to provide training to the Executives and other members who are closely related to Rural Industries, the Khadi and Village Industries Commission is charged with the responsibility of planning and organising training for persons engaged in Khadi and Village Industries activities. For this purpose, KVIC has organised four-tier structure of training programmes covering artisans, unit-level-workers, supervisory technical staff and management staff. The objectives of the training programmes are as follows :

1. to upgrade the skill of artisans.
2. to impart training for absorbing new techniques and technologies.
3. to bring the available equipments and technology within the reach of artisans.
4. to remove drudgery in cottage and village industries.
5. to increase productivity and enable artisans to earn higher income.

6. to provide training facilities to incumbents in the sector.

The artisans-level training is mostly organised at the production certres by voluntary agencies. The unit-level workers are trained in Khadi Gramodyog Vidhalayas and in other Village Industries training centres. The training courses for supervisory staff and managers are organised in Multi-Disciplinary Training Centres (MDTC) and the training of Officers is conducted in Zonal Training Centre.

Organisational Nature of Training Centres

Now the KVIC is implementing its training programmes through 48 departmental and non-departmental training centres which are organising training programmes under KVIC are classified below:

S. No.	Name	Organisational Nature	Number
1.	Multi Disciplinary Training Centre (MDTC)	Departmental	10
2.	Industry Directorates of Training Courses (IDTC)	Departmental run by respective Industry Directorate	13
3.	Board's Department Training Centres (BDTC)	Aided by KVIC run by KVIB	2
4.	Non-Departmental Training Centres (NDTC)	Aided by KVIC run by Institution	23

Source : Annual Reports 1988-89 KVIC-Mumbai.

Courses offered by the Training Centres

The various specialised training course offered by the departmental and non-departmental training centres is shown below:

S. No.	Name of the Courses	Duration of the Courses
1.	Village Industries Karyakarta	13 Months
2.	Area Organiser Course (Secretaries)	12 Months
3.	Integrated Management	2 Months
4.	Production Management	2 Months
5.	Financial Management	2 Months
6.	Marketing Management	1 Month
7.	Management Development	2 Months
8.	Industrial Co-operative Management	3 Months
9.	Marketing Assistance Course	6 Months
10.	Entrepreneurship Course (Neo Soap Industry)	2 Months

Persons trained under KVIC

So far KVIC has trained 8 lakh persons. The total number of persons trained in different Khadi and village industries programme from 1994-95 to 1998-99 is given in Table 9.1 and the performance of department and non-department training centres during the year 1998-99 is given in Table 9.2.

Table 9.1 : Number of Persons Trained under KVIC

Year	No. of Person Trained		
	Male	Women	Total
1994-95	12410	1352	13562
1995-96	16033	3169	19202
1996-97	6934	8563	15497
1997-98	4518	1955	6473
1998-99	5933	2932	8865

Source : Annual Reports from 1994-95 to 1998-99 KVIC Mumbai.

Table 9.2 : Performance of Departmental and Non-Departmental Training Centres during the year 1998-99

Category	Total	SC	ST	OBC	General	Women
MDTC	4131	437	88	547	3059	1085
IDTC	1094	115	84	282	613	314
BDTC	1812	359	256	92	1105	596
NDTC	1828	323	143	669	693	937
Total	8865	1234	571	1590	5470	2932

Source : Annual Report 1998-99 KVIC Mumbai.

Training Centres in Tamil Nadu

Tamil Nadu occupies a very high place in the production and efficient management of Village Industries. In Tamil Nadu the total number of persons trained are 359 during the year 1998-99. Of the 359 persons trained 50 persons constituted SC, 12 candidates are ST, 189 candidates are OBC and 108 candidates are general categories. In this year 102 women candidates are trained. The Institutions which are providing training for the executives in the rural industries in Tamil Nadu are mentioned here.

Sl. No.	Name of the Training Centres	Annual Intake	Training Courses being conducted	Duration of the Course
1	2	3	4	5
1.	Central Palmgur and Palm Products Institute. Khadi and VI Commission, No. 39, Arul Nagar, Madhavaram Milk Colony Madras-51 (T.N).	30	1. Advance Course Palmugur Technology	8 Months
			2. Confectionery & Indigenous Sweets making	3 Months
			3. Palm Leaf Articles Course	3 Months
			4. Palm Fibre and Brush Making Course	

Contd.

Contd.

1	2	3	4	5
2.	Khadi Gramodyog Vidyalaya, Tamil Nadu Sarvodaya Sangh, Post-Veerapandy, Tirupur - 638 605 (TN)	67	1. Poly, Karyakarta Course	6 Months
			2. Soap Artisan Training Course	6 Months
			3. Khadi Karyakarta Courses	6 Months
			4. Semi Automatic (Nepali) Loom Training	10 Months
			5. 12-Spindle Charkha Training Course	2 Months
			6. Soap Refresher Course	1 Month
			7. Orientation Course in A/C's and Audits	1 Month
3.	Dr. J.C. Kumarappa Institute of Rural Technology and Management Gandhi Niketan Ashram, P.P T. Kallupatti, Madurai Dist - 626 702	60	1. Artisan Course in pottery	5 Months
			2. Village Industries	13 Months
			3. New Weavers Course	12 Months
			4. Khadi Karyakartya Course	10 Months
			5. Semi-Automatic (Nepali) Loom Weaving Course	6 Months
			6. Refresher Course in Marketing	1½ Months
			7. Orientation Course in Marketing	1 Month
			8. Supervisory Course in Leather training	12 Months
			9. Supervisory Course in Leather goods Mfg. & Food wear	12 Months
			10. Design Weaving Course	12 Months

Contd.

Contd.

1	2	3	4	5
			11. Jr. Supervirosy Course. In Soap	4 Months
			12. E.D.P. Course for Detergent Cake & Powder making	1 Month
4.	Regional Pottery Training Centre, Sevapet, Tamil Nadu Khadi and V.I. Board, Tirur, Chengai MGR Dist., Sevapet, Tamil Nadu	50	Master pottery	10 Months
5.	Cottage, Tamil Nadu, Ambasamudram Sarvodaya Sangh, Gandhi Nagar, Veeravanallur, Tirunelveli Dist., Tamil Nadu.	—	Supervisory Course for Agarbatti,	2 Months

Future Approach

In the rural areas, individuals will be motivated to take up rural industrial programmes. For this purpose, training in entrepreneurship development is very important. It provided ever changing needs of the environment, the society and technology. Thus the training is an investment in human resources development. Training Programmes for developing rural entrepreneurship in village industries should be designed to the right persons having the quality of leadership and risk-facing capacity.

The artisans level training is mostly organised at the production centres. The traditional artisans are generally economically poor because, they do not get fair return in their profession for want of merchandising their product. The training to the artisans should aim at the upgradation of technical skills in new practices, product improvements and diversification of product, product-identification with the market demand. In production activity in providing training facilities to the workers in accordance with the requirements to take an active role in the working of the Institutions.

The first generation of self-employed persons in rural areas must be adequately trained so as to enable them to remain or continue in the business facing the competition successfully. Rural industrialisation constitutes the key-link in the process of socio-economic transformation of underdeveloped rural areas as well as social structure. In view of its importance and problems, it is necessary to take some corrective action to rejuvenate rural industries and rural artisans to play a pivotal role in the development process. By means of setting up training in agri-industrial service complexes and non-traditional industries in planned manner will lead to gradual urbanisation of the rural areas. On moving from protected economy to a market oriented economy, some amount of traditional changes seems unavoidable. The necessary changes in Technology, Product quality, factor productivity and competitive marketing techniques and management-practices alone seem to hold the key for the future of Indian Small Scale and Cottage Industries in the rural areas. Progressive expansion and modernisation of rural industry could be best brought out by the establishment of Small Scale Industrial Units along with the necessary services in large villages and small towns located all over the country.

References

Annual Reports KVIC, Mumbai.

A resume by Directorate of Training, Training progrmme and facilities offered by KVIC, *Khadi Gramodyog,* Vol. 34, No. 33, December 1992.

Bhairannavar, Kiran Ashok, What would be the appropriate form of Industries and Technology for the Indian situation, *Khadi Gramodyog,* Vol. 50, No. 10, July 1999.

Jalel, R.S., *Industrial Entrepreneurship and Small Scale Industries*, Anmol Publication, Delhi.

Kumar, Basant, 'Managing change in Trainig function', *Khadi Gramodyog,* Vol. 34, No. 3.

Nair, N. Kannan. 'Entrepreneurship Development in Small and Rural Industries', *Khadi Gramodyog,* Vol. 34, No. 3, December 1992.

Sharma, S.S., 'Multi-Disciplinary Training Centres' *Khadi Gramodyog,* Vol. 34, No 3, December 1992.

Srivastava, G.C., 1984, *Rural Industrial Development,* Chugh Publisher, Allahabad.

Waseen, S.M., *'Tiny and Cottage Industries : An Area for Entrepreneurship, Khadi Gramodyog,* No. 9, 1990.

10

TRAINING FOR THE EXECUTIVES IN RURAL INDUSTRIES

— *Shantha B. Kurup* and *A. Pankajam*

> The process whereby individuals acquire knowledge, skills and attitudes, through experience, reflection, study or instructions. Learning is the modification of behaviour through experience and training.
>
> — *Gates*

Training is a planned process to modify attitude, knowledge, skill, behaviour, etc., through learning to acquire effective performance in an activity or range of activities. The purpose of training is to develop the abilities of an individual, to satisfy current and future manpower needs, to supplement education or to train for taking up higher responsibilities. In days bygone it was 'training begins where education ends'; it is now, 'training with education'.

In a country where agriculture is the mainstay of a sizeable population and most of the people do not get work for more than 4 months in a year and have to suffer enforced idleness, there is no alternative, but to undertake a massive programme of rural industrialisation. At the same time there is need to adopt a common approach towards rural industrialisation. Similarly, rural industrialisation should not be considered in isolation. It should be part of overall strategy for rural development. Rural industrialisation would succeed only if it becomes part of the overall strategy of development of agriculture as well as industry.

Rural areas being the arteries of the Indian economy until and unless these are strengthened and developed, the nation cannot march on the road to prosperity. The strengthening can only be through industrialisation as the other alternatives, agriculture is ruled out for any more absorption of work force. And that too can be meaningful with taking up only village industries which can serve as the lifeblood and living vitality in the economic life.

Concept of Rural Industries

The industries in our country includes organised large and medium industries, small industries and unorganised traditional industries, small and unorganised traditional industries. Small and unorganised traditional industries constitute village and small-scale industries which constitute an important segment of the economy. The concept of rural industries include village and small scale industries, village and small scale sector divided into eight sub-sectors, namely Khadi, Village industries, handloom, sericulture, handicrafts, coir, modern small scale industry and powerlooms. The last two represents the modern small-scale industry and the other six sub-sectors constitute traditional industries which is a formidable part in rural industrialisation.

The concept of rural industries undergone changes from April 2nd, 1991, with the change in the structure and definition. A dynamic distraction has been created by central government. The small and village industries is distinguished between traditional industries and crafts and modern small oriented and ancillary gaining upto Rs. 75 lakhs each.

On the basis of scale and primary functions, there are 4 groups of industries which can be expanded as developed in rural areas.

1. Traditional village industries — khadi, leather, tanning, wood

work, artisan industry, coir, handicrafts etc.

2. Heavy industry — fertilizer plants with bio-mass, pesticides using biological inputs, mini-steel plants, ancillary engineering for medium and large farms like ploughs, threshers etc.
3. Medium group industry — mini cement plant for rural works, mini paper plants etc.
4. Large industries — animal feed and fodder industries, building materials like screens, doors, windows, roofing materials etc. agricultural implements and machineries for rural areas.

Importance of Training

Management is now recognised as a separate professional skill. The growing emphasis on professionalism, growing bureaucracy, competitive growth, rise in the educational level with demand for better leadership, all throw the need for a better equipped population. The pressure for better trained executive shortages, causes and emphasis for executive development programmes. The reduced work load on human on account of mechanisation, may mean pursuits leisure or an opportunity to seek additional secondary or multiple job holding. This would in turn require development of multi-disciplinary skills by multitudes and greater interdependence. In this robot age, the flights in space, the missiles and satellites controlled weather and automated factories, the increase in white collars is very perceptible.

A person may not possess the skills to do the required job at a required standard of performance or an operation team may not be meeting the targets. Performance may be inadequate to meet future objectives, e.g., improved cost control might mean improved skills in using planning techniques or the introduction of a new advanced system of computer may require retraining personnel in the use of the system. Performance problems arise because standards have not been identified, communicated or agreed, i.e., people are not clear as to what is expected of them and from them. People are also not sure about their level of authority and responsibility.

The adaptation to meet such situations is by training and

retraining. Managers of future have to develop new view points to open new vistas. The greatest problem in the field of management is and probably will continue to be for some time, the development of philosophy that supplies a practicable basis for the solution of business problems in consonance with public interest. The present day Business Executives, though continue to be responsible for Planning. Organising and Controlling the operations of job has not changed. The technological and social changes, the changing work force, and strong group pressures, makes the means of performing more difficult.

As Drucker has rightly said, 'competence in a speciality is of course not a barrier, however an excellent technocrat may not even make a reasonably good manager.' He has to be made one. This is where training comes in. Training is an activity since this helps in improving skills, attitudes and knowledge. The only area of possible different advantage for an organisation over the others is the quality of its human inputs, people's skills, capabilities, accomplishments and activities. Training is the process by which individuals acquire, through practical experience, knowledge, skills and attitudes. A major psychological process in humans, is learning. There is no human behaviour that is not affected by learning. Learning implies a conscious attempt towards imbibing knowledge. It brings about a noticeable change in behaviour. One of the principles of learning is 'reinforcement', which is defined as anything that increases the strength of response. Learning is the modification of behaviour through training. Training is a planned process to modify attitudes, knowledge, skill and behaviour through learning experience to achieve effective performance in any activity or range of activities. Its purpose in the work situation, is to develop the abilities of the individual and to satisfy the current and future manpower needs of the organisations. The purpose of training is to supplement education. Earlier it was 'training actually begins where education ends', but now it is 'training goes hand-in-hand with education'.

Training is always with a purpose. It is a means for maintenance and improvement of the level of performance of a person in a section or a department.

Training costs money in terms of time resource. Therefore, training as a tool of management should be used judiciously and the knowledge acquired should be applied in business. There must be direct relationship between performance problems that are business priorities and the training events that are used to overcome the problem. Training is a means of upgrading performance, e.g., improved layout of plant and equipment, improved systems and procedures, restructuring of jobs, etc. Any job has training implications but it should be ensured that when training is proposed it is cost effective. Young people, new entrants inducted to the company, will need special treatment when time comes to integrate them into working life. People new to the organisation, need help to adjust to their new surroundings, viz., those who have served as an apprentice in another industry may have to learn to apply their skills in a new technical field. The same applies to people who are transferred from another section, department, or location.

Relevance of Training

Flippo, lucidly discusses several advantages of training. These include increased productivity, high morale, and reduction in the level of supervision, increased organisational stability and flexibility as also reduction in accidents.

Yodder and others have described certain principles for effective training. Some of them are Training in a management function and therefore everyone is a trainer. Every individual requires training. There should be a differentiation between staff and training functions. Dayal, presents a comprehensive survey of studies on training in India. As he observes most of the issues confronting the field of training in India are not very dissimilar to those felt abroad. He also feels that training is effective only if the company is capable of using it. It is, however, not correct to say that training is effective only if the company is capable of using it. Training helps in development of a personality, which is of national significance too.

Training Needs and Objectives

Wherever there exists a gaping gap between the present performance and the desired performance, the need for training and development creeps in as the first priority. Involving the 'line' itself in training programmes instead of treating it as only a 'staff function would reduce conflicts.' Training should be aimed at a set objective. The objective should be clearly defined at the very outset.

We live in an age of change. Change is the only thing that is permanent. As they grow old, people themselves undergo changes. Therefore, people have to learn to cope with the change in their environment and with themselves.

People spend a lot of time working in groups, attending conferences, working in conjunction with other people from other sectors, in fact, interaction is the essence of any business, with the changing environment and the cultural revolution, the dynamics of a group also changes.

To meet this change, training and development of human as a resource to utilise other resources to its fullest extent is the solution. To decide whether or not training would help, one has to think of the situations.

There are some essential elements for the identification of a training need, they are:

Young People : New entrants, who are undergoing intensive training before posting. People new to the organisations, new to the job, new to the department of section will need special treatment when the time comes to integrate them into working life.

Newcomers need help to adjust to their new surroundings. Those who have served as an apprentice in another industry will have to learn to apply their skills in the new technical field. The same applies to people who are transferred from another department or location.

People who are established in the job: We live in an age of acceleration of change. People themselves undergo change as they grow older. The implication is that people have to learn to cope with the change in their environment and with themselves.

People in groups: People spend a lot of time working in groups, attending meetings, working in conjunction with other people from other department. Meeting are very often ineffective, or group problems occur on account of differences in objectives, e.g. operations department seek to maximise their throughput, maintenance department would want to keep the machinery in running condition at any cost, while the accounts department would like to impose cuts in expenditure.

Performance Problems

Training is always carried out for a purpose. It is a means of maintaining and improving the level of performance of a person, a section, or a department. It could be that a person does not possess the skills to do the job at a required standard of performance or that an operations team is not meeting targets.

Performance may be inadequate to meet future objectives, e.g. improved cost control might mean improved skills in using planning techniques or the introduction of new computer system will require retraining in the use of the system. Performance problems arise because of standards have not been identified, communicated or agreed, e.g. people are not clear as to what is expected to them and from them, they are also not clear about their levels of authority and responsibility.

Business Priorities

Training costs money in terms of time and resources. There is no point in sending people on a training course when there is little relation between what they learn through the course and the business needs of the department/section or when they cannot apply the skills and knowledge they have acquired. There must be a direct relationship between performance problems that the business priorities and the training events that are adopted to overcome those problems.

Training is a cost-effective way of tackling the problem.

Training is one of the many means of upgrading performance, e.g., improved layout of plant and equipment, improved systems and procedures, restructuring of jobs, etc. There will always be training implication when other means are used but it is essential to ensure that when training is decided upon, it is cost effective. For example, poor budget performance is a cause of concern. It is due to poor presentation of budget information, lack of clarity about what the budget holder controls, etc. The most effective means to correct this problem is to redesign the budget system so that it is useable and understood.

Training implications for this problem will be: (i) Introducing the new system and what is expected from job holders; and (ii) Training people in how the new system works and that they have to do to ensure its effective working.

Management of Training

There are four broad functions that characterise the work of the trainer who trains:

Planning

Based on the identification of need for training, the learning objectives should be established by analysing the task.

Organising

The trainer/teacher organises the work and arranges to relate the resources so as to realise the learning objectives in the most effective, efficient and economic way possible, i.e., by selecting appropriate training tactics, appropriate learning methods and the appropriate learning aids.

Learning

This is what the trainer/teacher does to motivate, encourage and inspire his participants so that they will readily realise the learning objectives.

Controlling

This is the work which the trainer/teacher does to determine whether his organising and leading capacities are successfully being realised to achieve the set objectives. If the objectives are not being realised, then the trainer/teacher must teach and regulate the situation. The objectives once set should not be changed. However, the methods can be changed.

Training for Executives in Rural Industries

Since today's organisations have to face

* Volatile market shares, including fluctuating segments within markets.
* Global competition, including fluctuating segments within markets.
* Global competition, including new players who break all the rules.
* Variety in production, including short runs, marked differentiation, briefer life cycles.
* Rapid changes in technology of product and process, generation sudden and decisive shifts in competitive advantage.
* Changing demands of customers dominating production and altering the nature of selling: distribution becoming a crucial component in the ultimate prices to customers.
* Economies of method and exploitation of powerful brands being the joint keys to superior profitability.

The executives should be capable of managing each and every situation. For this self-development through personal development is essential. For self-development first the person should understand himself better. The person can make you of the model from

"Everything you ever needed to know about training" to know the persons own perception. Lifetime leaving gives to executives the opportunity to explore the dimensions of themselves and they can build layers of knowledge as they work with others.

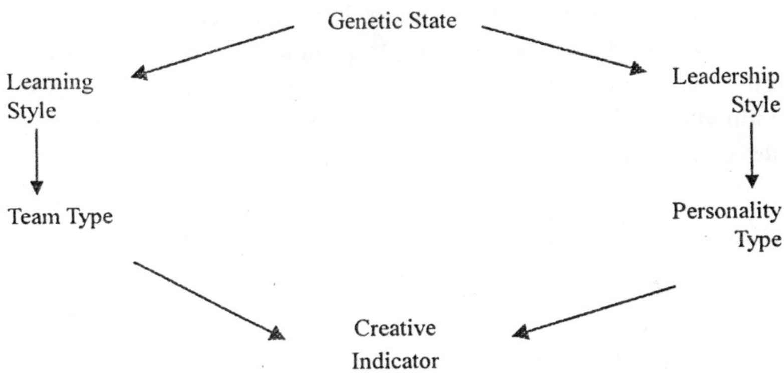

If one is able to develop a clear understanding about their own strengths and weakness then they can get easy training through training programmes.

The following are some of Training which will help the executives working in rural industries to improve themselves and in turn the concern in which they are working.

Training for Change

When introducing change the journey is at least as important as the destination. Change is a messy, iterative process. Just when you think you have arrived, you find you have hardly begun.

(Tony Turril: Change and Innovation - Challenge for the NHS)

Managing change involves dealing with the unexpected. When other people are involved we can never be entirely sure of this reaction. It means reviewing the process and intended outcomes as you go along. Tom Peter in his book, *Thriving on Chaos* (1989) goes so far to suggest that organisations cannot hope to survive if they are not able to respond to change — indeed to love it.

Since our country is a developing nation we have to change ourselves according to the changes in the environment. Rural industrial people should also change themselves to adapt to changes. For this purpose, we can provide the executives training for change. The module for this can be encouraging creativity, team building elements, provoking thoughtfulness, how managers might motivate and encourage, initiate in their staff, methods which reduce to a minimum the negative organisational and personal impact of redundancy, skills to act agents of change (i.e.) to help other acquire, develop or modify knowledge competence or attitudes, managing personal change, raising awareness of capability and skill strength, identifying the landmarks in the transition process, etc.

Interpersonal Skills Training

We all use interpersonal skills everyday in our lives and we have been using them almost the day we were born. The range of what constitutes interpersonal skills is vast. A short list of such skills would include at least the following — counselling, group membership skills, assertiveness, social skills, interviewing skills of various sorts, writing skills, using the telephone and group facilitation skills. Examples of how such skills are used in a range of setting are also numerous and would include the following among many others.

* Counselling skills: Counselling colleagues, friends, clients and customers.
* Assertiveness skills: returning faulty goods, saying "No" keeping to contracts and agreements.
* Social skills: Introducing yourself, attending meetings, working with the general public, with customers and clients.
* Facilitation skills: running meetings and groups, chairing discussions and organising planning meetings.

All professional people need and use a variety of inter-personal skills in every aspects of their work. Very often they are learned through the process known as "sitting with Nellie", the new professional is supposed to pick up various skills through observing older and more experienced colleagues at work. However skills alone will not suffice. Behind and alongside the practice of interpersonal skills must be set of values, a series of attitudes, all of which contribute to the human element of interpersonal behaviour.

Certain personal qualities are a prerequisite of effective interpersonal relationships. A basic cluster of such necessary qualities may be identified as: Warmth, genuineness, empathy, and unconditional positive regard (Rogers, 1967).

Only with the help of all these qualities an executive can shine in his career and improve his firm. For this the executives should be trained in acquiring assertiveness, group facilitation, counselling skills etc.

One should be assertive and not aggressive to get things done. Assertiveness can be useful in the following situations :

* When used by a colleague who feels he is being exploited by another colleague.
* When used by a person who has never been able to express her wants and needs in a marriage.
* When used by the professional, when facing bureaucratic processes in trying to get help for another person.
* In everyday situations (in shops, offices, restaurants, etc.) where a stated service being offered is not actually being given.

The assertive person comes to be seen an "adult" person who is able to treat other people reasonably and with recourse to either childish or loutish behaviour. So we should give training to the executives to acquire assertive skills to be a perfect executive.

Another type of interpersonal skill is group facilitation the process of enabling groups to run effectively.

The main work of the executives is to run the groups effectively to get the work done. Therefore training in group facilitation is also essential.

Counselling Skills Training

Counselling skills can be used in a variety of settings, they may be used to help the person who is suffering from a temporary emotional crisis or they may be useful in helping the person who has longer-term problems in living. Counselling skills are also useful in everyday business and administration situations when dealing with colleagues, clients or customers. They may also be practical and useful as a set of interpersonal skills for everyday use in every client-practitioner situation. Counselling skills, after all, are not skills to be turned on and off according to the need, but a way of being with the client to enable them to communicate their thoughts and feelings more effectively. Counselling skills form the basis of all consumers, whatever that relationship is. Further, the skills are essential ones for helping colleagues short list of situations in which counselling skills are useful in all professions includes:

* Helping people to make career changes.
* Helping people to make business decisions.
* Enabling people to make life decisions for themselves.
* Helping relatives to cope with bereavement.
* Working with children and adolescents.
* Helping families to work through problems.
* Discussing psychiatric difficulties and making decisions about when to refer on to other professionals.
* Teaching students to become counsellors.

It may be noted that the term 'counsellling' has different connotations for different people. In an everyday sense, the term seems to mean advising, helping giving guidance and so forth. In a more 'professional' sense, it is often used to describe a particular sort of helping the either person to stand on their own feet and make their own decisions, in my view, the debates about what counselling is and is not are sometimes rather sterile. The important thing is to be clear about how you are using the term when you engage in any sort of interpersonal skills or personnel training.

Counselling skills may be divided into two sub-groups : (a) listening and (b) counselling interventions. Listening involves not only giving full attention to the person being listened to, but also being seen to be listening by the other person.

Since in rural industries the executives have to come across the illiterate persons they have to counsel them often for that purpose the executives should often for that purpose the executives should possess the counselling skills to a great extent. Moreover only with the help of satisfied persons only we can produce a lot and improve our economy. Therefore counselling skills training is very much essential to the executives in rural industries.

A number of researchers in the counselling field have tried to identify the personal qualities that are necessary to effect therapeutic change in another person. Carkuff (1969) suggested that a climate of trust must be development in counselling in which the following characteristics are present: empathy, warmth, genuineness. Carl Roger (1967) added the following necessary qualities: positive regard, concreteness. Drawing from the considerable literature and research conducted in the field of counselling, the following other personal characteristics may be added: a sense of humour, a sense of tragic and self-awareness. At the time of giving training to the executives in the rural industries we should plan accordingly to incorporate the activities to improve their personal qualities.

Leadership Training

Leaders come in all shapes and sizes. They are army officers, fashion designers, managers, parents, politicians, sports coaches, etc. Only a proper leader can run an organisation in a better way. Therefore leadership training is a must for the executives.

The leadership training may be more effective with the help of small group discussions, role plays, games and simulations than traditional learning methods such as lectures and demonstrations. With the help of leadership training the executive can train his own industrial persons to compete in the global market. The Rural Industries Association can concentrate on giving training on leadership.

Role Plays

A role play, used for training purpose is a simulation in which trainees are required to act out of the role of an individual in a situation or in cirumstances that are relevant to the trainee.

Regardless of the precise situation, there are many common lessons to be learnt from role play. There are in the area of effective face-to-face communication. The manager's ability to coach, influence, persuade, advise or fully understand is crucial to the successful conduct of the interview or conversation whether the subject at issue is negotiation or handling grievances. Similarly the value of effective questioning and listening is fundamental to all management and workplace communication, as in an awareness and recognition of body language. All these aspects of face-to-face communication skills can be easily addressed by role playing. The ability to control conversation, handle conflict, reach agreement or gain commitment can also be improved through role playing.

So with the help of role play the executive can get more information about their work and about their people and they can manage their firm well. One of the training for them should be role play.

Survey and Findings

A survey was conducted among 200 executives who are working in rural industries to know about their opinion towards training. The following are the results of the survey. A questionnaire was framed and the data was collected on a four-point scale. The data was analysed with the help of mean scores and the results were given.

Majority of them prefer training. The respondents who gave their opinion are preferring the training for change, leadership training, interpersonal skills training, etc., The data is presented in the form of graph for easy reference.

69 per cent of the respondents felt that training is always necessary. 25 per cent felt that only sometimes it is necessary. 4 per cent felt that it is not necessary.

Opinion of the Rural Executives about Training

Query	No Idea	Never	Some-times	Always	Not used	No answer
Training is necessary	0	4.05	25.34	68.92	1.01	0.68
Training is useful	1.35	2.03	17.91	73.31	3.04	2.36
Training increases productivity	1.01	3.38	18.58	72.97	1.01	3.04
Improves organisational efficiency	2.03	4.73	23.65	63.85	1.69	4.05
On the job training	0.34	1.35	19.59	78.72	0	0
Off the job training	0.34	5.74	18.58	75.34	0	0
With training materials	3.72	3.04	20.61	70.95	1.35	0.34
Timely training	1.01	16.22	18.92	56.42	0	7.43
Role plays	2.36	10.81	20.61	62.16	0.34	3.72
Interpersonal skills training	5.74	4.39	24.66	57.77	3.04	4.39
Counselling skills training	3.04	7.43	21.62	61.49	1.69	4.73
Training for change	0	5.07	26.69	65.2	0.68	2.36
Leadership training	2.36	8.11	25.34	60.81	0.68	2.7

This picture considers 3 features, namely, usefulness of the training, increasing productivity and its efficiency. It is an encouraging picture where a big majority have positive attitude about the usefulness. 73.31 per cent found that the training is very useful. 73 per cent feel that the training increases productivity and 64 per cent show satisfaction that it improves organisational efficiency.

Majority of the respondents feel that timely training is needed while 62 per cent are for the use of role plays and so on.

Regarding the interpersonal skills training and the counselling skills training the response was moderate by the general standard. 58 per cent is feeling that interpersonal skills training is always needed while 62 per cent is feeling that the counselling skills training is always a must.

65 per cent of those approached felt that training should be for adapting to change. Similarly, 27 per cent felt that only sometimes training is to adapt to changes. 5 per cent seemed to feel that to adapt to changes training is not necessary.

60 per cent of the respondents are feeling that leadership training is always needed to the executives to run the firm in a better way.

Conclusion

Since to climb up in the ladder of economic development our country should be concentrating on the development of rural industries. To develop them first we have to develop the executives, then only we can develop the rural industries.

Therefore for the development of our country we train the rural Industries executives in Counselling, Leadership, Interpersonal skills, etc.

References

Bishop, Sue, David Taylor, *Training for Change,* Viva Books Private Limited, New Delhi, (1995).

Burnard, Philip, *Interpersonal Skills Training,* Viva Books Private Limited, New Delhi, (1995).

Debendra K. Das, *'Dynamics of Rural Development : Potential and Constraints,* Deep & Deep Publications, New Delhi, (1999).

Elizatet, M, Christopher and Larry E. Smita, *Leadership Training,* Viva Book Private Limited, New Delhi, (1995).

Khadi Gramodyog, The Journal of Rural Economy, Published by Khadi & Village Industries Commission, Bombay, Vol. XXXIII, No.1, October 1986.

Philip Burnard, *Counselling Skills Training,* Viva Books Private Limited, New Delhi, (1995).

Ramaswami, N., IRPS (Retd.), *A Handbook of Training and Development,* T.R. Publications, (1992).

Thorne, Kaye, Alex Machray, *World Class Training*, Kogan Page, London (2000).

Turner, David, *Role Plays,* Viva Books Private Limited, New Delhi, (1995).

11

EDUCATION AND TRAINING NEEDS OF THE RURAL POPULATION

— *M. Senthil* and *R. Mahesh*

Various government departments are responding to market demands very quickly. To name a few: Department of Telecommunication, Indian Airlines, Indian Railways, Department of Posts, etc. The focus here is the working of post office especially the Post Office Savings Bank (POSB).

The Post office will be the country's largest bank, both in terms of the number of branches and volume of deposits. The figures are startling enough now. Under its various savings schemes, the post office, which has 155,000 branches, has 115 million accounts with Rs. 1,80,000 crore in deposits. Contrast this with the country's largest bank. At Rs. 1,69,000 crore, SBI's (State Bank of India) deposit base is only slightly short of the post office's, but it has only 8,888 branches not even a fifteenth the size across the country. In fact, all the commercial banks put together have less than half (77,000 branches).

With 1,38,000 of these post offices in rural areas, the infrastructure is already in place. It is only a question of using it to optimum advantage.

The government has appointed a committee to restructure the operations of the post office savings bank. The committee's broad terms of reference: prepared a blueprint to convert the country's vast postal network into its largest modern bank — a bank that could offer services like postal girl, electronic money transfer, online electronic banking, debit cards and ATMs, and perhaps, even sell shares and mutual funds through its network.

As of now, the POSB in much like an agency attached to the Finance Ministry. The money it raises through various operations is passed on to the Finance Ministry, which pays the post office 1.7 per cent of the money as a collection fee. In turn, the Ministry lends 75 per cent of the money to State governments. The POSB manages various saving schemes — National Savings Certificate, Public Provident Fund, Kisan Vikas Patra, savings accounts, monthly income schemes and time deposits on the government's behalf. That is the end of POSB's role today.

POSB'S in other Countries

The Committee appointed KPMG as the external consultant. To find out what the POSB of tomorrow could look like, the committee studied POSB structure around the world. The largest POSB that is existing worldwide is in Japan and is also the world's largest bank. In fact, it was because most Japanese has enstrusted their savings to the post office that Japan was not hit by the huge financial sector bankruptcies that plagued most of south-east Asia during the not-so-distant meltdown. There's also the European model, where the Post Bank is usually a separate company allied with a commercial bank. While the commercial bank handles product development and asset management, the post office manages distribution and collection.

Futuristic Plan

The preview of POSB in India will be concentrated on: Electronic money transfer, Postal giro, Stocks and Mutual funds, Banking Services, Lending business.

Electronics money transfer : The post office is in the process of typing up with Western Union Financial Services International to offer electronic money transfer from anywhere in the world within 15 minutes. Western Union already has a tie-up for money transfer with 15 banks in the country, but again, the huge post office branch network makes it an ideal partner.

However, for this to happen, the post office's branches will have to be computerised and come on line. The drive is already on: 77 VSATs have been installed. These VSATs handle 1.5 million transactions, and have cut down the transmission time for money orders by about a week to 10 days, even as costs are down from Rs. 32 an order to Rs. 11. So far 271 branches have been computerised, and the number is expected to touch 848 by December 2001. The target for 2004 is 15,000. Amazing when you realise that no Indian Bank has 271 on line branches.

Postal Giro : The POSB is expected to provide a postal giro system to customers, offering them a simple and reliable facility for credit and debit.

In addition, institution like the department of telecommunications (DOT) could use postal giro accounts as bill payment centres; it need not then tie up with various banks across the country, Ditto with electricity bills.

Stock and Mutual Funds : The post office also wants to become the country's largest stock broker and mutual fund agent. Both these activities are primarily confined to the urban centres, as they are constrained by the lack of the distribution channels. Thanks to the post office's immense distribution potential, capital market activities could finally filter down to rural and semi-urban areas. The Internet would allow the post office to function as a countrywide broker, and the existing five lakh agents could deliver and collect mutual fund and stock application forms even in far-flung areas. In fact, the POSB is finalising a tie-up with a mutual fund to market its products across the country.

Banking Services : Then there are the benefit of online electronic banking with post offices. You would be able to operate your bank account at 155,000 banks across the country. Already, a window banking software, Sanchay Post, has been installed in 271 branches. Imagine 155,000 ATMs across the country with such a huge network of ATMS, wouldn't you prefer to bank with the post office, especially if your ATM card doubles up as a credit or debit card? Of course you would, and that's exactly what this grand plan is banking on.

Lending Business : Another big first, the post office also intends to get into lending. The huge post office database on people is leading Dak Bhawan bureaucrats to believe they can assess credit risk between than most banks when it come to rural lending. That's also where micro-credit comes in at the post office.

Training the Employees

It is true that today's population per square area has gone up from the past. But, recollect when you have written a letter last to your friend or relative? We bank more on telecom services like Phones, Internet, Fax etc. and courier services now-a-days. Mails through the Department of Posts have come down drastically. Even though, a post office today serves a higher population, the volume of transaction in real terms has come down.

This was realised by the government which resulted in no fresh recruitment since 1984. In spite of this, the membership of the National Federation of Postal Employees, which is the apex postal union, is six lakhs. Though every village of the country is networked through them, they have to be trained in the frontier areas of new services that are planned to be offered. Many employees in the rural area need to be exposed to the latest trend in technology, the corporate decides to bring in. For instance, it may be computers or ATMs or Internet services. If plan is there to offer uniform services in all parts of the country — whether urban or rural, then the training requirements will be very heavy and put tremendous strain on the financial front of the department.

Educating the Masses

For the POSB to be successful in the new *avtar*, the support of the rural masses is very important. Of course, today POSB enjoys the confidence for certain services that are offered. But when the new services like Postal giro, Stock and Mutual funds operation, e-money transfer and Banking services are offered, involvement of the POSB employees and their agents will be of very high order in educating the masses.

Rural population, in some areas have lot of disposable income, as agricultural income is not taxed. This potential can be tapped and corresponding required services offered. Zonation — identifying zones with different disposable income patterns — may be resorted to and correct positioning of services will lever the operations of the POSB in its new *avtar*.

Retraining

Unions in the department is strong but realised the importance and urgent need to expand their operations for their own survival. Similar situation was prevailing at Department of Telecommunication and the transition was smooth which was due to tactful handling of the issue.

For better working of POSB in the future, the culture has to undergo drastic change — from the department to corporate. The POSB employees so far involved only in collection of fixed deposit and operated savings bank accounts. The ambitious plan for the future requires them to perform all the functions of a commercial bank. This requires lot of financial burden on a loss-making organisation.

Conclusion

The postal services in the country, is slowly losing its grip over the society today compared to that of the past. The department has a numerous unmeasurable strength using which it connects one billion population with any difficulty. Now, it is time the department takes New *Avtar.* With the much needed change in the working culture, the POSB services can serve rural population in a better way, thereby bringing down the gap between the urban and rural India.

12

INDIAN SUGAR INDUSTRY DURING LIBERALISATION ERA

— *M. Soundarapandian* and *R. Jagadeswaran*

Introduction

With increasing population and urbanization, sugar consumption in India has been increasing from year to year. In order to meet the sugar requirements of the country, the Government of India adopts a policy of preferential licensing for sugar industry. With the help of Government assistance, private, public and co-operative sectors have started a large number of sugar mills throughout the country. The total investment in sugar industry has also increased considerably.

The sugar industry in India is one of the important agro-based industries occupying a pre-eminent position in the economy of the country. It ranks second among the agro-industries. Next to textiles it is the biggest industry employing 3.7 lakh workers and sustaining about 3.9 crore agriculturists who are engaged in the production of sugarcane. India is the original home of the sugarcane. It is also an important source of excise duty for the Central Government.

India's growth on sugarcane and sugar production has shown a spectacular increase in the recent years and the industry has come to occupy an important place among the foreign exchange earners of the country.

The main sugar production States in India are Uttar Pradesh, Bihar, Maharashtra, Karnataka, Andhra Pradesh and Tamil Nadu. The number of sugar factories in India has increased considerably. India is having 464 factories were installed up to 1997-98 seasons and sugar output of 12.9 million tonnes with installed capacity of 12 million tonnes. In 1997-98 about 416 sugar factories were in operation of which 229 were in co-operative sector, 127 were in the private sector and 60 were in the public sectors.

Sugar Factories in India

In 1950-51, the number of factories in India was 139, which has increased to 215 in 1969-70. It rose to 385 in 1989-90 and it has further risen to 416 factories in 1997-98. Table 12.1 represents the yearwise number of sugar factories in India.

Table 12.1 : Sugar Factories in Operation in India

Year	No. of Sugar Factories
1986-87	353
1987-88	356
1988-89	366
1989-90	377
1990-91	382
1991-92	392
1992-93	393
1993-94	394
1994-95	408
1995-96	412
1996-97	412
1997-98	416

Source : Kisan World, 2000.

Sugar Industry in India occupies a place of pride. In India there are as much as 416 sugar factories. In the First Five Year Plan, there were only 139 sugar mills, 174 in the Second Plan, 215 in the Third Plan and 416 in the Ninth Plan. 127 sugar factories in the private sector, 229 in co-operative sector and 60 in the public sector are at present operating in an economy.

The fluctuations in area and sugarcane production in the recent times are due to deviations in the actual rainfall, variations in production are also associated with variations in yield stemming from adoption of seed, fertilizer and technology. Moreover, the steady increase in consumption and the price of sugarcane paid to the farmers also significantly determine the production of sugar. The recent sugar crisis was caused by the shortfall in production in the main sugar production areas, delay in the payment of arrears to the farmers and the underestimation of the sugar requirements by the Government.

Government has introduced policies to promote the production of sugarcane. These policies related to development of new varieties and pesticides special programmes such as extension of area, institutional arrangements for production marketing provision of credit and insurance policies have initiated to strengthen the facilities for increasing sugar production.

This study attempts to explain the number of factories, area under cultivation, yield per hectare, sugarcane production, cane crushed, sugar production and the price of sugar in India. It also examines the problems faced by the sugar industry in the economy.

This chapter attempts to study the structure and trends of the sugar industry growth, of sugarcane production, sugar production, yield, areas under sugarcane and number of sugar factories and to study the problem faced by the sugar industry in India.

The study has covered a period of 12 years from 1986-87 to 1997-98. This would enable the researcher to examine whether the growth path of sugar industry with regard to Statewise number of factories, area under cultivation, yield per hectare, cane crushed, sugarcane production, price of sugar per unit.

This study is based on secondary data covering a period of 12 years from 1986-87 to 1997-98. The main sources of data are seasonal and crop reports. Tamil Nadu — An Economic Appraisal published by the Government of Tamil Nadu reports of the Directorate of Sugar, Indian Sugar Mills Association (ISMA), South Indian Sugar Mills Association (SISMA) and the Directorate of

Statistics. Data have also been collected from Indian Sugar Yearbook and from the journal of cooperative sugar etc.

Table 12.2 reveals that the installed sugar factories statewise and sectorwise as on 1997-1998.

Table 12.2 : Statewise and Sectorwise Installed Sugar Factories in 1997-98

S. No.	State	Co-operative	Private	Public	Total
1.	Andhra Pradesh	18	17	6	41
2.	Bihar	—	14	14	28
3.	Gujarat	20	—	—	20
4.	Haryana	10	3	—	20
5.	Karnataka	19	10	3	32
6.	Maharashtra	115	5	—	120
7.	Punjab	16	6	—	22
8.	Tamil Nadu	15	17	3	35
9.	Uttar Pradesh	32	55	35	122
10.	Other States	13	14	4	31
	India	258	141	65	464

Source : Directorate of Sugar.

India is expected to rise its supply mostly to 13.95 million tonnes and consumption forecast in 1999 was 15.80 million tonnes. Even though it has marked a record for three years from 1996-1997 to 1998-99, the total production of sugar during 1998-99 season was only 12 million tonnes.

India enters the world market only during years of surplus production and thereby bring down the prices in the world market. Likewise it seeks to import sugar from the world market during years of shortages. Along with the creation of a buffer stock of the magnitude of 10 lakh tonnes, the Government should adopt a policy of exporting a minimum of 5 lakh tonnes each year.

The sugar industry has a long and successful history and helped the country to emerge as the leading producer of sugarcane and sugar in the world. A bumper production of over 15 million tonnes of sugar has provided the Government with an excellent opportunity to make a firm decision on the long-felt demand for creating buffer stocks. The industry feels that fully catering to the domestic demand estimated to be 13.3 million tonnes and the Central Government could earmark 1.2 million tonnes for export. The plan period-wise sugarcane and sugar production with installed capacity is given.

Table 12.3 : Sugarcane and Sugar Production with Installed Capacity during the Plan Periods

Plan period	Year (end of plan)	Cane Production (million tonnes)	Installed Capacity (lakh tonnes)	Targeted Sugar production (lakh tonnes)	Actual Production (lakh tonnes)
I Plan	1955-56	72.7	17.8	18.3	18.6
II Plan	1960-61	110.5	24.5	22.9	30.3
III "	1965-66	124.0	32.2	32.4	35.4
IV "	1973-74	140.8	43.1	42.3	39.5
V "	1978-79	151.7	59.1	54.0	58.4
VI "	1984-85	170.3	72.7	75.0	61.6
VII "	1990-91	222.6	98.48	99.0	120.46
VIII "	1995-96	281.1	127.61	126.0	16.29
IX " (up to 1998)	1997-2002	277.0	134.59	121.0	129.05

Source : Indian Sugar Mills Association (ISMA) Yearbook 1998-99.

The above table gives the production of sugarcane and sugar and the annual installed capacity. During the plan periods, the country has witnessed a spectacular increase in these performance indicators upto VIIIth and IXth Five Year Plan has fallen from 164.29 lakh tonnes to 129.55 lakh tonnes.

About 39 million farmers (including their families) constituting about eight per cent of the rural population are engaged in growing sugarcane. The industry absorbs a sizeable portion of the crop and provides the farmers with resources to meet his commitments each sugar factory deals with thousands of cane farmers ranging from 8,000 to 10,000 in the southern States and from 40,000 to 45,000 in northern India.

Table 12.4 : Number of Sugar Factories in Different Sectors in Production

Year	Private/Govt. Sectors	Co-operative	Total
1950-51	137	2	139
1967-68	142	58	200
1972-73	143	85	228
1978-79	163	136	229
1984-85	161	178	339
1990-91	165	220	385
1996-97	183	229	412
1998-99	187	229	416

Source : Kisan World July 1999, p. 24.

In 1950-51 out of 139 sugar factories, only two belonged to the co-operative sector and the balance were in the private sector. The number of co-operative factories rose to 58 out of total of 200. Therefore, it continued to rise steadily out of 416 sugar factories, 229 are in the co-operative and 187 in private sector and public sectors sugar factories establishment over the years.

Table 12.5 : India's Performance in Sugarcane and Sugar Production

Year	Area (lakh hec.)	Production of Sugarcane (lakh tonnes)	Production of yield (t/hec.)	Sugar production (lakh tonnes)
1950-51	1.71	571	33.4	11.3
1960-61	2.41	1100	45.5	30.3
1970-71	2.62	1264	48.3	37.4
1980-81	2.67	1542	57.8	51.5
1990-91	3.69	2411	65.4	120.5
1997-98	3.96	2762	69.6	129.5

Source: *Yojana,* February 28, 1994, p. 6.

Indian Sugar Mills Association (ISMA) Annual Report : 1998-99.

Table 12.6 : India's Performance in Sugarcane and Sugar Production

Year	Production of Cane Lakh Tonnes	Sugar Production Lakh Tonnes
1950-51	571	11.3
1960-61	1100	30.3
1970-71	1264	37.4
1980-81	1542	51.5
1990-91	2411	120.5
1997-98	2762	129.5

Table 12.6 reveals that the sugarcane production which was only 517 lakh tonnes in 1950-51 had increased to 2411 lakh tonnes in 1990-91. The year 1998-99 witnessed a record production of 2762 lakh tonnes and coverage of 396 lakh hectares under sugarcane. There has been continuous increase in sugarcane production during the last decade. However the growth pattern has not been uniform throughout the period. India has made remarkable progress in sugarcane production and sugar production.

Profile of Sugar Industry in India

The number of factories in operation, area under cultivation, yield per hectare, sugarcane production, cane crushing, sugar production, average recovery in per cent, unit cost of sugar per quintal in India for the period from 1986-87 to 1997-98 are given in Table 12.7.

The number of sugar factories in India has increased from 353 in 1986-87 to 416 in 1997-98 were in operation. As far as area under cultivation is concerned, it has increased from 30,800 hectares in 1986-87 to 39,700 hectares in 1997-98. The yield per hectare increased from 60.4 tonnes in 1986-87 to 69.6 tonnes in 1997-98. The cane crushed during 1986-87 was 85.22 lakh tonnes and it has increased to 129.2 lakh tonnes 1997-98. The sugarcane production has increased from 186.1 lakh tonnes in 1986-87 to 276.2 lakh tonnes in 1997-98. The sugar production has increased from 85.01 lakh tonnes in 1986-87 to 129.05 lakh tonnes in 1997-98. The

Table 12.7 : Profile of Sugar Industry in India

Year	Area under cultiva-tion ('000 Hec)	Yeild per hec.in ('000 Ton.)	Sugarcane production ('000 Ton.)	Cane crushing ('000 Ton.)	Sugar production in 1996	Average Recovery in quintals	Unit cost Factori-es	No.of sugar Factories
1986-87	30.79	60.4	186090	85224	8501	—	393.70	353
1987-88	32.74	60.0	196737	93943	9110	9.70	439.21	356
1988-89	33.29	61.0	203037	85693	8752	10.21	440.92	366
1989-90	34.38	65.6	225569	111149	10988	9.89	496.86	377
1990-91	36.86	65.4	241045	122319	12047	9.85	523.88	382
1991-92	38.44	66.1	253995	133987	13404	10.02	577.17	392
1992-93	35.72	63.8	228033	103002	10609	10.31	688.21	393
1993-94	34.22	67.1	229659	98348	9833	10.00	746.06	394
1994-95	38.67	71.3	275540	147643	14643	9.92	813.19	408
1995-96	41.47	67.8	281099	174761	16451	9.42	909.62	412
1996-97	41.74	66.5	277560	130379	12905	9.90	1030.56	412
1997-98	39.67	69.6	276254	129188	12855	9.95	1959.4	416

Source : Indian Sugar Mills Association (ISMA) Yearbook 1998-99.

average recovery during 1986-87 is 9.7 per cent and it increased to 10 per cent in 1997-98. The cost of production (or) price per quintal in the year 1986-87 was 393.7 and it rose to 1050 in the year 1997-98.

Table 12.8 : Capacitywise Sugar Factories Installed in India

	Less than 1250	1250-2500	2500-5000	More than 5000	Total
Government	29	31	7	—	67
Private	18	95	23	6	142
Co-operative	12	213	29	1	255
Total	59	339	59	7	464

In the initial period, the new sugar factories installed small capacities and were below 1000 TCD. The factories completed expansion stages and increased their crushing capacities. New sugar factories were allowed with a capacity of 1250 TCD, defined as the minimum economic capacity. This was increased to 2500 TCD in 1987 onwards.

New Sugar Policy

The new sugar policy has been geared to raise production and productivity levels, particularly in view of the pressing need to export 10 lakh tonnes after meeting increasing home demand. The new policy seeks to raise the distance between factories to 25 km which could be reduced to 15 km provided enough sugarcane is available in the area.

To provide a larger supply of sugarcane, concentrated efforts have been made for increasing the yield per hectare of land and for improving the sucrose content and the same volume of cane would make possible larger production of sugar. To encourage the improvement of the quality, the new policy has laid down that the price of cane would be decided on the basis of sucrose content.

One can only hope that both the groups will now behave differently and co-operate to make the policy a success.

The new policy seeks to completely decline sugar mills from others and it provides for licensing of new units irrespective of cane availability or cane potential.

All expert bodies Gundu Rao Committee (1963), Sen Commission (1965), Tariff Commission (1969-74), Bhargava Commission (1974) and RBI study group on sickness in Sugar Industry (1980) have strongly supports adequate minimum spatial distance between the new and the existing mills.

In fact Bhargava Commission recommended that minimum spatial distance should be kept at 50 km. The RBI Report was in favour of raising it to 60 km. But blatantly ignoring all these recommendations the spatial distance has been drastically kept at 15 km, in the new licensing policy.

The new sugar factories would be licensed for a minimum crushing capacity of 2500 tonnes per day, new licences would be issued on the condition that cane prices would be payable on the basis of the sucrose content of the sugarcane and preference in licensing is to be given to proposals from the co-operative and the public sectors rather than from the private sector.

Both the Indian Sugar Mills Association (ISMA) as well as the National Federation of Co-operative Sugar Factories have represented to the Government as to find the way of a possible reversal of the present policy.

Problems of Sugar Industry in India

The problems of sugar industry can be divided into two groups, viz., external and internal. External problems are those which result from factors beyond the control of the entrepreneurs, while internal problems are those which are not influenced by external forces. These relate to organisational structure, production and distributional channels, technical knowhow, training, industrial relations and inadequacy of management. These two kinds of problems are correlated.

The cane supplies are fairly adequate, the sugar mills could not get their requirements because of diversion of cane to gur and khandsari manufactures with high prices for the two sweetening agents, it is possible for the producers in the unorganised sector to pay attractive prices to the cane growers. Recently, the diversion of cane to gur is very heavy and the mills have crushed a lower quantum of cane.

For sugar industry large capital investments and working capital are required. However, it is observed that there are limitations for the units in the co-operative sector to obtain such huge capital. Private units can raise finance from the general public. Central financing institutions cannot provide finance to the co-operative sector units, in the absence of default guarantee by the State Government.

More than one person to involvement in decision making unlike in the private industries, many times decisions are delayed in the co-operative sector. Professional managers also are in difficulty to obtain for the co-factor.

Cost of production is the another important factor affecting India's sugar industry. In the ever increasing cost of production, which itself is the result of high cost of inputs, inefficient and uneconomic nature of production in the sugar mill. Recently, it has been worked out that prices of sugarcane account for nearly 48 per cent of the cost of sugar followed by the cane seed, sales tax, income tax and excise duties which constitute about 35 per cent of the total cost of production and the labour alone accounts for nearly 151 per cent of the total cost of sugar production.

The problem of byproduct is an important problem of sugar industry i.e., the fuller utilisation of byproducts specially baggase and molasses. At one time, we do not know what to do with the accumulating molasses, a health hazard. At present, small paper plants are coming up to make paper and paper board, packing paper, etc. through using baggase, molasses is now being used for the manufacture of power alcohol, fertilisers, cattle feed, etc. The industry has indeed very bright prospects, as there is abundant supply of raw materials, cheap labour and local market.

References

An Economic Appraisal, Evaluation and Applied Research Department, Madras, 1999.

Datt, Ruddar and Sundaram, K.P.M., *Indian Economy*, S. Chand and Company Ltd., New Delhi, 1999, pp. 609-14.

Development of Sugar Industry, *Kisan World*, December 2000, Vol. 26, No. 7, p. 23.

Economic and Political Weekly, Libralisation under sovereign control, March 11-17, 2000, Vol. XXXV, No. 11, p. 929.

13

AN EVALUATION OF NEW ECONOMIC POLICY ON SSI

— *B. Shyamala*

Small Industries constitute a larger proportion of the industrial sector in India. It accounts for 50 per cent of the industrial production in the country and 80 per cent of the employment. Even with regard to exports SSI is responsible for 24 per cent and considering only non-traditional items, as much as 40 per cent of the total exports. The existence of SSI is justified by the fact that they are capital saving and can animate idle resources of labour and managerial talent. It is for these reasons the growth of SSI has been one of the most significant features of planned economic development. During the last three decades this sector has shown consistent growth rate in the sphere of production, employment and exports. In this study a modest attempt has been made to examine the existing state of SSI against the backdrop of the ongoing programmes of economic reforms, globalisation and technological changes.

This chapter is devoted to give an economic assessment of New Economic Policy on SSI sector. The chapter is organised in such a manner that it highlights New Small Enterprise Policy 1991, it analyses the performance of SSI before and after economic reforms, sickness in SSI, SSI in reality, challenges faced by the SSI and finally the promotional measures to improve the efficiency of SSI.

New Small Enterprise Policy, 1991

The primary objective of this policy is to impart more vitality and growth impetus to this sector. The packages are : (1) Ceiling of investment raised to Rs. 5 lakhs from Rs. 2 lakhs, (2) Locational restrictions on setting up of these industries removed, (3) Equity participation by other industrial units in SSI not exceeding 24 per cent of the total share holding, (4) Introduction of new legal form of organisation of business, namely restricted or limited-partnership, (5) Setting up of a monitoring agency to ensure that the genuine credit needs of this sector are fully met; review all regulations, procedures and modifications to ensure their operations, encouraging industry associations, expansion of Entrepreneurship Development Programmes and further liberalisation of schemes of National Equity Fund and Single Window loans.

Performance of SSI before and after New Economic Policy

For clear understanding of the achievement of New Economic Policy in the case of SSI, an attempt is made to have a comparative study of SSI before and after the Economic Reforms of Government of India. The period between 1983-84 to 1990-91 considered as pre-reform period, and the period between 1991-92 to 1998-99 is considered as the post-reform period. The variables chosen are number of units, output, employment and export. Table 13.1 depicts the performance of SSI in the above mentioned period.

The SSI sector is contributing 35.90 per cent to the GCP, 45 per cent to the country's exports and 35 per cent to the total exports. The number of small units rose from 1.15 million in 1983-84 to 1.94 million in 1990-91 (The compound growth rate is 8.44) and from 2.08 million in 1991-92 to 3.12 million in 1998-99 (CGR is 21.22). The output increased from Rs. 4.16 crore in 1983-84 to 15.53 crore in 1990-91 (CGR is 5.94) and further increased from Rs. 17.86 crore in 1991-92 to Rs. 52.75 crore in 1998-99 (CGR is 18.02). The employment increased from 84.2 lakhs in 1983-84 to 125.3 lakhs in 1990-91 (CGR is 19.27) and further increased for 129.8 lakhs in 1991-92 to 171.6 lakhs in 1998-99 (CGR is 12.91).

Table 13.1 : Growth Performance of SSI

Particulars	Pre-reforms period				Post-reform period			
	No. of Units	Out-put	Employ-ment	Export	No. of Units	Out-put	Employ-ment	Export
Compound Growth rate	8.44	5.94	19.27	17.20	21.22	18.02	12.91	15.77
't' value	57.44	79.93	45.16	13.77	76.05	18.35	15.16	11.27
R Square	0.997	0.998	0.995	0.955	0.997	0.998	0.995	0.993
S.E. of Estimate	0.0169	0.0086	0.0467	0.1209	0.1324	0.2795	0.1777	0.2137

The exports rose from Rs. 2350 crore in 1983-84 to Rs. 9664 crore in 1990-91 (CGR is 17.20) and further increased from Rs. 13883 crore in 1991-92 to crore 49481 crore in 1998-99 (CGR is 15.77). From the above analysis it is observed that a tremendous development has taken place in the SSI sector in recent times on account of the Government's policy of promotion of SSI through New Economic Policy.

Sickness in SSI

In spite of encouraging trends in small industry development, sickness has been rampant growing at an alarming rate in recent years. According to the RBI Report on Currency and Finance, the number of sick units in the pre-reform period increased from 78,363 in 1983-84 to 2,18,825 in 1990-91. The percentage change is 64.19. During the post-reform period the number of sick units increased from 2,21,423 in 1991-92 to 2,37,400. The percentage change is 6.73. The magnitude of sickness in SSI is clearly given in Table 13.2.

Table 13.2 : Magnitude of Sickness in SSI

Year	Number of Units (in lakhs)		Outstanding Bank Credit (Rs. in crores)	
	Small Units	Total	Small Units	Total
1980	0.23 (92.0)	0.23	0.31 (17.2)	1.80
1992	2.33 (98.7)	2.36	3.34 (26.2)	12.64
1996	2.62 (98.87)	2.65	3.72 (27.0)	13.74
1997	2.35 (99.16)	2.37	3.60 (26.1)	13.78
1998	2.22 (99.12)	2.34	3.86 (24.8)	15.68

Note : Figures in parentheses indicate percentage to total.
Source : RBI Report, 2000.

It is also observed that though the sickness in SSI accounted for 99 per cent at the end of 1998. Its share in total bank credit outstanding was only 24.8 per cent. In addition to the sharp increased in the number of sick units another serious problem is that a large number of small units are non-viable. For instance of the 2,21,536 sick small units, the commercial banks conducted viability studies in respect of 2,18,320 sick units and found 1,99,634 that is 91.4 per cent as non-viable.

The industrial sickness is attributed both to external factors such as power cut, market decision, erratic availability of inputs. Government policies etc. and internal factors such as problems in production, management and finance. Among these factors Government policy is attributed as more contributory factor because sudden change relating to imports, exports, industrial licensing, taxation etc.

For instance liberal import policy for a particular product can inflict serious on the domestic units producing similar and substitute products because the imported product is cheaper and of good quality. Similarly in the case of granting liberal licences to big industrial houses in the production lines reserved exclusively for the SSI sector is bound to affect the prospects of small units adversely.

The reservation policy is not of much help to the small units. In 1995 out of 836 items 233 were not even manufactured by small units, and over 80 per cent of small units produce just 5 per cent of the reserved items. By 1997 the number of products reserved for small units came down to 822 following the de-reservation of 15 items. Ironically the present system of incentives is used for tax evasion by the large units against whom the small units are seeking protection. The Abid Hussain Committee on SSI rightly felt that neither the investment ceiling nor reservation can guarantee efficiency.

Challenges faced by the SSI Section during Liberalisation

With the liberalisation of the economy the SSI sector is pushed to a peculiar environment to which it was not exposed earlier. So far these industrial units faced less competition, cared little about the product, quality and improved techniques of production and now with the new policy changes there is a threat to this character and the SSI sector is finding it difficult to carve a wayout.

Some of the important challenges that are faced by small units are identified.

(1) In spite of the impetus given to SSI, the industry has not crossed the take-off stage because these small units are not able to come out from the grips of recession which started in 1991. Therefore maintaining the growth rate in production, employment and export is really a challenge faced by SSI.
(2) Under New Economic Policy the SSI has to face a stiff competition both from domestic and international quarters. So meeting the global competition is an added challenge before SSI because so far concentration of these units on quality is very much limited.
(3) Small Units are less efficient in terms of cost, raw material use, production tchnique, marketing and finance. The cost of these units is very high in spite of abundant supply of cheap labour.
(4) The real challenge for these units now is the creation of a separate 'brand image' for itself. The task is gone to be more stupendous with the entry of Multi-national Companies (MNC) on to the Indian scene.

Promotional Measures

The promotional strategy suggested for SSI sector are :

(a) Ban on entry of medium and large units into the manufacture of such products which are reserved for SSI sector.
(b) Excise duty and sales tax exemption/concession.
(c) Government and PSU should make their purchase for SSI sector.
(d) Adequate infrastructure facilities like land and building, technical consultancy, and finance.

(e) Small units can adopt a group approach to ensure efficient management with a view to reduce the cost of production.

The Ninth Plan has recognised that the problem facing the SSI sector and suggested a proper strategy on the following lines: (1) Introducing a 'consortium' concept for consumer items to help SSI units in marketing their product, (2) Providing quality testing facilities, (3) Provision of training upgradation of skills, improvement in tool kit and production techniques, (4) Adopting appropriate policy measures to increase the export earnings, (5) Improving the data base for SSI sector.

To conclude, there are three areas of concern viz, finance, marketing and technology. The small units deserve protection but the future focus on the policy will be on competitiveness rather than protection. The present strategy is to shift to qualitative growth in a competitive environment. Also what is urgently required is a 'hassle-free' environment for small entrepreneurs.

14

FOREIGN TRADE PERFORMANCE DURING LIBERALISATION

— N. Mukundan

Indian Government has taken a lot of initiative measure to enhance the foreign trade. The 'U' turn in economic policy give a lot of significance to export promotion than import substitution, through the liberalisation of foreign trade policy during ninties.

The liberalisation of foreign trade policy is following :

1. Devaluation of domestic currency means of depreciating the currencies of leading industrial countries.
2. Convertibility of domestic currency for trade account and current account transactions.
3. Liberalisation of import regime.
4. Reduction of customs and tariff rates.
5. Decanalisation of many items of trade.
6. Providing heavy demand for exports.

The present study has the following specific objectives :

1. To examine the trends in India's Exports and Imports.
2. To estimate the average and marginal propensities to exports

and Imports.

3. To study the level of Exports and Imports before and after new economic policy.

The present study is based on the secondary data. That data regarding India's export and imports compiled from different publication Bulletins of Reserve Bank and Economic Survey from 1950-51 to 1994-95. The analysis is based on the secondary time — series data for 45 years. Net National product at factor cost is purely and solely based on 1980-81 price.

India's Foreign Trade since Independence

(Rs. crores)

Year	Exports	Imports
1950-51	647	650
1955-56	641	773
1960-61	631	1106
1965-66	783	1250
1970-71	1535	1634
1975-76	4043	5265
1980-81	6711	12524
1985-86	11578	21164
1990-91	35328	27658
1994-95	72806	69547

Source : Bulletins of Reserve Bank Economic Survey, 1999-2000.

Comparison of Exports and Imports before and after New Economic Policy

1. Considerable improvements in export performance between the pre-reform and post-reform period (While eighties cover the period 1980 - 91 to 1990-91, nineties cover the period 1992-93 to 1998-99 as the year 1991-92 is left out being an exceptional year) India's total agriculture and allied exports more than doubled in ninties from 15.4 per cent in 1990-91 to 34.2 per cent in 1998-99. It is the crucial emerging exports

during the nineties. The values of iron ore exports declined and that of primary and semi-finished iron and steel increased manifold. From 2.9 per cent to 11.9 per cent as between the two periods. On an average annual basis, export growth during nineties at 9.8 per cent was higher than that of 8.2 per cent registered during eighties.

In a similar way, the average level of import of manufactured fertilizers during 1992-99 was also higher by 77.7 per cent than that during 1987-91. The increase in the imports of consumption goods was relatively less pronounced (27.3 per cent) with its share dropping from 4.3 per cent during 1987-91 to 3.6 per cent during 1992-99. Among the industry related items, the import of capital goods recorded a relatively sharp rise of 56.9 per cent. The average import growth observed during the nineties at 12.0 per cent remained substantially higher than that of 7.8 per cent recorded during the eighties.

2. The period of nineties can be split into two sub-periods. The first sub-period covering the first-four years following the introduction of reforms, i.e. 1992-93 to 1995-96 and the second sub-period consisting of the subsequent three years (i.e. 1996-97 to 1998-99). During the first sub-period on an average basis, India's exports and imports increased by 15.7 and 17.5 per cent respectively. Which were significant higher than the rates of 8.2 and 7.8 per cent respectively registered during the eighties. However, the average rate of growth of exports and imports slipped to only 2.0 per cent and 4.5 per cent respectively during the second sub-period of the nineties.
3. India's share in world exports, which had declined from 0.52 per cent to 0.47 per cent between 1984 and 1987 improved to 0.53 per cent in 1992. Notwithstanding the slowdown in India's exports growth since 1996, its share in global exports increased to 0.62 per cent in 1997 reflecting the relatively better performance by India in the rest of the world.
4. India's trade GDP ratio showed substantial improvements during the nineties as compared with the eighties. On an

average basis, export GDP increased from 5.0 per cent to 8.2 per cent between eighties and nineties while the import GDP ratio increased from 7.7 per cent to 9.4 per cent.
Over the same period according to the Reserve Bank's report the noticeable improvements in the export-GDP and import - GDP ratios point to the increasing openness of India's foreign trade regime to global trade.

5. Along with the increase in trade-GDP ratio, there has been decline in India's trade deficit-GDP ratio between the two periods. This would be clean from the fact that the difference between export-GDP and import-GDP ratio, on an average basis, declined from 2.7 per cent in the eighties to 1.2 per cent in nineties and import performance was more pronounced during the eighties than in the nineties. Similarly, the export-import ratio increased substantially from 65.1 per cent during the eighties to 87.0 per cent during nineties, on an average basis.

Estimated Results and Discussion

The data are analysed through OLS method. The result of the present investigation is econometrically meaningful from the multiple regression analysis, which are presented and discussed as here-under.

1. Trends in exports and imports were estimated by using the following linear equations:
   (i) E = a + bt
   (ii) I = a + bt

Where,

E	=	Exports (Rs. crores)
I	=	Imports (Rs. crores)
a	=	Intercept, i.e the estimate value of E/I at t = 0
b	=	Regression Co-efficient
t	=	Time series (1... 2..n)

2. The average and marginal propensities to imports and exports were estimated using the following linear equations.

(i) Average propensity of export (ape) = E/Y
(ii) Average propensity to import (api) = I/Y
(iii) E = a + by
(iv) I = a + by
Where,
y = Net national product at factor cost (at 1990-81 prices)
b = Marginal propensity to exports
de / dy = mpe
di / dy = mpi

Table 14.1 : Trends in India's Exports

Period	N	Trend Equation Fitted	Value of r^2
1950 - 51 to 1994 - 95	45	E = 11715.05 + 945.47	0.83
			D.W. = 0.081

* Significant at 5 per cent level.

Table 14.2 : Trends in India's Imports

Period	N	Trend Equation Fitted	Value of r^2
1950 - 51 to 1994 - 95	45	I = 1172 + 1023.9	0.64
			D.W. = 0.1850

* Significant at 1 per cent level.

Table 14.3 : Marginal Propensity to Export

Period	Estimated Equation Mpi	r^2	api	ei
1950 - 51 to 1994-95	E = 11302 + 0.190y*	0.93	0.93	2.85

* Significant at 1 per cent level.

Table 14.4 : Marginal Propensity to Import

Period	Estimated Equation Mpi	r^2	api	ei
1950 - 51 to 1994-95	I = 1567 + 0.264y*	0.88	0.11	2.28

* Significant at 1 per cent level

Table 14.5 : Trends in Exports after Reforms

Exports	=	11302.0 + 0.190 Y* + 30269 D
R^2	=	0.88
$\bar{R}^2$	=	0.88
D.W.	=	0.9272

Table 14.6 : Trends in Imports after Reforms

Imports	=	15607.0 + 0.264Y* + 8968.5D
R^2	=	0.93
$\bar{R}^2$	=	0.94
D.W	=	1.07

The trends in export are presented in Table 14.1 and it indicates the significant increase in values of exports in India. On the average exports rose by about Rs. 945 crores per year. This is indicated by the slope of the least square trend line fitted to the time series data for the period 1951-95. The values of r^2 was 0.83 per cent, shows that 81 per cent, variation in exports in these periods are explained by time.

The trend values of India's imports are given in Table 14.2 and it indicates the significant increasing trend in imports. The annual trend value of imports during 1951-95 exhibited a secular rise by about Rs. 1023 crores per each year. Thus, the exports and imports exhibited significant increasing trends during the last four decades.

The linear regression results of exports function are presented in Table 14.3 and it shows that the regression co-efficient is not only positive but also significant at 1 per cent level. The marginal propensity to exports with respect to national income turns out to be 0.19 per cent during 1951-95. The income elasticity of demand for Exports comes to 2.85 per cent indicating that 1 per cent increase in national income leads to more than 2 per cent increase in exports during 1951-95.

The linear regression results of import functions are presented in Table 14.4. The regression co-efficient of income is positive and significant at 1 per cent level. The marginal propensity to imports with respect to income turns out to be 0.26 per cent during 1951-95. The income elasticity of demand for imports with respect to 2.28 per cent indicates that 1 per cent increase in national income leads to more than 2 per cent increase in imports.

Table 14.5 elicit that 1 per cent change in the national income leads to an increase of 30,269 units of exports. It is due to liberalised trade policy and devaluation of domestic currency.

Table 14.6 reveals that 1 per cent increase in the national income leads to 8968 units increased imports.

Conclusion

The researcher found the study of Impact of New Economic Policy on India's Trade who came to conclusion in the following way.

The real sharp increase in India's exports partly, due to the devaluation of domestic currency, the general improvement of world trade and little improvement in self-reliance in foreign trade and also due to the liberalisation in trade policy. After the post-reform period share of imports of capital goods have hiked upto 33.8 per cent. It helps that indirectly it will boost up the industrialisation of the Indian economy.

References

Datt, Ruddar, Sundaram, K.P.M., *Indian Economy,* New Delhi: S. Chand & Co., 1999.

Deshpande, Ashwini, Prabirijit Sarkar, Structural Adjustment in India, A Critical Assessment, *Economic and Political Weekly,* 1995.

Debes Bhowmik, M., Convertibility, Exchange Rate Behaviour and India's Trade during 1960-61 to 1992-93, *Southern Economist,* 1995.

Kumar, Arun, New Economic Policy, Instability and Policy Ineffectiveness, *Economic and Political Weekly,* 1996.

Kurien, C.T., *Economic Reforms and the People,* New Delhi Madhyam Public, 1996.

Misra, S.K., Puri, V.K., *Indian Economy — Its Development Experience,* New Delhi, Himalaya Publication, 2000.

Narasimha, Maruti, M. and Kasi, Sastri V., Elasticities of Demand for Certain Indian Imports and Exports *Sankhya,* March, 1951.

Panchamuki, V.R., Foreign Trade and Trade Policies, in Uma Kapila (ed), *Indian Economy since Independence,* 1991.

Partibandla, Murali, International Trade and Long-Term Economic Growth, *Economic and Political Weekly,* 1996.

Singh, L.P., Economic Reforms at the Crossroads, *Southern Economist,* 1999. Indian Economy Since 1991, Trade, Price and Exchange Rate Behaviour, *Economic and Political Weekly,* 1995

The Reserve Bank's reports on currency for the year 1998-99.

15

PERFORMANCE APPRAISAL OF GANDHIJI HANDLOOM WEAVERS CO-OPERATIVE PRODUCTION AND SALES SOCIETY, CHINNALAPATTI : An Analysis

— *Samwel Kakuko Lopoyetum*

Introduction

Promotion of socio-economic interest of the weavers through supplying raw materials and arranging proper marketing of goods produced by weavers is the basic premise and basic objectives of the Handloom Co-operative Society. The provision of full employment and promotion of the (quality), standard of living of the weavers will ultimately depend on the effectiveness and efficiency of the society to market the goods and products of the Member weaver's. The market demand for the textile goods/ products has undergone a dynamic and sea-change. The handloom cloth sales in India and overseas depends largely on its quality appeal and utilitarian value.

Handloom weaving being a cottage industry is not in a position to avail the advantages of the large-scale operations as seen in other textile industry. Along with this, the cost of production of handloom cloth is higher than mill/powerloom cloths, for it involves high human skills and specific specialisation. Most of the pre-looming and post-looming activities are done on small scale basis and therefore the high cost of labour gets reflected in the prices of the final products of the handloom textiles. There is a paramount need to introduce cost-effective methods and techniques of production and competitive pricing system.

The Need of the Study

The main objective of weaver's co-operative society is to proliferate the socio-economic lives of the weaving community. In order to meet this object, weaver's co-operative societies have to perform multifarious activities which are multifaceted and complicated by problem concerning with socio-cultural, traditional, political, personal and economical aspects of the weaver members who constitute the core of the weavers organisation. By realising this scenario, since independence greater accord has been given to the development of weavers' societies in all the Five-Year plans of the country.

Privileges and preferences in the National Textile Policy, provision and arrangement for raw materials and other appliances, creating strong infrastructure for better marketing of handloom products besides, paying adequate care on the non-business side of weaver members in general and weavers' co-operatives in particular would ensure success of weavers cooperative in the long-run. What are the activities undertaken by weavers' co-operative societies? How do they perform their operations? What are the problems with regard to production and marketing of handloom products and goods plus such other questions need field study and an indepth performance appraisal, hence the present study.

Objectives

The specific objectives of the study are :

* To study, the size and composition of the capital structure of the society;

* To analyse its performance in terms of production and sales operations of the weavers' society;
* To study the welfare schemes implemented by the weavers' society; and
* To offer suitable and practical suggestions to the weavers' society.

The society was registered under the Tamil Nadu Co-operative Society Act, 1983 (Act 30 of 1983). The society was registered on 7-12-1973 and started its operations on 12-12-1973.

The present study deals with the performance appraisal with reference to selected indicators applied suitably. The society was selected purposively. Subsequently, Chinnalapatti is a fast growing commercial centre famous and popular for art silk, cotton, handloom fabrics, textiles and its handloom weavers' communities. The area of operation of the society is confined to Chinnalapatti entire Town Panchayat and Kalikkampatti village which is approximately 4 km. from the centre.

Objects of the Weavers' Society

The objects of the Gandhiji Handloom Weavers' Co-operative Production and Sales Society Ltd. are

1. The principal object of the society is to improve the handloom industry and economic conditions of the weavers residing in the area of operation;
2. To purchase such required raw materials/appliances as may be required for handloom industry and rented the same either in cash or credit to the members residing in these places;
3. To purchase yarn and other raw materials and advance the same to weavers' members who shall convert them into finished goods and deliver them to the society and to pay wages for such conversion and to arrange marketing of the finished goods to the best advantage of the society;
4. To purchase and hold on common or let on hire improved appliances in connection with the industry.

Membership

The membership of the Weavers' Co-operative is made of individual membership and government. The members are made up of weavers. The position of the membership is indicated in Table 15.1. Membership indicated a mixed picture and trend. It recorded a negative compound growth rate of – 2.45 per cent during 1998-99 due to occupational shifts.

Table 15.1 : Membership Position and Share involved

S. No.	Co.op. Year	No. of members	Shares involved	Percentage Increase/decrease
1.	1994-95	274	16629	—
2.	1995-96	236	17418	4.74
3.	1996-97	244	17374	-0.26
4.	1997-98	236	17418	0.25
5.	1998-99	241	17425	0.04

Source : Office Records of the Society, 1999.

Share Capital Position

The authorised share capital of the society shall be Rs. 5,00,000 consisting of 5000 shares of Rs. 100 each. The paid-up share capital is made up of individual share capital and Government Share Capital. The position of share capital of the weavers' society is presented in Table 15.2.

Table 15.2 : Share Capital (in Rs.)

S. No.	Co.op. Year	Shares Capital (in Rs.)	Percentage Increase/decrease
1.	1994-95	1,84,440	—
2.	1995-96	2,66,340	44.40
3.	1996-97	72,000	-269.91
4.	1997-98	2,66,340	72.96
5.	1998-99	2,66,960	0.23

Source : Office Records of the Society, 1999.

From Table 15.2, the total share capital postition increased year after year except during 1996-97 which recorded Rs. 72,000 with percentage decrease of — 269.91. The share capital registered compound growth rate of 7.64 per cent due to admission of new members to the society.

Sources of Funds

The funds of the society shall comprise of (a) share subscriptions; (b) Borrowings from State Government, Financing Bank or other Co-operative Institutions by way of loans and advances; (c) Deposits, entrance fees and other fees, donations, gifts, grants, subsidies or other benefits as approved by the Registrar; (d) Other miscellaneous receipts.

Deposits

The Weavers' Society collects the deposits in the form of savings, deposits and thrift deposits. The deposits collected are thrift deposits under Savings Deposits Scheme, Security deposits, Members thrift deposits, Members S.S. Fund, Government S.S. Fund, Staff Security deposits, Employees P.F., house and members' contributions. The position of deposits is indicated in Table 15.3.

Table 15.3 : Deposits

S. No.	Co-op. Year	Deposit amount (in Rs.)	Percentage increase/ decrease
1.	1996-97	13,73,151.68	—
2.	1997-98	17,43,601.15	21.24
3.	1998-99	21,62,298.55	19.36

Source : Office Records of the Society, 1999.

From Table 15.3 the deposits showed increasing trend year after year inculcating the habit of thrift and savings among members.

The deposits at the discretion of the board can be received at any time from members and non-members. Deposits from members shall be given preferences to deposits from non-members. The Board of Directors has to frame regulations for accepting such class of deposits approved by the Registrar of Co-operative Society.

Statistics of Borrowings

The Weavers' Society borrows funds from the Dindigul District Central Co-operative Bank, Cash Certificate, advance from Dindigul DCCB, borrow funds from HUDCO, gets loans from Government. The status of borrowings is indicated in Table 15.4.

Table 15.4 : Borrowing Status

S. No.	Co-op. Year	Borrowings (in Rs.)	Percentage increase/ decrease
1.	1995-96	49,62,893.67	—
2.	1996-97	49,62,893.67	—
3.	1997-98	43,81,529.67	11.71
4.	1998-99	43,20,360.00	1.41

Source : Office Records of the Society, 1999.

The status of borrowings in Weavers' Co-operative Society was constant in the first-two years and less in the last two years.

The Working Capital Position

The working capital postition of the society is presented in Table 15.5.

Table 15.5 : Working Capital Position (in Rs.)

S. No.	Co-op. Year	Working Capital (in Rs.)	Percentage increase/ decrease
1.	1994-95	41,11,003.07	—
2.	1995-96	38,37,621.05	-7.12
3.	1996-97	53,98,906.40	40.68
4.	1997-98	64,36,791.22	19.22
5.	1998-99	68,04,599.55	5.71

Source : Office Records of the Society, 1999.

The working capital (W.C.) position of the society showed increasing trend for the past half-decade, however, there was a decrease of 5.71 per cent in 1998-99.

Reserve Fund

The Reserve Fund (R.F.) shall belong to the society as a whole and is intended to meet unforeseen losses. It shall be indivisible and no member shall have any claim to a share in it. It may be drawn upon with special sanction of the Registrar to meet unforeseen losses. The Reserve Fund (R.F.) position of the weavers' society is shown in Table 15.6.

Table 15.6 : Reserve Fund Position

S. No.	Co-op. Year	Reserve Fund (in Rs.)	Percentage increase/ decrease
1.	1994-95	2,06,054.88	—
2.	1995-96	3,10,683.56	33.67
3.	1996-97	3,01,596.28	-2.92
4.	1997-98	3,22,602.40	6.96
5.	1998-99	33,427.96	-89.63

Source : Office Records of the Society, 1999.

The Reserve Funds of the society shows a mixed trend within a half-decade. The Reserve Fund has been invested in the National Savings Certificate.

Cash Credit Facilities

The Weavers' Co-operative Society received the cash credit facilities from the Central Bank. The status of the cash credit is shown in Table 15.7. There was a reduction of the C.C. during 1997-98 and 1998-99.

Table 15.7 : Cash Credit

S. No.	Co-op. Year	Cash Credit (in Rs.)	Percentage increase/ decrease
1.	1994-95	28,09,350.40	—
2.	1995-96	35,16,000	20.10
3.	1996-97	35,65,000	1.39
4.	1997-98	33,00,000	- 7.43
5.	1998-99	32.9 (lakhs)	- 0.30

Source : Office Records of the Society, 1999.

Rebates

The Government Rebate as on 31-3-99 is indicated in Table 15.8. There was substantial amount of rebate given to the society by the Government in wholesaling and retailing operations.

Table 15.8 : Rebate

S. No.	Particulars	Amount (in Rs.)
1.	Society Rebate	
	(a) Wholesale	5,95,754
	(b) Retail	3,25,199
2.	HDC Rebate	
	(a) Wholesale	61,061
	(b) Retail	1,47,104
3.	Co-optex rebate	48,140
	Total	11,77,258

Source : Office Records of the Society, 1999.

The Co-optex supply yarns to the weavers' society whereas the society provides/gives 75 per cent of the products/goods to the Co-optex and the rest are sold locally.

Investments of the Society

After election of the BOD was conducted and assuming charge on

31-10-96, the investment performance has never improved in the weavers' society. Instead dwindled year after year. What does this portray and means to the weavers society? Further probe in this respect is certainly needed. The society reduced investments by large margin as seen in Table 15.9.

Table 15.9 : Investment Position

Sl. No.	Co-op. Year	Investment (in Rs.)
1.	1996-97	11,00,243.90
2.	1997-98	8,52,516.20
3.	1998-99	4,57,045.05

Source : Office Records of the Society, 1999.

Details of Wages given to Weavers

The wages given to the member weavers shows a fluctuating trend over a period of years. Further, it may be observed that majority of the weavers annual wages were between Rs. 6000 and Rs. 9000. The total wages given by the society rose from Rs. 16.38 lakhs in 1994-95 to Rs. 26.57 lakhs, in 1998-99 registering a compound growth rate of 10.16 per cent.

Stock Worth Position

The stock worth position of the society has declined from Rs. 34,862 in 1994-95 to Rs. 17,809. Thus, it may be stated that the society has made proper arrangements for marketing of its finished products, hence less stockpiles.

Production and Sales

Procurement of Yarn

The procurement of yarn made by the society shows fluctuating trend which stood at Rs. 41.35 lakhs registering a compound growth rate of 5.57 per cent. Further, in the year 1996-97 and 1997-98 purchase of yarn made by society was very low due to the withdrawal of membership from the society.

Processing Activities

The expenses incurred in processing activities shows a decreasing trend over the period under review. Further, the expenses incurred for the prelooming and post-looming activities declined in the year 1996-97 and 1997-98.

Production Details

Of the total production value, the proportion of production of polyester shirts formed the highest value in all the years. The production of cotton sarees shows decreasing trend due to less demand in the market. Further, the society started production of dhoties from 1996-97 onwards which shows increased trend as there was greater demand of dhoties in the market.

The sales performance of the society decreased from Rs. 52.92 lakhs in 1994-95 to Rs. 21.74 lakhs in 1998-99. Of the total sales made by the society, shirts formed the highest value as compared to dhoties and sarees.

Welfare Schemes

Savings and Security Scheme

Of the total amount of savings and security, government contribution was high in all the years compared to members' contribution. Further, the amount spent under savings and security scheme has increased from Rs. 7.60 lakhs in 1994-95 to Rs. 14.73 lakhs in 1998-99, which is a good sign of progress.

Weavers Pension Scheme

The amount given by the society under pension scheme has

increased from Rs. 4407, in 1994-95 to Rs. 8429 in 1998-99. Thus, it can be observed that very small portion of the members got benefited under pension scheme.

Weavers Housing Scheme

The society has been providing loans under housing schemes for both scattered and group houses to weaver members. The society spent major portion of its funds to construct group houses than scattered houses. Further, the amount spent under housing scheme declined from Rs. 7.52 lakhs in 1994-95 to Rs. 5.88 lakhs in 1998-99.

Share Capital Loan

The share capital loan provided by the society reduced from Rs. 2,750 in 1994-95 to Rs. 619 in 1997-98 and the society did not provide share capital loan in the year 1997-98 due to non-repayment of loan by the loanee members.

Quality Dyeing Centre and Handloom Development Centre

The society spent money for the development of quality dyeing centre and handloom development centre which increased from Rs. 8.80 lakhs in 1995-96 to Rs. 10.47 lakhs in 1998-99.

Health Packaging Scheme

The society introduced health package scheme from 1997-98. The society spent money under health package scheme amounting to Rs. 1 lakh each in the year 1997-98 and 1998-99.

Looms and Average Weaving Capacity

The average weaving capacity of each loom was 150 per month. The wages paid by the society is within the local rates. The society arrange for production by giving yarn to members and taking back the finished goods after paying wages to the weavers. The finished goods/products are sold to the TNHWCS by retail sales. The demaged goods are sold out at less than the cost price with the admission sanctioned by higher authorities. During 1998-99, the total number of looms were 3500. The weavers society looms were 240, HDC looms were 154 and the total number doing work were 150 (Society) and 55 (HDC). The idle looms were 90 and 99 in the case of HDC. There is an urgent need to revitalise and re-operate the idle looms, at the same time reduce the quantity of demaged products/goods to avoid losses to the weavers society.

Funds and Subsidies

A number of subsidies are given by the Government to the Weavers Co-operative Society. Some of the subsidies are: (a) Health Package Schemes; (b) Project Package Subsidy; (c) DRDA funds for the work-shed; (d) Margin Money; (e) Quality Dyeing Centre Funds; (f) Handloom Development Centre. Unfortunately, all these subsidies given by the government do not reach the beneficiaries directly and wholly. By the time, they (weavers) get the subsidy, the entire amounts have been splitted and misused by the so-called "Co-operative, Administrative Authorities". This matter needs to be looked into in a very critical and application of logical ways to obtain lasting remedial measures. The funds and subsidies position of the weavers society for the last two years is presented in Table 15.10 which indicates a quantum jump upto Rs. 18,55,000 in 1998-99.

Table 15.10 : Funds and Subsidies

S. No.	Co-op. Year	Funds and Subsidies (in Rs.)
1.	1997-98	13,88,600
2.	1998-99	18,55,000

Source : Office Records of the Society, 1999.

The Summary Status of Production Charges, Trade Charges, Sales Purchase and Trade Income

The purchases of the weavers society involves, polyester yarn, 80s yarn, Kora yarn, Jari, drill yarn, 60s yarn, art silk, finished goods from other societies and finished goods from HDC. Table 15.11 indicates the clear summary position of the transaction for three years.

Table 15.11 : Summary of Transactions

S. No.	Particulars	1996-97	1997-98	1998-99
1.	Production charges	1,70,256	14,75,877	31,49,892
2.	Trade charges	1,24,186	1,66,516	2,35,515
3.	Sales	45,85,510	42,30,924	1,17,03,137
4.	Trade Income	N.A.	10,475	N.A.

Source : Office Records of the Society, 1999.

Members' Loans and Advances

The amount of loans sanctioned for urgent purchase amounts to a maximum of Rs. 2,000 for purposes such as marriages, confinement expenses, funeral expenses, house repairs on surety basis. The loans are given to weavers' members of the society. The interest loans charged by the society to its members shall be 12 per cent per annum. The loans are secured on the joint and several responsibilities of members, or the borrower or one or two other weavers standing sureties for him provided the total amount for which a member can stand surety does not exceed 5 times his paid-up share capital whichever is less.

Recovery

The society can recover the loans on 10 monthly instalments within the period fixed for the loan. The members' loans and advances decreased for the last three years as seen in Table 15.12.

Table 15.12 : Loans and Advances

S. No.	Co.op. year	Loans and advances (in Rs.)
1.	1996-97	9,11,933.60
2.	1997-98	8,58,352.60
3.	1998-99	8,73,934

Profitability

The weavers society earned and sustained contiunous profit for the last five years under discussion. In Table 15.13, the profit position of the weavers' society decreased from Rs. 2,40,496 in 1995-96 to Rs. 57,083 in 1996-97 (–76.47). The decrease in profitability was due to increase in production and sales cost per unit of product. Further, the sales volume of the society was very low from 1996-97 to 1998-99.

Table 15.13 : Position of Profit earned

S. No.	Co-op. Year	Profit (in Rs.)	Percentage increase/ decrease
1.	1994-95	1,36,714.44	—
2.	1995-96	2,40,496.96	76.47
3.	1996-97	57,083.12	–76.47
4.	1997-98	45,801.50	–24.63
5.	1998-99	55,843.81	21.92

Source : Office Records of the Society, 1999.

Disposal of Net Profit

The procedures followed in the disposal of the profit by the weavers society are inscribed in the bye-laws of the society. Three per cent go to Co-operator Research and Development Fund; two per cent to co-operative Education fund the society pays honorarium to the Members of the Board, including President and Vice President, Dividend on shares is paid to members at a rate not exceeding 14 per cent per annum on the paid-up value of each share.

Promotion of Export of Handloom Products

By producing high quality handloom products, there is easy chance of exportation strategies in the Handloom Industry. The existence of Tamil Nadu Handlooms and Textile Directorate hoping to start an export promotion interaction centre to develop and promote export of handloom products would likewise encourage and improve handloom quality and add-value to the products. The Government has proposed to export at least Rs. 100 crores worth of handloom products/goods through the co-operative weavers societies. The weavers societies should produce quality products that suited the tastes and preferences of the foreign consumers. This would require the upgradation and modernisation of the looms apart from creating awareness among the weavers co-operative society.

Future Planning Strategies of the Weavers Society

The society intends to work on the following projects in the future:

(a) Opening up of new stores and sale points at Coimbatore in the Saibaba Colony area;
(b) The society is planning to install computerisation processes in the future. This will help and speed up the accounting procedures/processes.
(c) The weavers society are planning to improve and raise the quality of their products in order to match up with the cut-throat competition in the Textiles Industry.
(d) The society is planning to open up ways and means of pursuing exportation of the handloom products and by obtaining export orders/issues from overseas in the future.

Findings and Suggestions

1. The records of the weavers' society shows inherent weaknesses

in investments strategies adopted by the Board of Directors/ Management.

2. Unfortunately, the society is facing rampant and improper issuing of the "Government given subsidies to the weavers. They should target the right kind of beneficiaries and prepare accurate subsidies planning suchedules in a transparent manner.
3. Membership should be enlarged and improved by having comprehensive recruitment drive through co-operative extension education programmes.
4. The weavers society is presently having some agency showrooms at Luz corner, Chennai, Kurinjipadi, Co-optex Handloom Complex Shop No. 30, Egmore Chennai and Handloom Co-operative Marketing Complex, Pondicherry. These agencies should be strengthened and expanded to cater to the emerging needs of the weavers' members and consumers by adopting the latest modern marketing strategies and techniques.
5. The average weaving capacity should be increased and the overall efficiency of the looms to be streamlined.
6. The society should reduce the quantity of demaged/defective products or goods, because it fetches less than the cost price, hence loss to the weavers society.
7. The quality and value of the products must be improved from time to time. Keeping in mind, the competitive environment prevailing in the fabrics and textiles markets.
8. The society receives payment on elapsing of 4-6 months from Co-optex, Chennai, hence the payments are frequently delayed and the interest amount is lost. The society sells 75 per cent of the products or goods to the Co-optex and the remaining products or goods are sold locally;
9. The weavers, society should reduce production charges to enable them earn much higher income profit margin in the long run.
10. The finished products should have proper quality finish, design and patterns suited to the tastes of the ultimate consumers. The adoption of scientific and appropriate product strategy is the

need of the hour particularly in this era of liberalisation, privatisation and globalisation.

11. The saleability of the handloom weavers' society products are affected by the pricing strategy of the handloom fabrics, therefore, the Co-optex should adopt stable and sustainable pricing mechanisms, hence re-invigorates the handloom industry.
12. The society should further reduce the stockpiles position. They should improve the non-business and welfare schemes of the weaver members such as the savings and security scheme, weavers pension schemes, weavers housing scheme, share capital loan and health packaging schemes.
13. The quality of handloom fabrics should be improved scientifically whereas the distribution system and inventory management strategy should be streamlined at the weavers' society level and State level.
14. The handlooms fabrics enjoy seasonal demand, therefore, the information on the products, features, product price, the advantages, the places where they are stored and kept for sale to the consumers should unambiguously be communicated to the prospective consumers by promotional strategies through cable, TV advertisement, radio and newspapers. This shall resolve the problems of dead stock and unnecessary accumulation of handloom fabrics in the stores. Therefore, there is a need for integrated marketing strategies both at the production point and marketing phases of the weavers co-operative society and State level.

Summary and Conclusion

The Gandhiji Handloom Weavers Co-operative Society should adopt appropriate and modern marketing strategies, improve the quality and value of the products, pre-loom and post-loom operations must be updated and professionalised. The performance of the society is satisfactory and stable in terms of its capital structure, production and marketing, profitability and sales transactions. This society has been earning profit continuously from its inception. However, the society has provided continuous employment opprotunity of its members and implementing almost all the welfare schemes announced and pronounced by the government. Competitive pricing methods and marketing diversification/segmentations are highly imperative, particularly in the prevailing new commercial and economic order.

16

EXPORT PROMOTION IN HANDLOOM INDUSTRY : A Case Study of Handloom Export Promotion Council, Chennai

— *N. Thillinayagam* and *P. Muruganandan*

Introduction

The Handloom Export Promotion Council was set up in the year 1965 with prime objective of promoting exports of handwoven products of cotton as well as silk and readymade garments with the increase in the quantum of exports, the Council at present caters only to the exporters of cotton handloom fabrics and made-up, lungies and real Madras handkerchiefs and other items made from cotton handloom fabrics.

The Council has its head office at Chennai, its Regional Office at New Delhi and one-man office at Mumbai. The Council is governed by a committee consisting of elected representatives from the trade, ex-officio members and government officials.

The Council which started as an infant in 1965 with only 96 members has grown over the years to cover the entire country with a membership of about 1600 members. A special mention should be made here about the leap in the quantum of exports from a mere

Rs. 11 crores in 1965-66 to Rs. 1800 crores in 1997-98. This is due to the efforts taken by the Council for promoting exports. Merely 7000 million metres of cloth have been produced annually by the industry of which 10 per cent to 15 per cent is exported to over 100 countries. Two-thirds of our exports are to the European Union and U.S.A.

The following are the activities of the Council :

1. Dissemination of trade information and intelligence.
2. Publicity abroad for Indian handloom products.
3. Facilitating product diversification and adaptation to meet modern market requirements.
4. Providing impetus to modernisation of handlooms for the export market.
5. Provision for design inputs to promote exports of handloom products.
6. Organisation of business mission/buyer seller meet and participation in trade fairs abroad.
7. Consultancy and guidance services for handloom exporters.
8. Liaison with the Government of India on all procedural and policy matters relevant to the handloom export trade.
9. Dealing with trade complaints pertaining to handloom exports.
10. Liaison with import promotion and commercial agencies abroad for the benefit of handloom exporters.

The export figures of cotton handloom goods for the last five years are furnished in Table 16.1.

Table 16.1 : Export of Cotton Handloom Goods

Sl. No.	Year	(Value in Rs. crores)
1.	1993-94	1297.48
2.	1994-95	1500.82
3.	1995-96	1490.78
4.	1996-97	1621.81
5.	1997-98	1854.50
6.	1998-99	2007.91

Source : Reports HEPC, Chennai

Handloom provides mass employment to rural people next to agriculture. Several studies have indicated that the share of handlooms in Indian clothing has been reduced due to competition, price increase and lack of value addition. Therefore the alternative scope is to expand the exports market and sustain the handloom operations. These are lower products requiring little capital investment and simple technologies and hence analysis was undertaken to examine the present status of handloom exports and identify development strategies.

The specific objectives of the study are :

1. To find out the trends of cotton handloom fabrics and madeups to different regions.
2. To examine the growth rates in various items of exports to different regions.
3. To find out the percentage share of importing countries in different regions.

The present exercise uses analytical tools like linear equations, average, percentage growth rates, whole sale price index and trend analysis, to examine the level of performance of handloom exports for a period of five years.

Data Analysis

Analytical framework is the essential part of any case analysed. It is the inference and the indicators that will give suitable direction for the future course of action. These are several managerial tools that facilitate decision making process in complex situations. In this context HEPC and its performance for a period of five years from 1994-95 to 1998-99 were analysed through following tool :

1. Simple Average,
2. Marginal Revenue,
3. Linear Equation,
4. Average growth rate.

The presentations were represented through graphical charts, Bar charts and pie-charts.

The HEPC exports goods under two categories viz., fabric and madeups out of handloom goods.

Fabrics include items like, furnishings, real Madras handkerchiefs, handloom lunghies, saries, handloom towels, handloom curtains, napkins and mats and floor coverings.

Exports of Cotton Handloom Fabrics

The Table 16.1 presents the export of cotton handloom fabrics from 1994-95 to 1998-99. The quality of exports were declining steadily from 787.55 lakh sq.mts. to 399.99 lakh sq.mts. In the span of 5 years the quantity of exports were reduced by 50 per cent which is a very serious threat to exporters. Unless a niche market development undertaken by HEPC it can reach to scratch value. These low technologies products are in saturated markets which are operating under quota system.

Unless particular revival strategies are undertaken to expand the market base. These exports will continue to show a declining trend. In terms of value of exports the same trend to be observed where 30 per cent reduction was recorded in a five years period. The growth rate in actual prices for five years ranged from –20.42 per cent to + 1.7 per cent. It can be average of –8.24 per cent. The value of exports in actual prices are converted into constant prices to the price level of 1994-95 by using wholesale price Index this value will give actual value of exports ignoring the effects of depreciating money value. Under constant prices the average value of exports remained stagnant. The average value of exports ranged from Rs. 37.32 to 41.60 is an indication of exports. The average value of exports value per metre of fabric. It is quite nominal value and most the fabric exporters are motivated to undertake exports for the additional benefits given by the Government of India rather than profits. This trend should be changed and more and more value added items should be undertaken to have better profits and competitive in the international markets. In respect of the marginal revenue it ranged

Table 16.2 : Exports of Cotton Handloom Fabrics

Sl. No.	Year	Qty in Sq.mts	Value Rs. in crores	Growth Rate in %	Avg. value of Exports	WSPI	Constant prices	Growth at constant prices	Marginal Cost
1.	1994-95	787.55	320.22	—	40	262.9	40.00	—	—
2.	1995-96	596.34	254.82	−20.42	42	295.8	37.32	−6.7	0.34
3.	1996-97	476.87	232.42	−8.79	48	314.6	40.11	7.47	0.18
4.	1997-98	429.03	219.68	−5.48	51	329.8	40.65	1.33	0.27
5.	1998-99	399.90	223.49	1.73	56	353.7	41.60	2.30	0.13
	Total	2689.69	1250.63	—	—	—	—	—	—
	Avg		250.12	−8.24	—	—	—	1.12	—

Linear Equation $Y = 318.71 - 22.86 X$

Source : HEPC Annual Report.

from Rs. 34 to 18 per metre during the study period. Marginal revenue is the value of realisation for exporting additional metre of fabric. This could be attained by the following formula.

M.R. = Change in Sales value in crores/Change in Qty. of fabrics exported in lakhs sq.mts.

Higher realisation of marginal revenue will be advantageous to exporting countries. In the study period of five years, during 1995-96 the M.R. was Rs. 34 highest among all other years. The lowest was recorded during 1998-99 at Rs. 13 as the M.R. Fabric exporters should strengthen M.R. value and achieve a level equal to average value of exports. Lower M.R. will affect the export earnings in the country. In none of the years the M.R = average value of exports, where price equilibrium could not be achieved. The linear equation for handloom export was predicted as $y = 318.7 - 22.86X$ this indicates a (–) trend declining slope and confirms the earlier analysis. From the above analysis the following points could be inferred.

(1) Quantity of exports and value of exports of cotton handlooms are steadily declining.
(2) The average value of exports was around Rs. 40 to 50 per metre.
(3) The marginal revenue values are lower than average cost values which needs improvement in marketing value addition etc.

Exports of Handloom Madeups

Handloom made ups are the goods that involve certain value addition like, cutting, sizing, trimming, chemical processing, finishing, stretching etc. and use ready to use items. This value added products contribute to the higher earning and generate employment in India. In this respect the trends of handloom madeups was analysed. The overall trend from 1994-95 to 1998-99 was presented in Table 16.3 and this is an increasing trend in the volume of exports during the span of five years. In 1994-99 826.32 lakh kgs were exported and this has shown a steady

Table 16.3 : Exports of Handloom Madeups

Sl. No.	Year	Qty in kgs.	Value Rs. in crores	Growth Rate in %	Avg. value of Exports	WSPI	Constant prices	Growth at constant prices	Marginal Cost
1.	1994-95	826.32	1180.60	—	143	262.9	143.00	—	—
2.	1995-96	760.60	1235.96	4.68	162	295.8	143.98	0.68	0.83
3.	1996-97	855.14	1389.39	12.41	162	314.6	135.37	- 5.97	1.62
4.	1997-98	882.04	1634.82	17.66	185	329.8	147.47	8.93	9.12
5.	1998-99	958.65	1784.42	9.15	186	353.7	138.25	- 6.25	1.95
	Total	4282.75	7225.19	—	—	—	—	—	—
	Average		1443.03	10.98	—	—	—	- 0.652	

Linear Equation Y = 963.088 + 160.65 X

Source : HEPC Annual Report.

increasing trend and achieved 958.58 lakh kgs in 1998-99. In respect of values it ranged between Rs. 180.6 to Rs. 1784.42 crores with an average value and exports were Rs. 1445.03 crores per annum. The growth rate in current prices ranged from 4.6 to 12.41 per cent with an average growth rate of 10.98 per cent per annum as compared to fabric exports and madeups have shown positive growth rates with linear equation of y = 963.88+160.65X. These exports will have considerable future and requires additional government support mechanisms. The average future of exports per kgs causes to Rs. 169 which is 3 to 4 times higher than fabric exports. The marginal revenue also ranged from Rs. 83 to 912 during 1997-98 it has recorded maximum value of m.c. which may be fixed as the benchmark for madeups exports.

Among the years of study 1997-98 was the best year performance in both fabrics as well as madeups in respect of the marginal revenue. Considering the average value of exports at constant price level with base year of 1994-95 it showed negative at - 0.65 per cent. These base the real growth and suffers slightly in constant prices.

Exports of Cotton Handloom Goods

Table 16.4 presents a comprehensive trend of fabrics and madeups in respect of exports through HEPC. The total value of exports ranged from Rs. 1409.78 crores to Rs. 2007.91 crores in the year 1998-99. There has been a steady trend of growth of 8 per cent per annum in the span of five years looking at the trend after providing the cushion against wholesale price index. There has been a declining trend with negative growth rate of 0.142 per cent per annum. The linear equation in current prices is having a positive slope of 137.79 in the equation of y = 1281.79 + 137.79X. y is the value of sales in any year and X is the period (years).

Table 16.4 shows the growth percentage for different Regions based on the percentage shares except Europe all other regions, namely Asia, Africa, America and Oceania have recorded negative growth rates with an average of –6.97 per cent for Asia, –2.89 per cent to Africa, –1.82 per cent for America and –5.06 per cent for

Oceania. Europe has recorded positive growth rate of 16.05 per cent per amount on the whole the future products for handloom fabrics exports is quite unfavourable not contributing to the increasing demands. Many of the third world countries like Bangladesh, Pakistan and China are also trying hard to capture these markets because of low capital intensity and higher employment generation potentiality.

Table 16.4 : Exports of Cotton Handloom Fabrics and Madeups

S. No.	Year	Value in crores	% Growth	% Share	WSPI	Constant Prices	Growth Rate in Constant Prices
1.	1994-95	1500.82	—	17.71	262.9	1500.82	—
2.	1995-96	1490.78	-0.66	17.59	295.8	1324.96	-11.72
3.	1996-97	1621.81	8.78	19.13	314.6	1355.29	2.29
4.	1997-98	1854.50	14.34	21.88	329.8	1478.31	9.08
5.	1998-99	2007.91	8.27	23.69	353.7	1492.0	0.92
	Total	8475.82	—	100	—	—	—
	Avg.	1695.16	7.68	—	—	—	0.142

Linear Equation Y = 1281.79 + 137.79 X
Source : HEPC Annual Report.

Trends in Handloom Furnishings

Among the total handloom fabric exports handloom furnishing occupy 8 per cent. During the study period of five years during 1994-95 only highest value of exports was recorded at Rs. 25.95 crores. In 1995-96 it has made a sharp decline by about 50 per cent due to the reduction in exports to Europe and Asian nations from 1996-97 onwards it is showing a steady trend at about 20 crores per annum.

Among the regions Europe contributed to the major imports at 35.58 per cent followed by America and Asia. So these are the major markets for Indian handloom furnishings and strengthening strategies can be constructed in the following three regions : Europe, America and Asia.

Table 16.5 : Exports of Regionwise Percentage Share and Growth of Handloom Fabrics

S. No.	Year	Region									
		Asia		Africa		Europe		America		Oceania	
		% Share	% Growth	% Share	% Growth	% Share	% Growth	% Share	% Growth	% Share	% Growth
1.	1994-95	32.31	—	11.30	—	21.86	—	25.49	—	09.03	—
2.	1995-96	35.69	10.46	11.54	2.12	29.06	32.94	15.44	-39.42	8.26	-8.53
3.	1996-97	34.27	-3.98	10.87	-5.81	33.96	16.86	15.68	1.55	4.78	-42.13
4.	1997-98	31.11	-9.22	10.54	-3.04	35.28	3.88	17.70	12.88	5.36	12.13
5.	1998-99	23.78	-25.17	10.03	-4.84	38.99	10.52	20.84	17.70	6.34	18.28
	Avg	31.43	-6.977	10.86	-2.892	31.83	16.05	19.03	-1.822	6.54	-5.062

Source : HEPC Annual Report.

Trends in RMHK

These are fancy products that has earned name by certain special characteristics. The same trend as observed in furnishings could also be noted in handkerchiefs with an average export value of Rs. 24.09 crores per annum.

Among the five regions African region was resource for major imports with an average value of Rs. 27.4 crore per annum. These products cannot have demands in the ensuing years because of the low profile.

Trends in Handloom Lunghies

Handloom lughies occupy 18.55 per cent of the total handloom fabrics — a higher percentage than furnishing and RMHK. In the span of five years during first three years the value of exports recorded a steady constant trend at Rs. 51 crores in the fourth and fifth year drastic reduction has been recorded due to following reasons :

1. Lunghies are mainly worn by Muslim people. The consumers for this product are from Malaysia, Singapore, Indonesia and UAE.
2. After the demolition of the Babri mosque, these Muslim nations have reduced the imports as a vindictive action for the above political problem.
3. The competition from Pakistan and Bangladesh are very severe in this cultural products.

Trends in other Handloom Products

Other handlooms are silk goods, saries, dhoties and other special goods. Among all exports in fabric side this is the major area that contributed to 63 per cent of the total export earnings with 155.39 crores per annum. Among the regions Europe, America and Asia are the major importers due to the dupion silk products. These markets are very volatile in nature and at any time this could be taken by China, Philippines and other South East Asian nations.

These four exporters should add more value to the products and strengthen competitive advantages.

Table 16.6 presents the Regionwise share of madeups for five years. Asia contributed to 20 per cent of total madeups exports. It ranges from 15.2 per cent to 23.2 per cent with an average of 18.22 per cent. There is a declining trend in the share of Asian exports with negative growth rate of 12.8 per cent and it implies that there is a severe competition from China, Pakistan and Bangladesh. In these exports that have the advantage of lower transportation cost. The exporters from India gain advantage only when the price per piece of export is reduced considerably to gain over the competition and this can be done only by undertaking adequate cost reduction methods. Africa occupied 0.92 per cent of the total exports which is quite insignificant and any statistical inferences could not be drawn. Europe contributed to the major share among the five regions at 40 per cent. It has also shown positive growth rate of 7.84 per cent and majority of the exports of European countries are quota exports which will be affected from 2003 onwards. Therefore realistic measures are to be undertaken to tide over the ensuing problem and more of Asian countries in this direction to prepare a long term plan to retain and sustain the European share. The government should also prepare a master plan to tackle this situation. The American nations have occupied second major share of around 35 per cent with an average of 34.44 per cent per annum as stated above and these are also quota exports which could be affected in the future for America. The per cent growth rate is positive with 1.53 like Africa, Oceania countries have also contributed to very small share in total madeups exports. There are many untapped markets in this region which have to be exported through periodic buyer-seller meets and appointment of market promotional officers in the regions.

Trends in Bed Linen and Bedsheets

Table 16.7 presents the export trends of one of the madeups items that is Bed linen and Bedsheets. It occupied 8 per cent share and total madeups exports. Europe and Asia are the major importers

Table 16.6 : Exports of Regionwise Percentage Share and Growth of Handloom Madeups

S. No.	Year	Region									
		Asia		Africa		Europe		America		Oceania	
		% Share	% Growth	% Share	% Growth	% Share	% Growth	% Share	% Growth	% Share	% Growth
1.	1994-95	23.23	—	0.47	—	36.79	—	34.06	—	5.45	—
2.	1995-96	22.06	−5.04	0.67	42.55	35.89	2.45	34.91	2.49	6.46	18.53
3.	1996-97	15.20	−31.09	1.28	91.04	43.57	21.40	33.29	−4.64	6.65	2.94
4.	1997-98	19.75	29.93	1.2	−1.56	39.33	−9.73	33.46	0.51	6.20	−6.76
5.	1998-99	10.87	−44.96	0.93	−26.19	48.04	22.15	36.06	7.77	4.11	−33.71
	Avg.	18.22	−12.79	0.92	26.46	49.72	7.842	34.45	1.532	5.77	−4.75

Source : HEPC Annual Report.

of bed linen and bedsheets. The major importers in Asia are NRIs which has shown a fluctuating dealing trend in the study period of five years. In case of Europe these are quota exports which has shown a steady growth with average value of Rs. 66.7 crores per annum. The existing European markets has to be strengthened in order to achieve growth in the exports of Bedlinen.

Table 16.7 : Exports of Bedlinen/Bedsheet

Sl. No.	Year	Total	
		Qty. sq.m.	Value
1.	1994-95	44.41	83.08
2.	1995-96	28.88	58.32
3.	1996-97	26.30	51.58
4.	1997-98	62.24	220.25
5.	1998-99	82.49	167.69
			116.18

Source : HEPC Annual Report.

Trend in Floor Coverings

These are floor mats that are mainly sold in cold climatic countries like America, Japan in Asia and many of the European countries. Indian carpets occupy a major share in total madeups export at about 31.38 per cent. In respect of Asia the value of exports are steadily declining. China, Pakistan and Bangladesh are again the major competitors for supplying floor carpets to Japan and other Asian nations. China has the merit of precision to Japanese markets and they compete on prices with the Indian goods. If Chinese and Japanese relations are strengthened further these markets may entirely be scrapped. Therefore Government of India should take efforts to strengthen this export. North America and Europe are the major importers of Indian floor mats to the tune of Rs. 200 crores per annum. In case of America the quantity of exports is declining steadily. This is due to the constrained and using child labour in vertical looms of carpet making. Unless sufficient measures are taken to eradicate in floor carpets the trend could not be revived. This is a 'U' trend in respect of exports to European nations it started at 158.9 lakh kgs and decline to 111.53 lakh kgs then it has shown steady increase and this market can be strengthened further (see Table 16.8). The African region and Oceania are contributed to very small share in floor coverings.

Table 16.8 : Exports of Handloom Floor Coverings

Sl. No.	Year	Total	
		Qty. sq. m.	Value
1.	1994-95	471.56	519.73
2.	1995-96	378.52	450.84
3.	1996-97	373.80	431.29
4.	1997-98	373.09	443.91
5.	1998-99	381.68	421.28
			453.51

Source : HEPC Annual Report.

Table 16.9 : Exports of Handloom Mats and Napkins

Sl. No.	Year	Total	
		Qty. sq. m.	Value
1.	1994-95	113.86	192.35
2.	1995-96	155.02	282.59
3.	1996-97	179.77	314.87
4.	1997-98	162.16	339.69
5.	1998-99	120.01	291.03
			284.11

Source : HEPC Annual Report.

Trends of Handloom Mats and Napkins

Tables 16.9 presents the exports of handloom mats and napkins. It occupied 19.66 per cent of the total madeups exports. America, Europe and Asia are the major importers of the mats and napkins. In respect of Asia the quantity as well as the value of exports are steadily declined. China, Pakistan and Bangladesh are the major competitors for supplying mats and napkins to Asian nations. America was the major contributor of mats and napkins exports earning. American trend has been steadily increasing in the quantity as well as value of exports during the study period. In case of Europe it comes next to the America's exports. Europe achieved with an average value of exports at Rs. 100 crores per annum and it has shown increasing trend in terms in quantity as well as value of exports. It started at 24.16 lakh kgs and increased upto 65.86 lakh pieces and this market can be strengthened further. The African region and Oceania region have contributed to very small share in mats and napkins.

Table 16.10 : Exports of Handloom Towels

Sl. No.	Year	Total	
		Qty. sq. m.	Value
1.	1994-95	39.80	60.19
2.	1995-96	36.62	62.37
3.	1996-97	49.97	84.10
4.	1997-98	31.35	47.82
5.	1998-99	31.99	47.77
			60.45

Source : HEPC Annual Report.

Trends in Handloom Towels

Table 16.10 presents the export trends of Handloom towels. It occupied 4.18 per cent of the total handloom madeups. In this respect Asia contributed with an average value of exports of Rs. 1.7 crores per annum. Most of the Asia's customers were NRIs and Muslims and it has been steadily increasing with fluctuating trend. Europe has the major share of the Towel imports of Rs. 35 crores per annum. The major reason is asofree dyes, Quota, Quality and timely delivery of the products. In case of America was the second largest country to import the Towels and it has steadily increasing trend from 1994-95 to 1996-97. But in the 1997-98 and 1998-99 it has the declining trend due to the reason of Africa and Oceania these contributed to the very small area in the towels imports.

Table 16.11 : Exports of Handloom Curtains

Sl. No.	Year	Total	
		Qty. sq. m.	Value
1.	1994-95	22.34	43.68
2.	1995-96	18.85	43.89
3.	1996-97	25.94	61.60
4.	1997-98	56.13	149.98
5.	1998-99	72.04	201.35
			98.1

Source : HEPC Annual Report.

Trend in Handloom Curtains

Table 16.11 shows that the exports trends of the handloom curtain goods and it has occupied 6.84 per cent of the total madeups exports. Europe and America are the major importers of the Indian handloom towels. The major importers in Asia are NRIs which has shown a fluctuating declining trend in the study period of five years. In case of Europe, the quota exports which has shown an increasing growth with an average value of Rs. 60 crores per annum. America is the second largest country to contribute the exports share of Indian handloom towels. Oceania comes to next in Asia's contributors, which has contributed Rs. 3 crore per annum and Africa has the very small contribution to the exports of handloom towels.

Exports Trends of Other Handloom Product

Table 16.12 shows that the exports trends of handloom madeups products like silk madeups, cotton readymade shirts, cotton shirts, trousers etc. which has contributed the exports value of about 25.58

Table 16.12 : Exports of Handloom Madeups Products (Silk, Cotton Readymade Shirts, Shorts, Trousers)

Sl. No.	Year	Total	
		Qty. sq. m.	Value
1.	1994-95	95.55	197.10
2.	1995-96	160.68	269.09
3.	1996-97	157.30	364.47
4.	1997-98	197.07	433.14
5.	1998-99	270.44	584.77
			369.71

Source : HEPC Annual Report.

per cent share of the total madeups exports. Europe, America and Asia are the major importers of the other handloom madeup items. The major importers in Asia are the NRIs and Muslim peoples which has shown a fluctuating increasing trend in quantity as well as value of exports and it has occupied the exports value of Rs. 65 crore per annum. Europe was the major importer of the other handloom madeups which has contributed to the exports value of Rs. 160 crores. P.A. due to the reason Quota, Asofree dyes and prompt delivery of the goods. America has recorded its exports share of Rs. 112 crores per annum which is the second largest country to import to the other handloom madeup items. Due to the reason of cold the Oceania country has contributed its share of Rs. 28.72 crores per annum and also Africa has recorded very small contribution of the other handloom madeups.

Regionwise Share in Handloom Exports

In 1994-95 Asian nations purchased 25 per cent of the total exports of Handloom fabrics and madeups. This has declined to 12.3 per cent in 1998-99 for the reasons described earlier. In Asia both fabrics and madeups have shown negative trend which needs immediate attention to improve the positive trend. NRIs and Muslims are the major users of the Indian handloom products.

Among the five countries Europe has the major share of the imports of total Indian handloom products, which contribute with an average growth of 9.5 per cent. The main reason was due to quota, quality of goods, asofree dyes and timely delivery of the goods. And it has the positive increasing trend of 33.61 to 47 per cent during the study period of five years. America has the second largest contributor of the Indian handloom goods imports which has contributed of 2 per cent and also it has the increasing trends during the study period.

Africa and Oceania has very small contribution of the Indian handloom goods imports.

Among the five nations which has the steadily increasing trend of during the study period of five years. In 1994-95 it has contributed Rs. 1500 crores and in the year 1998-99 it has shown Rs. 200 crores (see Table 16.13).

Table 16.13 : Exports of Handloom Products

Sl. No.	Year	Total	
		Qty. sq. m.	Value
1.	1994-95	1500.82	100
2.	1995-96	1490.79	100
3.	1996-97	1621.80	100
4.	1997-98	1854.50	100
5.	1998-99	2007.90	100

Source : HEPC Annual Report.

Recommendations

1. In order to improve the earnings by the exporting of handloom goods, more quantity of madeups need to be exported.
2. New areas of market should be created for these goods which involve high value addition. These value added products will generate more employment opportunities in the country.
3. Europe is the major importer of Indian handlooms followed by America and Asia. However there is a declining trend in

their import which is due to the export policy of the government. The government should encourage the exporters by providing incentives and also to reduce the exports duty on handloom goods.

4. In order to meet the competition from other countries, viz. Pakistan and Bangladesh. New variety of handloom goods must by produced by the manufacturers. Steps should also be taken to reduce the cost of production by introduction of appropriate technology.
5. In order to attract foreign buyers eco-friendly coloured handloom cloth should be introduced. For these purposes asofree dyes and vegetable dyes can be used.
6. Arranging frequent buyers and seller meets will provide more interactions between these groups and improve the market.
7. India should participate/conduct trade fairs inside country and abroad to exhibit our handloom products.
8. More advertisement in internal and international level is needed for increasing the market.
9. Government should come forward for a bilateral agreement with various countries in order to increase the exports.
10. A market survey must be conducted by the government in order to find out the diminishing trend in the marketing of handloom goods.

Conclusion

Handloom industry which is a traditional industry of our country provides large scale employment opportunity in the rural India. A declining trend in its production and marketing is prevailing in the country at present. Finding of the cause of this trend and suggesting suitable remedial measures are the immediate requirements. The suggestions given above will certainly contribute to solve most of the problems faced by this industry at present.

References

Handloom Export Promotion Council, 1998-99 — Annual Report.

Handwoven Textiles, published by HEPC, 18, Cathedral Garden Road, Nungambakam, Chennai.

HEPC Newsletter, Published by HEPC.

Indian Journal of Fibre and Textile Research, Published by National Institute of Science, Communication, CSIR, New Delhi.

Saravanvel, P., *International Marketing*, Himalaya Publishing House, Bombay.

South India Textile Research Association, *Handloom Readymade Garments Exports*, The Seshan Printers, Coimbatore.

Textile Magazine, 'Trumae Engineering Co. Ltd., Ahmedabad.

17

DINDIGUL WOMEN POLYTHENE WORKERS INDUSTRIAL CO-OPERATIVE SOCIETY : An Evaluative Study

— *N. Lalitha*

Introduction

The segments of co-operative movement like service co-operatives, thrift and credit co-operatives and industrial co-operatives prove a lot of opportunities for women. From gender point of view co-operatives can be classified into (a) exclusive women co-operatives and (b) mixed gender co-operatives. Realising the need to provide supplementary income to women especially those below poverty line, a number of women industrial co-operatives came into existence during 1987-88 and 1990-91 in Tamil Nadu.

The main objectives of the Women Industrial Co-operatives Societies are to provide employment and improve the social and economic conditions of the women workers living below poverty line and residing in the area of operation. For fulfilling this objective it shall be competent for the society (1) to raise the funds required for its business, (2) to purchase such raw material and appliances as may be required for the industry and retail the same either for cash or credit to members, (3) to get raw materials converted into finished into products by issuing them to members and paying them wages for such conversion, (4) to establish workshops where members can carry on their industry jointly or where the member artisans can be employed by the society as labourers for the manufacture of articles on its account, (5) to obtain contracts from the Government public bodies or others for the supply of goods and get them executed through or with the help of the members, (6) to impart business and technical training to members and to provide dwelling houses or house sites to worker members and staff.

As the products manufactured by these societies are supplied to Government Departments and its agencies, the schemes are being implemented as the government sponsored schemes. It is necessary to study the structure and organisation of women industrial co-operatives, growth pattern, their financial performance, production, marketing linkages, distribution of income among the members and their participation and to examine how far they have contributed to empowerment of women.

It is against this background that a study was undertaken to evaluate the performance of Dindigul Polythene women industrial cooperative society. Evaluation of the performance of women co-operative society will provide valuable insight into the weakness and strength of the societies and will enable to draw more ambitious plan for the replication of women's co-operatives in other areas and sectors. Hence this study.

The specific objectives of this study are as follows :

(a) to measure the progress in production and sales of the selected women co-operative society;
(b) to gauge the efficiency of operations;
(c) to evaluate the management of finance in these societies;
(d) to identify the problems faced by the members of selected society; and
(e) to study the participation of women in the activities of the selected women co-operative society.

The investigation is based on case study method studying the overall functioning of the Women Polythene Industrial Co-operative Society in Dindigul. The secondary data for the study was collected from the records, annual reports, audit reports which are maintained by the society. The period of study covers1989-99. Based on census method the whole universe constituted the respondents of the study the members have been interviewed to collect primary data. Bearing on the objectives of the study, two interview schedules were prepared, one for the officials of the society and the other for the employees. Primary data were collected by means of the pretested interview schedule. The study employs tools pertaining to disciplines of economics as well as management for the purpose of analysis of data. Besides simple averages, concepts like capital output ratio and rate of return have been used in the study. Further price indices have been used as deflators for the removal of inflationary effect from money value.

Findings of the Study

Dindigul Women Workers Industrial Polythene Co-operative Society under the control of Department of Industry and Commerce was registered on 18-11-1959 and started functioning from 21-11-1959. The society buys raw materials from the Indian Petro Chemical Corporation, Baroda. The women workers are engaged in sheet cutting, handle pressing and sealing work. The details of share capital of the society is given in Table 17.1.

As observed from Table 17.1 the Government contributes Rs.10,000 towards the share capital of the society. Festival advances are given to the women workers of polythene society at 16 per cent interest. They enjoy facilities like Employees State Insurance (ESI) and Employment Provident Fund and Gratuity. The polythene bags produced by the society are sold to district forest office, Ayyalur waste land development scheme, social forestry division in Kunoor, Villupuram, Viruthachalam, Government rubber corporation, Madurai Pandyan consumer societies etc.

Table 17.1 : Polythene Society — Share Capital Details

Year	No. of workers	Individual share	Government share	Total
1988-89	63	85403	10000	95403
1989-90	62	90745	10000	100745
1990-91	57	87365	10000	97365
1991-92	72	85213	10000	95213
1992-93	72	81158	10000	91158
1993-94	72	85933	10000	95933
1994-95	69	97017	10000	107017
1995-96	62	100317	10000	110317
1996-97	60	99112	10000	109112
1997-98	55	86912	10000	96912
1998-99	50	79912	10000	89912

Source : Records of the society.

Particulars of the production for Women Polythene Workers Industrial Society are furnished in Table 17.2. Particulars of value of production are furnished in both current prices as well as in price level of 1989-90. Wholesale Price Index with base year of 1980-81 been used for deflating the value of production in current prices to the price level of 1989-90. The value has been deflated to remove the inflationary effect and measure the real growth rate.

Table 17.2 : Production Particulars — Polythene Society

Year	Production in current prices	Production in price level of 1989-90	Variation (%) in current prices	Variation (%) in the price level of 1989-90
1989-90	31.08	31.08	—	—
1990-91	33.95	30.79	9.23	(–) 0.93
1991-92	50.61	40.36	49.07	31.08
1992-93	75.25	54.35	48.69	34.66
1993-94	75.25	50.32	—	(–) 7.41
1994-95	65.28	39.38	(–)13.25	(–)21.74
1995-96	30.52	17.64	(–)53.21	(–)30.37
1996-97	30.43	16.53	(–) 0.32	(–) 0.17
1997-98	33.9	17.58	11.53	5.98
1998-99	5.57	2.46	(–)83.77	(–)86.01

Source : Records of the Society.

In current prices, the value of production reach the peak in 1992-93, stagnated there in 1993-94 and recorded a fall in 1994-95. Thereafter the production level declined to such a level that there seems to be remote chances of recovery. In 1998-99 the production reached the bottom level of 5.57 lakhs. The real growth rate came to a halt in 1993 and thereafter the decline set in. In respect of sales, the performance reached the peak in 1992-93 and declined thereafter both in current and constant prices. In current price level, the sales declined from 94 lakhs to 5.4 lakhs in 1998-99 and in constant prices, from 70.32 lakhs to 2.42 lakhs during the same period. The reason for fall in performance after 1992-93 can be attributed to the mushrooming of competitors encouraged by simple technology and modest investment in the activity.

Capital Output Ratio

Another important criteria in the evaluation of business operation is the efficiency in the utilisation of scarce capital. In capital output ratio, capital is represented by all long term own funds of the business consisting of share capital, reserves and surpluses and output by gross value added by manufacture. In the ensuing analysis both capital and output are furnished in the price levels of 1989-90. The capital output ratio for the society is furnished below:

Table 17.3 : Capital Output Ratio

Year	Capital	Gvam	Cor
1989-90	37.72	9.50	1:3.97
1990-91	44.10	9.41	1:4.96
1991-92	54.82	15.46	1:3.55
1992-93	67.76	26.29	1:2.58
1993-94	60.03	15.87	1:3.78
1994-95	49.79	13.01	1:3.82
1995-96	40.20	9.15	1:4.39
1996-97	43.69	4.35	1:10.04
1997-98	47.04	4.60	1:10.22

Source : Office Records, Industrial Cooperative Society.

The table reveals that amount of capital required for producing one rupee output varied between Rs. 2.58 and Rs.10.22 during the ten period according to the level of activity represented by GVAM. The sharp decrease in the amount of GVAM and the consequent increase in the capital output ratio shows that the rate of utilisation of long term funds will have to go up in order to make full use of the long term, funds locked up in this unit.

Rate of Return

Rate of return on investment is the most widely used yardstick for measurement of success of business in general and profitability in particular. Computation of rate of return on investment relates profit to long term funds or fixed capital employed in the business.

Net profit in the price level of 1989-90 has been used for the estimate of rate of return. The rate of return has fallen from 35.75 per cent in 1989-90 to 3.64 per cent in 1995-96 and afterwards the society meets with loss only. It was already noted that production and sales declined even in current and more sharply in constant prices, thanks to competition. Consequently profit rose and declined in course of the study period almost the same way as production and sales did. One deviation from the trends of production and sales on the one hand and trend in profit is that the net profit reached its maximum in 1991-92 while production and sales reached their peak only in 1992-93 a year which recorded a fall in net profits. Thus the increasing and production and sales in 1992-93 did not produce any rise in profits but caused a reduction in surplus because of the increase in expenditure on establishment and provision for depreciation. Thus the benefits of rising unit price were largely absorb in depreciation, establishment and expenditure resulting in fall in profits. The stagnation and decline in production and sales produced a decline in trends of profitability.

Participation of Members

Basically the rural women form co-operative societies in order to improve the socio-economic conditions of the members, to develop internal leadership to handle and control the activities of the society and to take part in decision making process and to provide employment opportunities to local talents and to avoid exploitation in the marketing process. The members can exercise control in two ways in co-operative societies. Firstly, by attending general body meeting and secondly, by exercising visiting rights in the elections to the Board of Directors. But mere attendance at a meeting or voting does not ensure democratic control. It is necessary for the members to have sufficient knowledge of the working of their co-operatives and of its policies to be able to form a rational judgement upon them. They should participate in the meetings and discuss the problems and find ways of solving the problems. This requires adequate information to the members and opportunities for discussion of the society's affairs with those responsible for its management.

The interview with the women workers of polythene industry reveals that they used to get job for 5/6 days/week till 1989-90. Thereafter however competition from other producers forced reduction, production and consequent shrinkage of employment. Thus the workers find work only for 2 days/week at present. The society has to find new market not only to improve the profitability but also to enhance the duration of employment of those women workers who are totally dependent on the society for their livelihood.

18

A STUDY ON MINERAL BASED INDUSTRY IN DINDIGUL DISTRICT

— *M. Ponniah*

Introduction

Rural industrialisation is important in the case of developing countries like ours. It is a means of generating employment opportunities in rural areas with low capital cost and raising the real income of the people. It contributes to the development of agriculture and urban industries. Without rural Industrialisation, it would be difficult to solve the problem of agricultural unemployment and widespread under-employment. The development of rural industries increases the level of income in rural areas, and tends to create opportunities for youth, women and the labourers. Rural industrialisation should be looked upon not merely as a way of containing the rural workers and stopping them from migrating to urban areas by providing them some kinds of remunerative employment in the villages, but also as a dynamic element in the process of raising the productivity and income levels of the workers in rural areas.

The main characteristics of these industries are to develop local initiative, co-operative and spirit of self-reliance in the economy and at the same time to help in the utilisation of the available manpower. Processing locally available raw materials by adopting simple techniques is another characteristic.

Statement of the Problem

Rural industrialisation being the most important for creating employment opportunities, a national programme for rural industrialisation NPRI, with a mission to set up 100 rural clusters every year, to give boost to rural industrialisation, was announced in the Union Budget for 1999-2000 presented on 27th February, 1999. KVIC has been accorded an important role in this area. There are so many schemes, concession and subsidies announced by the State and the Central Governments for promoting mineral based industry in the State and district level in general. The State Government of Tamil Nadu and the Central Government have played a very vital role for promoting mineral based industry in different districts. But the introduction of new schemes and system however did not culminate into a positive boost to this sector in Dindigul district. That is why the researcher has chosen this topic and tries to identify by the causes and reason. In pursuance of the above problem, certain objectives have been set for the present study.

* To study the problem faced by the mineral based industry in Dindigul District.
* To analyse the performance of the mineral based industry in Dindigul District.
* To find out the various suggestions and recommendations for the improvement of mineral based industry in Dindigul district.

Review of the Previous Studies

1. Gupta and Inderjit Gupta in a study on financing of the small industry in Jammu & Kashmir based their observations on the survey of 50 artisans and 200 small units at random from different line of manufactures.
2. Patel is of the view that in India there is much scope for the

development of village industries. He has recommended, setting up of raw material banks, marketing outlets, training centres, demonstration centres, technical guidance and financial facilities to artisans for meeting the capital expenditure and working capital needs.

3. Pandit Rao has conducted a study on financing KVIC in the changed economic scenario suggest that KVIC should pay greater attention to the development activities and refinance may be entrusted with NABARD whose act should be amended to enable it to sanction working capital loan to institutions from commercial banks.
4. Chauhan and Parthasarathi have studied KVIC - Export promotion strategy and their suggestions to the government to establish a separate merchandising house in the country specialising exclusively on export promotion of KVI items, is worth considering.

Methodology

In order to study the performance of mineral based industry in Dindigul district, only secondary data have been used.

The secondary data have been used for analysis to the extent of employment opportunities provided to different sections of the society. The Annual Report of KVIC, state KVIB Chennai. Journals and periodicals are served as the major source of secondary data. The present study covers the performance of mineral based industry through KVIC assisted units.

Trend, percentage and 'F' test techniques have been used to analyse the performance of mineral based industry in Dindigul district over a study period of 1994-95 to 1998-99.

District Profile

Dindigul district spreads over an area of 4217.36 sq.km. As per the 1991 census, the total population of this District was 17,60,601, out of which males constitute 8,90,783 and females 8,69,818. Next to farming a sizeable population depends on industrial activities. Dindigul district is the important industrial centre. A number of spinning mills are coming up in Vedasandur and Vadamadurai block, besides a few paper mills in Swaminathapuram. A steel industry has been established, Tobacco, Lock, Metal, Dyeing, Iron Industry, Cotton Spinning and Weaving are the other promising industries.

Results and Discussions

There are a number of agencies involved in Rural industrialisation either directly or indirectly and one among the important agencies are Khadi and Village Industries Commission (KVIC). The KVIC has broadly re-grouped various village industries under seven heads for the purpose of implementing its programme.

- — Mineral based industry.
- — Forest based industry.
- — Agrobased and food industry.
- — Polymer and chemical based industry
- — Engineering and non-conventional energy industry.
- — Textile industry (excluding Khadi).
- — Service industry.

There are about 119 village industries among the seven groups of village industries which come under the purview of KVIC. A variety of products are manufactured under this group which includes earthenware, terracotta, stoneware, glazed tiles, modern decorative art pottery, handicraft items made from conch and shells, plaster of paris utensils, washing powder etc. The major industries under this group are cottage pottery and lime manufacturing. Under pottery industries Maharashtra State has contributed the maximum, i.e. 33 per cent in the total production, while Uttar Pradesh with 8 per cent was the next State with significant contribution followed by Rajasthan with 7 per cent.

Under the lime manufacturing industries the States which contribute major portion in production are Rajasthan, Andhra

Pradesh, Tamil Nadu and Kerala with 24 per cent, 16 per cent, 9 per cent and 9 per cent respectively. As per the 1998-99 data, Tamil Nadu stands fifth in production (Rs. 3808.19 lakhs) and sale (4008.93 lakhs) in mineral based industry. It also holds the first place in employment (1.39 lakhs persons) and third place (Rs. 2198.28 lakhs) in earnings.

Mineral based industry group recorded a maximum growth of 33 per cent in the national level during the year 1998-99 over the year 1997-98. During the year under the report maximum additional employment was generated by the mineral based industry group, i.e. by 92000 persons.

Mineral Based Industry Performance Over A Period

Production	1994-95	95-96	96-97	97-98	98-99	Growth rate
Rs. in crores	388.53	428.13	473.09	470.08	622.94	12.50%
Employment (in lakhs persons)	6.10	6.52	6.78	6.40	7.40	4.95%

It could be seen from the above table that the production and employment of mineral based industry over the different years show an increase. One of the reasons could be that the eco-friendly nature of its product and their usages.

Table 18.1 : Industrywise Progress in National Level (1998-99)

(Rs. in crores, Employment in lakhs persons)

Sl. No	Industry	Production	Sales	Employment	Earning
1.	Mineral based	622.94	769.04	7.40	253.09
2.	Forest based	310.30	392.28	3.16	120.72
3.	Agro based	1635.04	1840.78	20.90	492.13
4.	Polymer based	934.25	1162.54	7.23	329.79
5.	Engineering based	771.65	620.00	4.29	208.90
6.	Textiles	108.80	118.54	0.95	50.85
7.	Service industry	93.50	—	0.51	64.80

Source : Annual Report 1998-99.

Table 18.1 reveals that out of seven classifications of village industries the Mineral based industry stand fourth place in terms of production (Rs. 622.94 crore), third place in sales (Rs. 769.04 crore), and Earnings (Rs. 253.09 crore), and second place in employment (7.40 lakh persons). It is also observed that this industry contribute the major portion of village industries in national level.

The performance of mineral based industry in Dindigul district, is shown in Table 18.2.

Table 18.2 : Mineral Based Industries in Dindigul District

(Rs. in lakhs, Employment in lakh persons)

Sl. No.	Year	Production	Sales	Employment			
				Women	SC & ST	Others	Total
1.	1994-95	134.15	142.76	696	412	5440	6548
2.	1995-96	141.33	178.08	776	708	5538	7022
3.	1996-97	129.07	140.76	1017	471	5396	6884
4.	1997-98	37.80	38.55	915	548	5424	6887
5.	1998-99	101.89	118.21	640	512	3732	4884

Source : KVIC Regional office annual report.

It could be seen from Table 18.2 that production, sales and employment over the study period are fluctuating in nature, the reason being lack of awareness, of this industry and mushroom growth of spinning mills in Dindigul district. In textile Industry the worker will get a decent salary than the activities. In the case of sales this product shall face the competition from large scale sector, and in proper sales outlet.

Table 18.3 shows the analytical information about production, sales and employment of mineral based industry in Dindigul district. The value with parenthesis are SE values.

It could be understood from Table 18.3 that, production, sales and employment classification were found to be not significant in all the three models. The reason behind this was that people in this

Table 18.3 : Growth Rate of Mineral Based Industry in Dindigul District

	Linear Model	r^2	Semi-log	r^2	Log-log	r^2
Production	– 16.8049 (12.08)	.3922	–.1869 (.1701)	.2763	–.4591 (.4253)	.2798
Sales	– 18.8630 (15.64)	.3267	–.1908 (.1916)	.2483	–.4611 (.1224)	.2343
Total Employment	– 346.3 (256.20)	.3785	–.0606 (.0433)	.3951	–.1120 (.1224)	.2181
Women Employment	–2.7 (56.82)	.0007	–.00029 (.0697)	.000006	–.5409 (.1705)	.0324
SC & ST	– 4 (40.65)	.0032	–.0178 (.0728)	.0196	–.0865 (.1760)	.0745
Other Employment	-353 (19367)	.5255	–.0774 (.0428)	.5216	–.1565 (.1248)	.3440

district are not giving much importance to this industry. Dindigul district has a unique feature of having a number of industries, like lock, tobacco, leather, textile and other units.

The same data can be analysed by F test using mean value.

Table 18.4 : Mineral Based Industries in Dindigul District (1999-2000)

(Rs. in lakhs, Employment in lakh persons)

	Production	Sales	Employment			
			Total	Women	SC & ST	Non SC & ST
	108.848 *	123.672 *	6445	808.80 **	530.20 **	5106 **
F	102.586	319.25	1.21	88.76	132.80	108.02
SE	17.26	9.27	438.44	64.87	31.16	379.68
CD	49.906	28.007	—	187.892	90.253	1099.66

** Significant at P = 0.01.

Table 18.4 reveals the production, sales and classification of employment of mineral based industry. The mean value were, 108.848, 123.673, 808.08, 530.20 and 5106 respectively. The analysis of variance of mean value revealed that it was significantly different. The mean value was the highest in total employment, followed by non SC & ST employment and so on. The reason for the variation is that the KVIC and the State government did not take much effort for implementing so many schemes about the mineral based industry in Dindigul district. Rural people are not interested in the schemes offered by KVIC and the State government did not take much effort for implementing so many schemes about the mineral based industry in Dindigul district. Rural people are not interested in the schemes offered by KVIC and government. Dindigul is a fertile land for agricultural purpose. It is surrounded by Sirumalai and Kodaikanal hills and this district gets normal rainfall throughout the year and the people in rural areas are always engaged in agricultural and allied activities. If they are properly motivated the industry would come up in the near future.

In order to ensure large scale employment to the people in this area, KVIC brings so many schemes for providing funds for development activities. In this context the rural people who mainly depend upon agricultural and other non-farm sector, like mineral based industry. These rural people are passing through a phase of economic transformation along with the rest of the country.

Problems and Suggestions

Due to their poor economic condition the artisans working in the Mineral based industry are not much educated. Even if opportunity comes, they are not willing to go of their place outside for training. Potters are very conservative in nature. It is also seen that those who have got training in improved production practices do not have the scope to start their work in the new direction due to non-availability of sufficient funds and lack of market for their products. The artisans working in mineral based industry in Dindigul district have failed to grow because of its inability to get adequate capital and finance. It has been depending on money lenders who charge high rate of interest, imposing heavy burden on the part of the workers.

The new products introduced in the market are attractive and non-breakable and thus durable, though they are much costlier compared to earthenware produced by village potters. Today mineral based industry's production are sold only to a limited segment of the society, for this reason, children of the potters are trying to shift to other occupation.

The problem of the workers involved in mineral based industry in Dindigul are so complex that they are not easily amenable to ready-made sophisticated solution involving the economists and planners. Apart from the economic factors, the social and political features of the society too become very relevant. To overcome the above mentioned problems the following suggestions are found out:

KVIC and State government should create awareness among the village people as well as educated youth about the self-employment scheme.

District authorities should come forward to provide marketing assistance to village artisans for their products.

Mineral based industry's product are to be sold through Khadigram, Sarvodaya Sangam and Co-operative stores etc.

Proper training facility at their door steps should be given regularly about the design, technology of the product.

Government should list down the articles produced by small and village industry and it should not be produced by large scale industries. If they do so severe action should be taken.

Financial aid should be provided to the needy, and the officer should see the necessity of the scheme and its importance.

Mineral based industry's production is an eco-friendly activity with a touch of creativity and skill.

Aggressive publicity campaign have to be launched to create awareness and educate the people about the inherent values of the product.

Prospect

It is estimated that there are about 7.40 lakhs traditional skilled persons in India and among them 4884 skilled persons are in Dindigul district. Raw materials of mineral based industry like clay and limestone are available in abundance in all the parts of the country. The traditional activities are using locally available raw materials. This industry has great scope and potential for development in view of its unique features and inherent qualities of the products which have helped to keep the traditional heritage and artistic beauty of the product in tact.

Conclusion

The mineral based industry has tremendous scope for development. Introduction of modern design of pottery activities can surely pave the way for speedy progress of this craft contrary to the belief that it would uproot the artisans. What is required is a well planned strategy to impress upon the potters the urgency to acquire knowledge about the production of modern mineral based industry products (Modern Pottery wares) which have a ready market. They should avail of the facility offered by various agencies, including KVIC. Simultaneously their skills ought to be sharpened, so that they can undertake the production of various utility articles which are needed by the society.

In view of the extremely backward and isolated nature of the rural area of Dindigul district, the regional disparity can only be removed and exploitation of rural masses be mitigated through the setting up of the mineral based industry in KVI Sector. Moreover these industries are specially labour-intensive and they should be directed to benefit the targeted rural people exclusively.

People of this district are generally hardworking. Lack of awareness of government incentives and concession to the industries, resulted in the stagnation of industrial growth. If they are properly motivated, guided and trained, this district will come up as one of the industrially developed districts in Tamil Nadu in general and Dindigul (Mineral based industry) in particular.

References

Chauhan, B.R., *Khadigramodyog* (January 1997).

Gupta, N.S., Inderjit Gupta, *Financing of SSI*, S. Chand & Co, Ram Nagar, New Delhi - (1947).

Pandit Rao, Y.A., "Financing of KVIC in the changed scenario, *Khadi Gramodyog*, December, 1999.

Patel, A.R., "Financing Village Industries Problems and Prospects", *Khadi Gramodyog*, October 1978.

19

AGRO BASED AND FOOD PROCESSING INDUSTRY : A Study in Theni District of Tamil Nadu

— *S. Maria John*

Growth of Small Scale Industries in India is a significant feature of the Indian Economy. The Small Scale Sector covers wide range of activities. It is also playing a pivotal role in employment generation with low capital investment. At present it has provided employment opportunities to around 18 million people. The Government of India, recognising the importance and role of rural industries, has been allocating large amounts during the plan periods (*vide* Table 19.1). In India small scale industries include traditional and modern small industries, cottage industries, tiny units, business and industry related services etc. Consequent to the provisions during the plan periods, there has been tremendous growth of small and rural industries (*vide* Table 19.2).

Cottage Industries as feeder units to other industrial units, are mostly managed by artisans and skilled craftsmen and are involved in traditional activities such as agriculture, khadi, handlooms, handicrafts etc. These are generally associated with part-time or full-time occupations in rural and semi-urban areas utilising locally available resources and/or human skill.

Table 19.1 : Plan Outlays for Rural Industrialisation

Sl. No.	Plan Period	Outlays Rs. in crores	Cumulative Percentage
1.	First Plan	42	0.34
2.	Second Plan	187	1.86
3.	Third Plan	241	3.81
4.	Annual Plan	126	4.83
5.	Fourth Plan	293	7.20
6.	Fifth Plan	592	11.99
7.	Sixth Plan	1780	26.41
8.	Seventh Plan	2753	48.70
9.	Eighth Plan	6334	100.00
	Growth rate in percentage	15081	—

Growth rate is calculated as $\frac{yt}{y0} \times 100$

Table 19.2: Growth of Small and Cottage Industries (1980-81 to 1998-99)

Period	No. of Units (in lakhs)	Production (Rs. in lakhs)	Employment (in lakhs)	Exports (Rs in crores)
1980-81	4.48	28060	71.0	1643
1984-85	8.50	50520	90.0	2580
1988-89	11.59	106400	113.0	5490
1992-93	22.35	209300	134.0	17785
1996-97	28.57	412636	160.0	39249
1998-99	31.21	538357	175.2	57488

Source : Tamil Nadu Economic Appraisal, 2000.

Tiny Units are the enterprises having an investment limit of less than 5 lakhs, whereas ancillary units have Rs. 75 lakhs. These ancillary units are engaged in manufacturing parts, components, sub-assemblies, toolings or intermediaries rendering services units to large industries. The small and tiny units account for 35 per cent of the gross value of the output in the manufacturing sector, about 80 per cent of the total industrial employment and about 40 per cent of the total exports of the country.

Service establishments are units involved in all industry related service and business enterprises, irrespective of location with recognised potential for generating employment. The investment ceilings correspond to those of tiny units.

The cottage industries are more or less household industries depending on local resources catering only to a limited local market. These industries may be classified into :

1. Part-time rural cottage industries,
2. Whole-time rural industries, and
3. Urban cottage industries.

The part-time rural cottage industries cover all such industries which provide supplementary occupation to agriculturists and which are mostly processing industries, Handloom Weaving, Tadi, Palm gur, Jaggery making and basket and rope making etc.

This study relates in general to groundnut industries which are agro-based processing industries. Groundnut is used in two types of village industries. They are

1. Groundnut decorticating industries, and
2. Oil industries.

In a decorticating industry groundnut is processed, i.e., the outer shell or covering is removed. This decortication is done by machines by employing some persons in the premises of the entrepreneur. The other activities included in processing groundnut are drying, storing, packing etc. This processed kernel is sold to the following (*vide* Table 19.3):

1. Small business people, i.e., those who carry on cottage business at their homes;
2. Other business people, i.e. those who carry on provision type of business;
3. Wholesalers who deal only in kernel business;
4. Sent to oil industries (cottage); and
5. Large oil units.

Table 19.3: Pattern of Distribution of Processed Nuts by Entrepreneurs

Sl. No.	Category	Percentage
1.	Small business people	16
2.	Other business people	38
3.	Wholesalers	14
4.	Oil industries direct — cottage	15
5.	Large oil units — own	17

Oil industries indulge in extracting oil from the processed kernels. These industries take oil not only from groundnut but also from other types of Dhals and seeds. The reason behind this is that of inconsistency in supply of groundnut to these entrepreneurs. They get cake too which is sold separately.

Oil industries are of two types. They are:

1. Oil Industries carrying on business at large scale; and
2. Oil Industries which are carried on at very small scale, i.e. these types of industries are run either at their own residence of the entrepreneurs or at a small hired place and employing a very few workers. They use one or two machines. These people extract oil from various duals and nuts.

This research was carried on in Aundipatti Taluk (Theni District) which consists of many types of industries (*vide* Table 19.4) and nearly 20 groundnut industries. These industries comprise both decorticating and oil industries. Theni district has 5 Taluks, viz., Aundipatti, Bodinayakanur, Uthamapalayam, Periyakulam and Theni.

In all these Taluks there has been groundnut production every year. During some years the production in one Taluk exceeds the production of the other Taluk. Among all these Taluks, the production of groundnut in Aundipatti Taluk, often exceeds the production of other Taluks, has three significance, viz.

(a) Large production in quantity,
(b) Large production in quality (size of the nut), and

(c) More oil content.

The nature of the soil of Aundipatti and the climatic conditions have proved more productivity of groundnut in the locality.

As there is more demand for the groundnut cultivated in and around Aundipatti Taluk, this area has been selected for the study. On the basis of the maximum turnover of groundnut in the industries of the sample area, 10 industries (5 decorticating industries and 5 oil industries) were selected and a survey has proved that the sample respondents have been facing many problems in connection with handling of the kernel.

The very object of the study is to probe into the various problems (both economical and technological) faced by the respondents and to suggest to possible recommendations that require immediate action.

Table 19.4 : Factories and Industries located in Theni District

Sl. No.	Nature	Number
1.	Registered Working Factories	301
2.	Large Scale Industries	18
3.	Medium Scale Industries	12
4.	Small Scale Industries	582
5.	Cottage Industries	150
6.	Unregistered Cottage Units	NA

Source : District Industries Centre, Theni.

Table 19.5 : Sickness in Small Industries

Sl. No.	Year	Units	Percentage of sick small units to total small units
1.	1980 December	23149	5.67
2.	1983	78363	11.40
3.	1986	145776	15.34
4.	1990	218828	11.28
5.	1991	221472	11.07
6.	1998	358915	11.50

Source : *Economic Survey*, 1999.

Findings of the Study

Shortage of Raw Materials

The cottage worker suffers from acute shortage of raw materials. The groundnut industry is wholly dependent upon the supply of raw groundnut. The groundnut growers are unable to supply the nut, throughout the year, to the industries, as this crop is seasonal. Hence the shortage of raw groundnut is always felt. In the study area there are two types of industries, viz.

(a) Industries at large scale of operation,
(b) Industries at low scale of operation.

The industries which indulge in huge business operations are rightly categorised as health business enterprises. They buy more raw materials, produce more, sell more and enjoy more. They also procure and hoard groundnut in bulk and operate the market. They fix the price of the groundnut (raw materials) and act as middlemen in the field. The average industries and low scale operating industries have to depend largely on the market operators. Thus the artisan does not get enough of what he wants, what he gets is of poor quality and that too has to be bought at higher price.

Lack of Credit and Finance

The financial disability of small artisans is beyond doubt. Their financial needs consists of the purchase of raw materials working expenses and accommodation between production and sale of the products. The internal sources are quite inadequate. This leads to instability of their profits which deters banks from giving unsecured loans. Their requirements are met by village money lenders who charge high rates of interest. The total amount of loan granted to them by the commercial banks forms a very small part of the total loans to the industry.

Low Level of Technology and Skill

The development of the village and small scale industries is hampered by the present low level of technology and shortage of trained and experienced supervisory personnel. So that the methods and art of production technique especially the producers for want of information, know very little about modern technologies which have revolutionised production in small units in advanced countries. There is little research and development in this field in the country.

Competition from Large Scale Industries

Large scale industries, organised as they are on modern lines, using latest production technology and having access to many facilities can easily outsell the small products. The small producers cannot, therefore, stand up against them in the market.

Sickness and Inefficiency

Quite a large proportion of small industries has fallen sick (*vide* Table 19.5). Their number run into lakhs. At present as many as 2.96 lakhs units are sick. This is exclusive over a lakh sick units which are not traceable or are not in existence. The reason for such sickness is that in many of the units 45 per cent to 60 per cent of its capacity remains unutilised. The reason may be incompetent manager, improper location, insufficient technology, skill, inadequate infrastructural facilities etc.

Inadequate Cost Analysis

Inadequate product-cost analysis binds entrepreneurs to the losses incurred by adding new products willy-nilly. As the sample members deal with many products, viz., coconut, neem seed, gingely seed etc. they could not calculate the cost per product. Usually, there are one or more products or product lines that should be dropped.

Another common failing is gearing the operations to the income statement and ignoring the other financial statements. Lack of concern with cash flow and the productivity of capital employed can be fatal to the small company, that is on its own. Entrepreneurs can make better use of the funds which they already have by making use of financial statement rather than seeking for new funds. Thus entrepreneurs need to realise that the surest test of their business success is sufficient and profits growing from year to year.

Cost of Electricity

Separation of oil and cake from the concerned raw materials requires the use of machineries. Machines now-a-days are not operated by men, but by electricity. The cottage entrepreneurs, who use machineries, are charged the commercial rate (Rs. 3.20 per unit) by the electricity boards. This is a great burden to these small entrepreneurs which prevent their growth and expansion.

Collection of Debts

A businessman cannot depend only on cash sales. He has to depend on credit sales too. Credit sales is profitable as well as a risky affair. Most of the entrepreneurs face the problem of debt collection. It has been proved that there has been an average of 25 per cent bad debts on credit sales which is made to small household businessmen. This occurrence of bad debts is due to the downfall of small cottage units, diversification of business (change of business), loss in business, family commitments, etc.

No business can operate without inventories. It needs protection. Guarding inventory thus becomes essential and forms strength to the units.

Inventory comes in various forms such as supplies, raw materials, goods in process of manufacture, finished goods and floor stock (display).

It is always prudent to guard inventory as well as the inventories cost money in several ways.

Groundnut occupies vast floor area. So a businessman has to allocate a major portion of the industry for keeping the raw groundnut, semi-finished and finished stock. Maintenance of the whole area for keeping of the goods results ultimately in high cost.

Groundnut production is purely seasonal. So a large volume of raw groundnut is to be preserved till it is used for the process of production. The harvesting season lasts just for 2 months only. So the businessmen dealing in groundnut have to invest a lot in procuring raw groundnut. As, within a short period, their raw groundnut has to be procured for storing, the businessmen are unable to generate the fund from their own business. Hence they borrow. Thus, by this process money is tied up. This tie up of money causes payment of interest.

Raw groundnut has to be stored for a very long time in the factory. So risk is more in preservation. So to get rid of the risk, the entire stock is insured. Insurance in this respect is considered to be costly as premium is paid on the basis of the area of storage.

Storage is done is large areas. Hence it is bound to pay property tax on them. Cost of protection from pilferage and weather, pests and insects also cause damage. So to destroy them some cost is incurred.

Marketing Problem

Marketing the groundnut oil is the major problem faced by the small and large entrepreneurs. The sample members are of the opinion that, if at all they could sell one kilogram of groundnut oil atleast for Rs. 40, it will be of benefit to them. At this situation, it is very difficult, it is not impossible to sell them at this required price. It is due to the globalisation policy of the government (bilateral agreement). As the price of groundnut oil is more, consequently the demand decreases. Another reason for such fall in demand for this oil is that of the import of palmoline (Palm oil) by the government even at Rs. 21 per litre. So the middle income group as well as the people below and at poverty line switch over to the substitute. At present the price of Gingely oil has also fallen down to a certain extent.

Suggestions

There are many problems which stand as an obstacle on the improvement of groundnut industry. In this study the problems with regard to inventories are mostly highlighted and some suggestions for optimising the inventory have been made.

The businessmen can opt for a nearby source of supply that gives prompt delivery too. The supplier may be asked to carry the inventory. Sometimes one may charge for transportation. But this arrangement will save lot of money tied up in long-term inventory.

When suppliers offer quantity discounts one must see that the savings is not offset by other costs. One can negotiate a year's supply in order to get quantity discounts, then demand that the goods be supplied in small quantities as and when one needs them.

One can look for faster quick and cheaper transportation modes.

It is better to keep the inventory only as finished goods.

One can expand the concept of time. If it takes six weeks for delivery one do not need a six-week supply, as one can order smaller quantities for weekly or daily delivery.

The businessmen have to shop around for best price and group purchase are suggested. In case a rented warehouse is established by the supplier one can prefer such a supplier.

Other Suggestions for Improvement

It has been found that large scale industries dominate the market and they do not allow the small industries to come up. Purchase of raw materials can be made on co-operative basis. Regulated markets functioning in the districts can also render services of this nature.

The civil supplier corporation can establish warehouses to preserve groundnut at a very meagre rate of rent to the agricultural farmers.

Revolving credit facility system could be followed in this

connection. Commercial banks can give guarantee to the supplies who extend revolving credit system.

Electricity can be supplied at a concessional rate.

Subsidy may be granted to the cultivators which may reduce the cost of production in total.

The government can allot more funds towards Research and Developments in the field of agriculture in general and commercial oil seed crops in particular. Western pattern of production (cultivation) could be introduced by the Department of Agriculture in every district by selecting unemployed graduates who have atleast little property for cultivation. Co-operative farming to a certain extent can also be thought of with the help of establishing cooperative societies in this regard. Training the graduates can be imparted at a low cost quickly.

The impact, on implementation of the above said suggestion may be that, there will be more employment generation, more benefit to the agriculturists and entrepreneurs, and more income to the nation. This may also prove that the rural area itself will get developed economically and socially.

References

Agarwal, A. N., *Indian Economy Problems of Development & Planning,* 21st Edition, Wishwa Prakashan, 1995.

District Profile Department of Statistics.

Entrepreneurship Development Centre for Research & Industrial Staff performance, Tata McGraw Hill Publishing Co. Ltd., New Delhi.

Memoria, C.B. & Tripathi, B.B., *Agricultural Problems of India,* Kithab Mahal.

Small Industries Development Organisation and Eighth Five Years Plans, 1992-97 and 1998-99.

State Directorates of Industries, Chennai.

20

A STUDY ON REVIVAL OF SICK SMALL SCALE INDUSTRIAL UNITS IN MADURAI CITY

— *R. Varadarajan*

Small Scale Industries play a very significant role in the economic development of our country. Promotion and growth of the Small Scale Industrial sector has been a cardinal feature of Indian Industrial Policy. SSIs in India have been given a destined indentity and the government has accorded high priority to this sector on account of vital role it plays in balanced and maintainable economic growth. It plays a crucial role in the process of economic development by value additions, development generation, equitable distribution of national income, regional dispersal of industries, mobilisation of capital and entrepreneurial skills and contribution to export earnings.

It has all the characteristics of the decentralised sector such as small size and emloyment's intensity and the entire lot belongs to private sector. The contribution of SSI sector for employment is next only to agriculture. At the end of March 1999, there were 27.24 lakhs SSI units in the country. They contribute 40 per cent of the total industrial output; employ 1.54 crore persons and accounts for 35 per cent of the total exports from India. Since independence, Government of India has been giving impetus on the development of this sector. The Industrial Policy Resolutions of 1948 to till date have stressed the importance of SSIs. New Industrial Policy Statement 1990 has taken lot of measures to develop SSI in India.

The SSI covers a wide range of enterprises with diverse characteristics. There are tiny or micro entrepreneurs on one hand and there are sophisticated modern small scale units on the other.

Small scale industrial undertakings are those which are engaged in the manufactures processing or reservation of goods and in which investment in plant and machinery does not exceed Rs. 3 crore. These would include ancillary industrial undertakings, tiny enterprises, small scale service/business enterprises, the decentralised sector, artisan, village and cottage industries and women enterprises.

A SSI unit is considered as sick when any of its borrowed accounts has become doubtful advance, i.e. principal or interest in respect of any of its borrowed accounts has remained overdue for a period exceeding 2-1/2 years.

There is erosion in the net-worth due to accumulated cash losses to the extent of 50 per cent or more of its peak net-worth during the preceding two accounting years.

The study of revival of sick units in Madurai city is undertaken to pursue the following specific objectives:

1. To identify the position of sickness in SSI units in Madurai city.
2. To identify the possibility to revive the sick SSI units in Madurai city.
3. To summarise and suggest the measures to revive the sick units.

Sickness in the industrial units is a bane to the society. It blocks up the very vital and scarce resources such as capital, machinery, skill and expertise. The entire goes out of gear and remains as a black patch in the economy. It is like a virus, which spreads widely and leads to frustration. This calamity can be overcome by reformulating all the concerned entrepreneurs, Government Corporations, Industrial Associations, Financial Institutions, Commercial Banks and other concerned officials. This study is an attempt to develop a matching concept. There is a need to find out the possibility of reviving the sick units is the need of hour. Hence, the study probe into reviving the sick small industrial units. Madurai being the district headquarters has become a place of SSI conglomeration. Madurai city is the target place for the study.

Descriptive and Exploratory method of research has been adopted in this attempt. A descriptive analysis is made to find solutions to the problem stated. The primary data collected with the help of structured questionnaire from SSI owners.

Madurai city is the oldest city with lot of rural face. It has only one small scale industrial estate in K. Pudur and lot of small scale units in and around the city. Nearly nine hundred (900) units registered with SIDCO. There are quite a good member of unregistered units in and around the city. Hence, the apt universe is Madurai city.

As the universe to be studied consists of 250 respondents, the author conducted a survey. The author has taken non-probability and convenient random sampling of handloom textile units, auto ancillaries, service sector, steel product manufactures, wax products manufactures and electrical units. Out of 250 units, only 180 units' responses were considered finally for analysis.

The questionnaire has been prepared by the author for identifying the variables. He had made comprehensive study of the literature directly and indirectly connected. He had also discussed the problems with government officials and some financial institutions before finalising the questionnaire. The field work cover a period of nearly 10 days from October 10, 2000 to October 20, 2000.

The questionnaire has been checked and edited. Data thus obtained have been grouped into meaningful classes and master table was prepared. Sub-tables have derived from it for further analysis and interpretation. Average and percentage analyses were used for making a detailed discussion of data collected from the respondents.

SSI Units in India

In line with the trend all over the world, micro-enterprises constitute the largest blocks in terms of numbers in India. It is estimated that 'tiny enterprises' form about 96 per cent of the total number of small scale enterprises. Their contribution in terms of production and employment is about 58.5 per cent respectively. The small size of investment in an industrial unit is considered to be a disadvantage in a market economy characterised by intense competition, guilty upgraduation. However, small investment and size need not be a handicap if such an enterprise is in a cluster of enterprises engaged in a particular sub-sector. If small enterprises are in a cluster, the out reach of promotional and developmental agencies is enhanced.

In 1991-92, the number of registered small scale industrial undertakings was 22.35 lakhs. Of these, the five States of Uttar Pradesh, Madhya Pradesh, West Bengal, Punjab and Tamil Nadu accounted for 8.43 lakh units. Small scale industrial enterprises also exhibit a characteristic of agglomerations near urban areas and metropolitan cities. Of course, there are clusters of industries in terms of product groups like cotton hosiery at Tirupur (Tamil Nadu), Woollen Knitwear at Ludhiana (Punjab), Leather footwear, readymade garments, glass industry, foundry industry, chemical industry and the like at different locations. It would appear that the developed infrastructure facilities, availability of skilled labour, strong consumer demand etc. have worked as magnets.

In India, small scale industries employ all levels of technology. It has been observed that the percentage of enterprises using modern technology is quite small. This observation is based on the process of manufacture used, investment in plant and machinery, installation of testing equipment, R&D facilities, adoption of quality making etc. In a publication of the Federation of Indian Chambers of Commerce, a study conducted by National Council of Applied Economic Researh, has been quoted which indicated that, out of a sample of 657 units, those units using manual process numbered 372 (56.62) and those using semi-automatic processes were 254

(38.7). In enterprises employing less than Rs. 2 lakhs of capital, 81.5 per cent are manual processes. Low level of technology employed in small enterprises hinders linkages with large industry.

Sickness among SSI units is also large. As per the data collected by the Reserve Bank of India (RBI), the number of sick SSI units at the end of March 1991 was 0.22 lakhs and this increased to 0.25 lakh units by the end of March 1992 registering an increase of 10.9 per cent. The amount outstanding in bank loans increased during this period from Rs. 2792 crores to Rs. 31,011 crores, an increase of 11.1 per cent. It is interesting to note that the number of sick SSI units fell to 0.23 lakhs by the end of September, 1992, that is a decline of 4.9 per cent. However, the amount of bank loans outstanding increased to Rs. 3,344 crores, an increase of 7.9 per cent. The above description of characteristics include the vast diversity in the number of products manufactured in this sector such as low power intensity, poor capital base, great employment intensity per unit of fixed capital, lack of access to capital, greater use of local resources and local skills.

Government of India announced a separate industrial policy for Small Enterprises for the first time on 6 August, 1991. The primary objective of the policy was stated to be to impact more vitality and growth impetus to the small-scale sector, so that it could contribute fully to the economy in terms of output, employment and exports. Along with the new industrial policy, the major policy measures were continued. These related to reservation of items produced in the small scale sector, priority sector lending and excise relief. At present 836 items are reserved for exclusive production in the small scale sector. Similarly, 409 items are reserved for purchase from this sector. In matters of Government purchases, price preference to products from this sector is 15 per cent payment of small industries bills and legislation for Limited Partnership Act, introduction of a new scheme of integrated infrastructure. Development to promote industrialisation in rural and backward areas, setting up of Technology Development cell, setting up of Exports Development centre, recognition of industry related service and business enterprises as small scale industries, Promotion of marketing of ancillary units, promotion of entrepreneurship, quality upgradation.

The small industry sector has been given considerable importance in the Five Year Plans. The allocation of funds to this sector has been increasing steadily over the years. The outlay approved for small scale sector, including industrial estates, Central and State Plan Schemes during the successive periods are presented in Table 20.1.

Table 20.1 : Five Year Plans — SSI — Central and State Plan Schemes

Plans	Period (in years)	Total outlay (Rupees in crores)
I	1951-56	5.20
II	1956-61	56.00
III	1961-66	113.08
ANNUAL	1966-69	53.48
IV	1969-74	96.19
V	1974-80	221.74
ANNUAL	1979-80	104.81
VI	1980-85	616.10
VII	1985-90	1120.51
ANNUAL	1990-91	392.13
ANNUAL	1991-92	182.86
VIII	1992-97	2862.14

Source : Report of SIDO, Govt. of India, Eighth Five Year Plan.

In the post-independence period, the Government at the Centre and in the State established a number of specialized institutions to cater to the varied needs of small scale units. These promotional institutions assists all and sundry in setting up small with a view, either to fulfilling their objectives or over-reach their target. But they neither ensure the provision of adequate working capital, raw materials, power supply nor do they help them in developing marketing outlets for the sale of their products. This situation has arisen because of the absence of a meaningful coordination among the concerned agencies. Besides these, Government have also taken a very important role in establishing Industrial Estates, on a rental basis in order to provide good accommodation and basic common facilities to a group of small entrepreneurs. The following are the major objectives of the industrial estate programme:

1. To shift small scale industries from congested areas to estate premises.
2. To encourage the growth of small scale industries.
3. Decentralised industrial development in small towns and large villages.
4. To encourage the growth of ancillary industries in the townships.

The number of industrial units in the small scale sector in 1993-94 was 23.85 lakhs. These provided employment to about 138 lakh persons. Their value of output estimated to Rs. 241,648 crores. As per Industrial Policy 1991, small scale industrial units contribute to the extent of 35 per cent of gross industrial production within the country. In employment, their contribution only second to agriculture and in exports, they account for about 40 per cent of the total exports. This sector produces more than 7,500 products. In terms of growth, the performance of this is much above the manufacturing sector. For example, in 1992-93, the manufacturing sector grew by 1.2 per cent whereas, small scale industries recorded a growth 5.6 per cent in 1994-95, this sector is expected to have grown by about nine per cent. In a year, about 1.5 lakhs registered and unregistered small scale industrial units took birth.

According to a report, tiny enterprises received bank credit only equal to 2.8 per cent of its output. Despite financial returns, bank credit to SSI's does not exceed 14-15 per cent of their total advances. The financial condition of state financial coporations is not happy marketing is another area of their weakness. There are about 45 central laws applicable to small scale industries. Technology is an area which needs urgent attention. Despite governmental efforts, the programme of modernisation has not picked up.

Some critics, blame the policy of reservation for high cost of production and indifferent quality of products of the small scale sector. While this may be an exaggerated view, the need for upgradation of abilities in technology, skills of workers, management of enterprise and marketing is recognised. Poor non-financial support and poor infrastructure available to small scale industries are well known. The growth rates recorded by the small scale industries during the last years, that is, 5.6 per cent, 7.1 per cent and 9.5 per cent all above those recorded by the manufacturing sector. It is hoped that this trend will continue and give a greater scope for small scale industries in future (Wasme News Letter — April 1995).

In India, small industry is a State subject. Programmes for the development of small industries are implemented by State Directorates of Industries, State Financial Corporations and State Small Scale Industries Development Corporations. District Industries Centres (DIC) have been set up at district level as a single window interacting agency with the entrepreneur. There are 422 DIC's covering 431 districts. The growth of SSI units in India, over the year (1990-91) are shown in Table 20.2.

Table 20.2 : Small Scale Sector Growth over the Year (1990-96)

Year	No. of Units	Employment (lakhs)	Investment (crores)	Exports (crores)	SSI Shares (percentage)
1990-91	19.38	124.30	19302	9100	28.20
1991-92	20.82	129.80	20438	13883	31.50
1992-93	22.35	134.10	21816	17785	31.10
1993-94	23.85	138.40	22934	25307	36.30
1994-95	25.38	146.00	24874	32555	39.50
1995-96	26.78	151.00	26726	38036	39.80

Source : Office of the Development Commissioner (SSI — New Delhi).

Small Scale Industries in Tamil Nadu

In order to avoid various indifferences in development of Small Scale Sectors, the Government of Tamil Nadu has taken a separate policy for Small Scale Sectors to improve their overall living standards.

Tamil Nadu Government has introduced both 'temporary

registration application' form comprising of seven sections and 'permanent registration application' form comprising of eight sections with all simplified means using both Tamil and English as the medium of communication. This has shown some sort of easy accessibility on the part of people who wish to start their business at any means. Moreover, for making their registration on legal grounds, it is enough if the person signs in affidavit (legal document). This will make their registration immediately effective without taking much of their time.

In order to make a 'Standard growth' in Small Scale Sector, the Government of Tamil Nadu has fixed a standard target for their achievement. The following Table 20.3 shows exactly the level of standard target and their achievement in growth of SSI sector in Tamil Nadu concerned to the particular year from 1992-93 to 1995-96 respectively.

Table 20.3 : The Growth Level of SSI Units of Tamil Nadu (1992-96)

Year	Standard Target Fixed (in numbers)	Actual Target achieved (in numbers)
1992-93	20,100	23,577
1993-94	24,100	25,719
1994-95	28,900	31,052
1995-96	30,000	30,470

Source : Annual Report, Government of Tamil Nadu, 1995-96.

The total number of SSI Units registered in Tamil Nadu at the end of every financial year from 1992-93 upto 1995-96 respectively are shown as follows:

Table 20.4 : Number of Registered Unit in Tamil Nadu and Madurai 1992-96

Year	Number of registered units Tamil Nadu	Number of SSI units Madurai
1992-93	1,57,892	1192
1993-94	1,78,114	1827
1994-95	2,07,357	1479
1995-96	2,34,663	2601

Source : Annual Report, Govt. of Tamil Nadu, 1995-96.

Apart from this, the Government of India has formulated 20 points of programmes for want of enriching the industrial growth in India. Accordingly, they formulated two different projects namely, I(J) and II(A). The project I(J) is concerned to those who are educated but unemployed and the project II(A) is concerned to those who have started small industries belonging to scheduled castes only.

Table 20.5 shows, exactly the level of standard target fixed and their achievement in growth of SSI sector in Tamil Nadu concerned to those who are educated but unemployed during the particular year from 1992-93 to 1995-96 respectively.

Table 20.5 : Growth of SSI Units among Educated but Un-employed Persons

Year	Standard Target (in numbers)	Actual Target achieved (in numbers)
1992-93	12,000	15,983
1993-94	13,200	14,203
1994-95	13,300	15,945
1995-96	14,700	16,410

Source : Annual Report, Govt. of Tamil Nadu, 1995-96.

SSI in Madurai District

On the basis of the primary data collection through questionnaire from the sample size, the analysis is made.

Table 20.6 : Age Pattern

Age	No. of Respondents	Percentage
Below 25 years	38	21.1
Above 25 years	142	78.9
Total	180	100

Source : Primary Data.

Out of 180 respondents, 142 were the age group of more than 25 years which contributed 78.9 per cent and 38 consisting less than 21.1 per cent belonged to the age group less than 25 years.

Table 20.7 : Marital Status

Marital Status	No. of Respondents	Percentage
Married	116	64.5
Unmarried	64	35.5
Total	180	100.0

Source : Primary Data.

It can be seen that about 64.5 per cent are married and only about 35.5 per cent are unmarried. Out of 180 respondents women respondents is very low and it is 20 per cent.

Table 20.8 : Educational Background

Qualification	No. of Respondents	Percentage
Graduates	80	44.5
Postgraduates	14	7.8
Professional/Technical (BE/ME/M Tech)	189	10.5
Diploma	55	30.5
Certificate	12	6.7
Total	180	100.0

Source : Primary Data.

Table 20.9 : Entrepreneurship Background

Background	No. of Respondents	Percentage
Family Background	106	59.0
Relatives	44	24.5
Friends/Others	30	16.5
Total	180	100.0

Source : Primary Data.

About 44.5 per cent of them of Graduates, 7.8 per cent of Post Graduates, 10.5 per cent are professionally qualified like B.E., M.E., B.Tech 30.5 per cent of them are Diploma holders. Among them 6.7 per cent illiterates are in the field.

It can be observed that about 59 per cent are influenced by the family background, 24.5 per cent of them are from relatives background and 16.5 per cent of them are from the friends and other contacts. It should be noted that 59 per cent are having some entrepreneurship link.

Table 20.10 : Motivational Factors

Factors	No. of Respondents	Percentage
Only pull factors	57	31.7
Only Push factors	40	22.3
Both Pull & Push factors	83	46.0
Total	180	100.0

Source : Primary Data.

The pull factors identified are challenge or adventure, urge to do something and a liking for business and 31.7 per cent of them are influenced by pull factors. The push factors are to get over financial difficulties, due to family circumstances, unemployment, and forced to take over from others. If consituted 22.3 per cent of the respondents. Majority (46%) of them are coupled with both the factors.

Findings of the Study

Threat from MNCs: In spite of the onslaught of MNCs, the small scale industry sector met with some problems. It has been accepted by 72 per cent of the respondents.

Raw Material Shortage : Dependency is a *sine qua non* for SSI units. Majority of units depends on the supply of raw materials from the government nodal agencies. Ministeel product, manufacturers of wax supply, supply of yarn and etc. suffer from shortage of raw materials. Delay in supply is another impediment in the way 80 per cent of the respondents accepted as true.

Inadequacy of finance : Many SSI units have hand to mouth existence especially in the initial stage. Harshness meted out the units by the financial institutions adds fuel to the injury. Frequent lapses on repayment of installments put them into red. They find it difficult to come out from this vicious circle. 75 per cent of the respondents accepted this as a serious problem.

Non-payment by big industries : Many SSI units supply their outputs to big industries and government requirements. Lack of payments by these big industries causes a great hardship to SSI units. Bureaucratic delay from government department is also not uncommon. 62 per cent of the respondents emphatically accepted this as fact.

Demand recession : Every business is subject to cyclical effects. A SSI unit finds it difficult to sustain depression with the increase of competition, market share dwindles, which ultimately reduces the sales revenue. 86 per cent of them accepted this problem, e.g. Weavers societies and terry towel handloom units closed in Madurai.

Trade wars : With limited resources, SSI unit cannot survive the threat of competition. Law of jungle prevails in business. 76 per cent of them accepted this fact.

Underutilisation of capacity : Plants might have been installed with the hope of expansion in future. This may not be materialised due to several factors. Similarly, capacity of labour force might have been underutilised due to lack of work, innovativeness. It is found that 65 per cent of the respondents significantly accepted for underutilisation of capacity.

Obsolete machinery and technology : For a SSI unit, replacement of a machinery is a difficult task. Technologies both for products and processes are rapidly changing. A SSI unit with outdated technology cannot survive. But this is not only a scarce resource but also an expensive one, which a SSI Unit may not afford to have. 90 per cent of them accepted this problem.

Managerial incompetence : Many SSI units have been commenced by the entrepreneur who have not been backed up by proper training skills. A momentary decision, without proper support system and foresightedness may lead to land in trouble. Professionalisation in Management has become expense and so many units (83%) may not afford to avail the same. This results in failure of the venture.

Incompetent marketing : Improper assessment of demand non-judicial investment in sales promotion activities, non-provident strategies, and plans are leading factors contributing for sickness. 65 per cent of them accepted as a great problem. Lack of awareness of symptoms of sickness. Prevention is better than cure. There are no standard techniques or measures or awareness to identify the symptoms of sickness in early stage. 90 per cent of them accepted this fact.

Inferences

This is an important segment of the questionnaire. The respondents were asked to give their opinion about the possibility of reviving the sick unit.

70 per cent of them prefer to make necessary changes before being taken over. The reason is to mould the unit according to their desires, liking and choice. 30 per cent of them are interested in taking up the sick units "as is where is condition".

It is found that 50 per cent of the respondents prefer to take over because the plant is available at lesser price. 35 per cent of them willing to take over because financial facility is available. 15 per cent of them accepted that all facilities are already existing.

It is observed that 64 per cent of the respondents prefer package from both government and private agencies. 24 per cent of them are not interested in the government interference to take over the sick units.

It is pointed out that 82 per cent of the respondents favour financial assistance at concessional rate of interest, whereas 18 per cent of them are at regular rate of interest to take over the sick units.

It is seen that 58 per cent of the respondents prefer the repayment period to be between 3 and 5 years, 21 per cent prefer above 5 years and remaining 21 per cent of them prefer less than 3 years.

It can be noted that 90 per cent of them want to change the employees whenever required. 8 per cent of them want to retain the same and only 2 per cent want to completely replace the labour force.

74 per cent of the respondents revealed that they want to market their products by themselves. 26 per cent of them willing to market through others.

73 per cent of them are willing to avail the tax benefits in one form or the other. It can also be seen that 27 per cent of them don't want any concession.

92 per cent of them preferred the institutional support, only 8 per cent of them don't want any support from anybody.

Conclusion

The study encompasses a review of the plethora of existing revival packages and the possible awareness that could be suggested to tackle the situation of sickness. Thus, the study has been a concerted effort to throw light on the persisting problem which has all ingredients for hindering the development of SSI sector and also to find the possible avenues that could solve as powerful instruments to solve the problems, as well as to contribute to the creation of strong, healthy and prosperous economy.

References

Annual Reports, DIC, SIDCO, Madurai.

Business India, June 2000.

Desai, Vasant, *Small Scale Industries and Entrepreneurship*, Himalaya Publishing House, Delhi, 1996.

RBI Bulletins : 1990-1999.

RBI, "Small Scale Industry - Policy and Guidelines", 1996-1999.

Schumpeter, J. A., *The Theory of Economic Development*, Oxford University, New York, 1967.

SISI, Government of India.

The Hindu, Madurai Edition.

21

INDUSTRIAL SICKNESS IN TEXTILE INDUSTRY IN TAMIL NADU

— *P. Solomon Raj*

Introduction

The Cotton Textile industry may be considered as the real *swadeshi* industry of India built under Indian Management. In addition to providing means of livelihood for nearly 10 million handloom weavers, the mill industry provides direct employment to nearly 8 lakh workers representing about 20 per cent of the total industrial population of the country. Moreover, considerable foreign exchange is also obtained by exporting textile products, which helps to attain economic development of the nation. Today textile industry in India has also gained stature among the world textile industry occupying second rank in terms of capacity.

The textile industry occupies a pre-eminent place in the economy of Tamil Nadu in the country. In Tamil Nadu, there are 800 textile mills functioning now. They produce 50 per cent of the total yarn production in India, out of which 35 per cent are exported to foreign countries and thereby gets 2500 crores of foreign exchange every year. Moreover, Government of Tamil Nadu collects Rs. 190 crores through sales tax. About 4 lakhs of labourers are getting employment in textile sector.

Such an important industry is now passing through recession. Therefore, the cotton textile industry is rightly considered as a sick industry or a problem industry. Hence, an attempt is made to study the industrial sickness in textile industry in Tamil Nadu. The conclusions that are arrived in this study may be useful for the policy makers to initiate necessary steps to overcome the problems encountered by the textile industry in Tamil Nadu.

The textile industry in India has a complex and varied structure. The fairly well accepted way of viewing the textile industry and its problems for policy making and scholarly analysis in terms of sectoral differentiation of the three sectors being - handlooms, power looms and mills.

Table 21.1 highlights the fabric production of various sectors in textile industry in India. The fabric production statistics clearly establish the extent of decline of the mill sector due to the expansion of the cost-effective powerloom sectors, which could also be the consequence of the mill owner's entry into and encouragement to the powerlooms. It would be necessary to note that the contribution of the mill sector to the total textile production has steadily declined over the years, while the share of powerlooms has recorded a phenomenal increase before the National Textile Policy (1980-81 to 1984-85). This shows a decline of mills share from 37.93 per cent in 1980-81 to 28.57 per cent in 1984-85, while during this period the powerloom share had recorded 7.64 percentage point increase.

The decline in mill production can obviously be traced to the restrictions on capacity and fibre-use, imposition of heavy excise duties, controls on the import of polyester fibre and of technology for modernisation of the mill sector by the earlier policy regimes. Though National Textile Policy, 1985 intervention was intended to protect handlooms, its unintended consequence was the expansion of the powerlooms. The mill owners are the beneficiaries of the modernisation schemes, brunt has to be borne by the workers. By the end of the 5th year of the National Textile Policy (1985-89) around 567 mills (both spinning and composite) were closed

Table 21.1 : Sector-wise Production of Textile Industries in India

(in meters)

	Mills		Powerloom		Handloom		Total	
Years	Cotton	Total	Cotton	Total	Cotton	Total	Cotton	Total
'80-81	3434 (41.03)	4168 (37.93)	2334 (27.9)	4140 (37.68)	2600 (31.07)	2680 (24.39)	8368 (100)	10988 (100)
'81-82	2923 (36.61)	3808 (34.68)	2520 (31.57)	4547 (41.41)	2540 (31.82)	2626 (23.91)	7983 (100)	10981 (100)
'82-83	2393 (30.09)	3132 (29.51)	2830 (35.58)	4694 (44.22)	2730 (34.33)	2788 (26.27)	7953 (100)	10614 (100)
'83-84	2704 (30.93)	3487 (29.66)	3148 (36.02)	5315 (45.20)	2889 (33.05)	2956 (25.16)	8741 (100)	11758 (100)
'84-85	2619 (28.97)	3432 (28.57)	3348 (37.04)	5445 (45.32)	3073 (33.99)	3137 (26.11)	9040 (100)	12014 (100)
'85-86	2587 (28.18)	3376 (27.1)	3435 (37.43)	5886 (47.10)	3156 (34.39)	3236 (25.89)	9178 (100)	12498 (100)
'86-87	2470 (25.95)	3317 (25.54)	3676 (38.60)	6222 (47.91)	3376 (35.45)	3449 (26.55)	9522 (100)	12988 (100)
'87-88	2234 (23.77)	3027 (23.3)	3734 (39.72)	6547 (49.7)	3432 (36.51)	3508 (27.00)	9400 (100)	12992 (100)
'88-89	2021 (22.25)	2808 (21.14)	3680 (40.52)	7008 (52.76)	3381 (37.23)	3466 (26.1)	9082 (100)	13282 (100)
'89-90	1957 (16.64)	2667 (14.64)	5965 (50.73)	11632 (63.83)	3837 (32.63)	3924 (21.53)	11759 (100)	18223 (100)
'90-91	1859 (14.32)	2589 (12.80)	6887 (53.05)	13348 (65.97)	4237 (32.63)	4295 (21.23)	12983 (100)	20232 (100)
'91-92	1651 (13.64)	2376 (12.03)	6383 (52.76)	13262 (67.11)	4065 (133.6)	4123 (20.86)	12099 (100)	19761 (100)
'92-93	1407 (10.5)	2000 (09.15)	7306 (54.53)	14644 (66.98)	4686 (34.97)	5219 (23.87)	13399 (100)	21863 (100)
'93-94	1356 (9.4)	1990 (08.35)	7836 (54.29)	15994 (67.1)	5241 (36.41)	5851 (24.55)	14433 (100)	23835 (100)
'94-95	899 (8.57)	1370 (07.67)	5845 (55.72)	12303 (68.9)	3746 (35.71)	41.85 (23.43)	10490 (100)	17858 (100)

Note : Total includes Cotton, blended and 100 per cent non-cotton fabrics only. Percentage are given in the parentheses.

Source : Economic and Political Weekly, vol. xxx 1 no. 49, Dec. 7, 1996.

affecting 727 lakh workers.

Employment Potentials of Textile Industry in India

One of the factors that make the textile industry so vital to the country's economy is the employment potential it has generated. The sector-wise details of employment for the years 1988-89 to 1990-91 are given in Table 21.2.

Table 21.2 : Sector-wise Employment Potential in Textile Industries

Sector	Employment (in lakhs)		
	1988-89	1989-90	1990-91
Mill Sector	11.04 (7.5)	11.6 (7.5)	11.0 (6.7)
Handlooms	84.25 (57.6)	88.64 (57.0)	96.87 (58.8)
Powerlooms	57.07 (34.9)	55.20 (35.5)	57.00 (34.5)
Total	146.36 (100)	155.44 (100)	164.87 (100)

Note : Figures in brackets indicate percentage to total.

Table 21.2 shows that although there was stagnation in the organised mill sector, employment in the decentralised weaving sector has been steadily rising.

Cloth Production in Textile Industry

The sector-wise production of total cloth during 1987-88 to 1991-92 has been given in Table 21.3.

Table 21.3 : Cloth Production in India

Year	Total cloth production (million sq. mts)			
	Mills	Powerlooms	Handlooms	Total
1987-88	37.78 (18)	10429 (58)	4370 (24)	17977 (100)
1988-89	29.02 (14)	13123 (65)	3993 (21)	20018 (100)
1989-90	2667 (13)	14007 (68)	3924 (19)	20598 (100)
1990-91	2589 (11)	16044 (70)	4295 (19)	22928 (100)
1991-92	2376 (11)	16089 (71)	4123 (18)	22588 (100)

Note : Figures in brackets indicate percentage to total.

Table 21.3 shows that the share of organised sector in the total production of cloth has been continuously declining and dropped to a mere 11 per cent in 1991-92. This fall in the share of the organised mill sector was made up entirely by the power looms whose share went up from 58 to 71 per cent during the period 1987-88 to 1991-92. Handlooms lose their share from 24 per cent to 18 per cent of the total cloth production.

Textile Industry in Tamil Nadu

The premier status of this industry in Tamil Nadu is, however, now threatened as the industry is encountered with innumerable problems which in turn, have led to closure of a number of mills. Of the 133 mills lying closed in the country as on March 1988, 37 mills were in Tamil Nadu. The major problems facing the industry today is the ever-rising input costs and the slump in the market for textile products. The textile mills in Tamil Nadu consume about

27 lakh bales of cotton every year. Against this, the State produces only 6 lakh bales of cotton. The mills are, therefore obliged to buy the cotton from States as far as Punjab, which in turn necessitates additional cost on transportation. Similarly, of the total yarn produced by the mills, only 60 per cent is consumed within the state, the rest being sold out in country markets adding to the cost of transportation to the mills.

Table 21.4 : Performance of Textile Mills in Tamil Nadu

Particulars	1990-91	1991-92
1. No of Textile mills		
(a) Spinning	438 (41.2)	449 (40.5)
(b) Composite	413 (53.2)	424 (51.5)
2. Installed Spinning Capacity	77.3 (29.0)	79.4 (29.1)
3. No. of looms installed ('000)	9.0 (5.1)	9.0 (5.1)
4. Yarn production	529.0 (29.5)	534.0 (30.0)
5. Cloth production (million metres)	167.0 (6.4)	160.0 (6.7)
6. Employment	1.84 (16.6)	—

Table 21.4 outlines the contribution made by the textile industry in Tamil Nadu. Despite contributing to nearly 41 per cent of the total 'number of textile mills', 29 per cent of total 'installed capacity' and 30 per cent of total 'yarn production' at the all-India level, Tamil Nadu's share in total cloth production in 1991-92 was less than 7 per cent (160.0 million metres) only.

Performance of Handlooms and Powerlooms in Tamil Nadu

Handlooms are a gift of the Indian subcontinent to human civilisation. The share of handloom cloth in the total production gradually declined from 60.51 per cent in 1900, to 45.4 per cent in 1910, to 37.3 per cent in 1920, to 32.6 per cent in 1930 and to 28.3 per cent in 1938. The steady declining trend induced the authorities to take suitable measures for strengthening the handloom sector in the interest of weavers. In Tamil Nadu, 5.56 lakh handlooms are still functioning.

In Tamil Nadu, the powerlooms in the unorganised sector has been on the increase. Tamil Nadu has about 2.27 lakh powerlooms out of which only 3,000 powerlooms are in the co-operative sector. Tamil Nadu had late start in the case of powerlooms, because of the State government's policy of preference to handloom sector. The mounting handloom cloth has forced the government to change its policies. Future demand for the textiles in the country could be met only by powerlooms sector.

Statewise Industrial Sickness in Textile Industry in India

The Statewise number of cotton mills, closed and affected workers shows that Gujarat is most affected State in terms of closure of textile mills, 66 out of 227 (29 per cent) and workers 1,04,513 out of 2,61,524 (40 per cent). The next comes Tamil Nadu in terms of closure of textile mills, 49 out of 227 (22 per cent) and workers 17,797 out of 2,61,524 (7 per cent). The less affected both by closure of mills (0.4 per cent) and workers is Kerala State.

Problems of Textile Industry in Tamil Nadu

On the day of independence, there were 370 textile mills in India. At present we have 1624 Textile mills. We could see enormous development in Textile mills, handlooms and powerlooms in Tamil Nadu. Anyhow, 80 per cent of raw cotton is purchased from other Sates and most of the cloth produceed is marketed in northern States

Table 21.5 : Statewise Number of Cotton/Man-made fibre Textile Mills (Non-SSI) closed and affected workers as on December 31, 1997

State/Union Territory	Spinning		Composite		Total	
	Closed mills	Workers	Closed mills	Workers	Closed mills	Workers
Andhra Pradesh	16	5899	2	1345	18	7244
Assam	3	571	0	0	3	571
Bihar	2	501	0	0	2	501
Gujarat	9	4761	57	99752	66	104513
Haryana	7	3988	0	0	7	3988
Karnataka	8	2676	2	5617	10	8293
Kerala	1	2178	0	0	1	2178
Madhya Pradesh	4	2401	5	18690	9	21091
Maharashtra	14	9969	7	18022	21	27991
Orissa	1	48	0	0	1	48
Punjab	2	2317	0	0	2	2317
Rajasthan	9	11085	0	0	9	11085
Tamil Nadu	45	9147	4	8650	49	17797
Uttar Pradesh	9	13930	6	15369	15	29299
West Bengal	2	1541	7	164000	9	165541
Delhi	0	0	3	6117	3	6117
Pondicherry	1	75	0	0	1	75
Manipur	1	0	0	0	1	475
Total	134	71562	93	189962	227	261524

Source : Government of India (1998), Monthly Closure Report, Ministry of Textiles, Office of the Textile Commissioner NIC-TXC, Mumbai, February 28.

only. In earlier days textile market was a seller's market and the quality of the product was not bothered much now-a-days, textile market is a buyer's market.

The important factors, which are responsible for the recessionary trend of textile industry in Tamil Nadu are such as hike in the prices of raw materials, fall in the price of textile products, capital incurred for modernisation of textile mills, interest for capital, depreciation of Rupee, economic crisis, financial shortage, stagnation of textile product, shortage of power, hike in electricity tariff, shocking changes in textiles field, loss in export market and reduction in cotton production etc. The above factors ultimately increase the cost of production of the products. The only remedy is to improve the quality and thereby minimising the cost and to avert recession in textile industry.

Impact of External Policy on Textile Industry

The present external policy affects our textile industry to a large extent. The Central Government has announced the policy on the assumption that a minimum of 5 lakh bales in any year will be necessary to keep the international community interested in importing Indian cotton. While the heavy rains in Punjab, Gujarat and Maharashtra during the flowering season have dampened crop production. At least a 5 per cent drop in harvest is now projected. Under these conditions, it is reported that no cotton exports should be finalised before all the cotton is pressed.

Last year, prices of cotton went above international prices, forcing many mills to import. Further, it is surprising to know on which basis export quotas were given to the trade even before actual cotton arrivals, which chose to create shortage of cotton internally. As a consequence the capacity utilisation covers nearly 50-70 per cent only, which results in the closure of textile mills. The marked show down in cotton production is attributable to the noticeable fall in area under production of cotton followed by unprecedented rise in cotton prices, which affected cotton consumption considerably. It is clear to know that there is a steady increase in the prices of cotton yarn since 1994 onwards.

The textile policy of the Government is a document that makes plenty of promises but does not give any clear ideas about how to deliver on them. The policy merely becomes a statement of intent and is not action-oriented. The textile trade is one of the most regulated industries in the world governed by the multi-fibre agreement (MFA). This was integrated into GATT and the WTO. From 1 January, 2005 there will be no quantitative restrictions on textiles and garments. A 10-year period was given to allow countries to restructure their industries and prepare for a free trade regime. We have lost almost 7 years. Unless this policy is immediately followed up, the textile industry in India, which is already on the verge of death, will eventually die and then it will be impossible to revive it.

Suggestions

The following suggestions are given with a view to enable the policy makers to initiate necessary steps to overcome the recessionary trend in textile industries in Tamil Nadu.

1. Government of India should stop the export of cotton and lift the ban on the export of yarn.
2. Government should consider cotton growing as an agricultural work like sugar-cane provide low interest bearing loans to textile mills through commercial banks.
3. Government should permit procurement of cotton across the State.
4. Government of Tamil Nadu should regulate the sales tax on textile products uniformly.
5. Government of Tamil Nadu should grant exemption of excise duty to products that are produced for export in all parts of the country.
6. Hike in the electricity tariff for textile industries in Tamil Nadu should be reconsidered.
7. Cotton textiles also earn foreign exchange for India. Therefore,

suggestions have been made that the Central Government might set up some cotton textile mills in the public sectors as well as suitable sites for purposes of export.

Conclusion

It is concluded that Government should initiate measures more urgently to save the textile industries in Tamil Nadu from a major disaster in future. The Central Government has to pay a vital role to change the export policy according to the present need.

References

Deepak, 'Textile Components modernisation, crying need', *The Hindu, Survey of Indian Industry*, 1991, pp 361-362.

Government of India (1998), Monthly Closure Report, Ministry of Textiles, Office of the Textile Commissioner, NIC-TXC, Mumbai, February 28.

Guruajan, S., 'RBI against liberal bonus', *Indian Express,* Dated 13-08-98.

Jeyaraman, C.J., 'Textile machinery: Rising technology level', *The Hindu, Survey of Indian Industry,* 1990, pp. 362-367.

Krishnaraj Vanavarayat, 'Prevent the closure of textile mills in Tamil Nadu', *Daily Thanthi*, Dt. 27-09-98.

Mehtra, S.S. and Dinesh Harod (1998), Industrial sickness and workers — case of Gujarat textile industry, *Economic and Political Weekly*, Vol. XXXIII, No 26, December 26.

Perumalsamy, S., *Economic Development of Tamil Nadu*, S. Chand & Company Ltd., New Delhi, 1996, pp. 118-144.

Radhakrishnan, C.V., Textiles: Gaps in modernisation thrust', *The Hindu, Survey of Indian Industry*, 1991, pp. 357-359.

Radhakrishnan, C.V., 'Textiles: Will recovery phase continue,' *The Hindu, Survey of Indian Industry*, 1991, pp. 349-354.

Singhal Arvind, 'Textile policy is just a statement of intentions', *The Economics Times*, 28 November 2000, p.9.

Tamil Nadu — An economic Appraisal, 1983-84, pp.23-24.

Thiyagarajan, K.M., 'Textile exports : Mills gear to tap potential', *The Hindu, Survey of Indian Industry,* 1990, pp. 355-356.

22

STATUS OF RURAL INDUSTRIES IN NEW PANCHAYATI RAJ SYSTEM

— *G. Umashankar* and *G. Uma*

In a country like India rural industries play a key role in economic development. As majority of the population residues in the rural areas and almost all the resources are found deposited in the rural areas, rural industries becomes inevitable to utilise the resources of various kinds. The lack of knowledge, i.e., technical know-how, recent advancements, ignorance and poverty makes these rural industries to be in dol-drums. Though it is the condition rural industries particularly Khadi and Village industries are playing the crucial role in the economic development of the rural areas.

The estimated amount of production from these industries tunes to a sum of more than 5000 crores of rupees and an estimated 6 million people are employed either directly or indirectly in these industries. As said these industries are in a deplorable stage, it has become inevitable to have an alternative arrangement. Because the existing principles of globalisation, privatisation and liberalisation has not achieved the desired ends.

In addition, the five revolutions green, blue, white, brown, pink and yellow has yielded the results and today's environment find it difficult to cope up with the already established achievements.

Today we are on the threshold of looking for an alternative or the so called Doosri Ajadee, i.e., second independence. Independence from the evils curtailing human development. So the democratic decentralisation came in the last decade of the last century is expected to achieve economic development and social justice. Thus it is looked in the limelight of rural industries in the following way.

The concept of rural industry is not new in the Indian context. People were leading a self-sufficient and self-reliant life for the centuries together. The concept of Swadeshi and Sarvodaya are evolved only after the experiences of the living examples. Even after fifty years of independent democratic governance and implementation of various kinds of schemes and plans are not able to achieve development.

The industrialisation process took place in rather negative side. Wherein it provided opportunities for a portion of the population and resource utilisation in a more negative side. Therefore the industrial revolution is all that disaster because of its urban orientation. This is stated as,

> "The industrial revolution in India has not achieved the desired ends. As the resources are scattered and the pattern of large scale industry is unfit to the Indian context, it happened so that the majority of the population's interests and sustainable utilisation of resources are totally rejected."

Thus the alternative for the existing different scenario is establishment of rural industries in the limelight of New Panchayati Raj System, which aims at " Economic Development and Social Justice". The conditions laid here can be stated as,

(a) The preparation of plans for economic development and social justice.
(b) The implementation of schemes for economic development and social justice as may be entrusted to them including those in relation to the matters listed in the eleventh schedule.

The Need

For a developing country like India, where two-third of the populations residing in the rural areas and seasonal unemployment is a most common feature. Rural industrialisation has become inevitable in the path of economic development of the country. The industrial revolution on a larger scale is not able to provide ample employment opportunities to the existing human resource. This takes into consideration both the public and private sectors.

Two different dimensions are considered here. First, in the public sector, the majority of the industrialisation takes place on large scale. Whereas in the private sector 80 per cent of the industries are of small scale. The existing chronic unemployment cannot be solved by the large scale industries because in order to have cost effectiveness and added quality mechanisation becomes a must, finally, this adds degree to the existing chronic unemployment.

It is only the small scale rural based industries which can feed the people in the rural areas. The unskilled labour force in an unorganised manner can be developed through the rural industries. Thus the development of human resources can be done on a massive scale. The other important features are :

1. The existing socio-economic differences among the rural community can be established.
2. Provision of additional employment opportunities both in agricultural and its allied sector.
3. Additional income leading to increase in quality or standard of human life in the rural areas.
4. Enhance the economic development of the country.
5. Organisation and optimum utilisation of various kinds of resources in the rural areas.
6. Enhance agricultural operations.
7. Empowerment of women and the weaker sections.
8. Social development and social justice could be established.
9. Self-employment becomes more primitive.

10. Local technology, local resources and local utilisation leads to local development.
11. Instant or immediate investment which is small is more adequate leading to generation of more employment opportunities.

The above discussions helps us to derive a chart which gives a clear picture about the existing rural situation :

Quality and Quantity Resources

↓

Improper Utilisation and Preservative Methods

↓

Partialised distribution

↓

Partial Development

↓

Socio-Economic Problems

↓

Underdeveloped Nature

New Panchayati Raj System

The new panchayati raj system which came out as a panacea for the existing conflicting situation in the rural areas. It came out through the 73rd Constitutional Amendment Act in the year 1992. Simultaneously the State Conformity Act was passed in the year 1994. This Act has created new history in the polity of India. A paradigmic shift was experienced in the grassroots governance through the decentralisation of political power. This new system aims at economic development and social justice is not unilateral in its functioning. It is multidimensional in its functions. It probes into each and every aspects of rural life.

Salient Features of the New Panchayati Raj System

The salient features of the New Panchayati Raj System which empowers and enhances the people to participate in the management of the affairs relating to their governance are

(i) the Gram Sabha
(ii) uniform three-tier system
(iii) one-third reservation of seats at all levels in all positions for the women
(iv) reservation for SC/ST based on their population
(v) separate finance commission
(vi) separate election commission
(vii) 29 subjects under article 243(G) in Part XI of the Constitution of India.

Status of Rural Industries

As said the dual aim of this system is to achieve economic development and social justice. It has its own significance related to the 29 subjects entrusted to it. The discussion is made with the help of the Tamil Nadu Panchayts Act of 1994 and the status of the rural industries in this system is learnt as,

Powers, Functions and Responsibilities entrusted on the subject Small Scale Industries including Food Processing Industries, Khadi Village and Cottage Industries.

1. *Village Panchayats*

a. Assist in identification of beneficiaries for Entrepreneurs

Development Programmes.

b. Identification of beneficiaries for setting up industries in the backward areas.

c. Identification of beneficiaries for sanctioning of loans under schemes implemented through Director of Industries and Commerce.

d. Village Panchayats may assist to give publicity through media so that the scheme announced by the Central and State Governments reach the beneficiaries who are interested to start industries in rural areas.
(G.O.Ms.No. 75, Rural Development Department, Dt.24.4.98)
(G.O.Ms. No. 66. S.I (ST) Dept, Dt. 21.6.99)

e. Assist in identification of village level potential activities and formulation of projects.

f. Identification of beneficiaries for skill development and transfer of technology.

g. Advise the artisans about the training centres suitable for their trades and crafts and marketing of their finished goods.

h. Identify the beneficiaries, inform about the training centres and impart training by formulating the projects.

i. Village Panchayats should assist the establishment of marketing centres and for making necessary arrangements for starting industries using locally available raw materials and also fixing the prices of the goods produced by them.

j. Village Panchayats may implement new schemes for the development of Khadi Industries in consultation with Tamil Nadu Khadi Board.

k. Village Panchayats may plan, monitor and supervise the modernisation of the khadi and handloom weaving in consultation of the officials of Khadi and Handloom department.

l. Village Panchayats may assist for providing beehives boxes to the Adi Dravidas and Tribals living in the village to supplement their income and to supervise the implementation of the scheme.

m. Village Panchayat may formulate the schemes for the Khadi Silk weavers for providing jacquard boxes in consultation with the department concerned and supervise the scheme.

n. Village Panchayats may seek the assistance of the officials of the Khadi and Handloom Department to formulate the schemes for producing khadi based industries to improve living conditions of the people below the poverty line.

o. Village Panchayats can formulate the schemes for the people engaged in palmrya tappers by providing necessary equipments and supervise the scheme.
(G.O.Ms. No.75, Rural Development Department, Dt.14.3.97)
(G.O.Ms. No. 107. S.I HT & K Dept, Dt. 21.6.99)

2. *Panchayat Union Council*

a. Advise and assist in formulation of industrial estates and development centres.

b. Advise and assist in entrepreneurs development programmes.

c. Advise and assist in setting up industries in backward areas.

d. Advise and assist in the issue of loans to groups controlled by Director of Industries.

e. Assist in the establishment of Common Facilities.

f. Identification of the industries that can be started at the union level and providing basic requirements.
(G.O.Ms. No.75, Rural Development Department, Dt.24.4.98)
(G.O.Ms. No. 66. S.I (ST) Dept, Dt. 21.6.99)

g. Formulation of new trade centres or improving the existing centres for upgrading the skills of rural artisans and to impart technical skills.

h. Assist in the marketing of the products through cooperative societies.

i. Assist in the issue of loans for rural artisans.

j. Assist the village panchayats selection of beneficiaries for technical training and development schemes.

k. Panchayat union may action for integrating the schemes of the agencies for formulating schemes for handicraftsmen and others engaged in khadi and other rural small industries and supervise the schemes.

l. Panchayat union can assist the village people engaged in various units, trades and other works by enlightening them about technology.

m. Panchayat Union can assist for infrastructure development such as construction of common work places, workshops and market complexes.

n. Panchayat Unions can make necessary arrangements and supervise to avail loans and financial assistance for the establishment of rural industries.

o. Panchayat union can supervise whether rebate has been allowed on sale of khadi cloth produced in the panchayat union.

p. Panchayat union can supervise the implementation of schemes for modernisation of looms for khadi weaving.

r. Panchayat union can formulate new schemes for khadi development and to supervise the scheme.

s. Panchayat Union may take necessary action for supply of beehives to the Adi Dravida and scheduled tribes and to get the income increased.

t. Panchayat Union can formulate the schemes to supply palm tree climbing device for palmyra tappers and to monitor and supervise the same.
(G.O.Ms.No. 75, Rural Development Department, Dt.14.3.97)
(G.O.Ms. No. 66. H.H. T & K Dept, Dt. 7.6.99)

3. *District Panchayats*

a. Planning and review of the formulation of industrial estates and growth centres.

b. Advise and assist the entrepreneurs development programmes.

c. Advise and assist the setting up industries in backward areas.

d. Assist in the establishment of common facilities for the small scale industries.

e. Preparation of a plan on the feasibility of starting of industries in the district and to conduct conference on industrial development.

f. At the time of constitution of District-level Standing Committee on Industries and Labour, the General Manager, District Industries Centre may be included as a member of this committee.

(G.O. Ms. No. 75, Rural Development Department, Dt.24.4.98)
(G.O. Ms. No. 66. S.I (ST) Dept, Dt. 21.6.99)

g. District-level planning and identification of appropriate training centres for khadi silk, village and cottage industries/handicrafts development.

h. District Panchayat may draw up district plan for development of khadi, handicrafts, sericulture, cottage and village industries.

i. District Panchayats can identify the training centres and institutes suitable to impart appropriate technological training and disseminate such details to the panchayat unions and village panchayats.

j. District Panchayat may advise the KVIB about the infrastructures needed for exploiting available potentialities in the district.

k. District Panchayat may design suitable credit flow to the sector in the district as part of overall district credit plan.

l. District Panchayat may plan and suggest the implementation of schemes like modernisation of looms for khadi weaving, supply of beehives to the Adi-Dravidas and tribals. Schemes for jacquard provision to khadi silk weavers, free supply of loom kit to tappers, schemes for village industries promotion under Western Ghat development project and promotion for village industries, beekeeping in Nilgiris.

(G.O. Ms. No. 75, Rural Development Department, Dt.14.3.97)

What Could be Done ?

With the above said provisions the panchayats are expected to carry out the following activities. Here the need is stressed on people's participation. As this decentralised institution is an institution based on transparency and intimacy on the threshold of people's participation the steps evolved here are :

1. *Assessment of the Environment*
a. Identification of the resources available in terms of their quality, quantity and durability.
b. Identification of the entrepreneurial potential.

2. *Information*

Information about facilities, programmes, schemes, productivity and market potentials.

3. *Plan Preparation, Implementation and Evaluation*

Target setting and establishment with the assistance of various groups in terms of resource utilisation and preservation.

4. *Assessment*

Assessing the productivity and marketing potential and assisting for the improvement of the same.

The activities of the panchayats does not end here. It has a series of activities to enhance the process of rural industrialisation. In a nutshell the characteristics of panchayat institutions towards the rural industries can be listed as below.

1. Providing shelter for production and market.
2. Assurance of supply of quality and quantity resources available in the panchayat area for the industries.
3. Recommend financial assistance through the various rural development schemes.
4. Can provide technical knowledge through extension services.
5. Prepare map and report of the various kinds of available resources.
6. Encourage establishment of institutions for the development of the locality.
7. Can integrate the non-governmental organizations working in the locality.
8. Can establish resource banks for raw materials.
9. Create awareness on rural entrepreneurship among the mass

through Gram Sabha.

10. In its advertisements the panchayats can include the products of the rural industries.

Hence the expectation arising out of this can be expressed as,

QUALITY AND QUANTITY RESOURCES

↓

OPTIMUM UTILISATION AND PROPER PRESERVATION

↓

NEED BASED DISTRIBUTION

↓

SOCIO-ECONOMIC CHANGE AND POSITIVE GROWTH

↓

SUSTAINABLE DEVELOPMENT

Conclusion

Hence we experienced that the new panchayti raj system is going to achieve the desired ends and the rural industrialisation process can get its start in more positive way. The ultimate thing to make this process is to educate the people and create awareness. This can enhance the process of development in the rural areas. For the purpose an integrated effort by the academic institutions, government and non-governmental organisations can be made. Hence with the efforts as said above we can achieve development and harmony.

References

Government of Tamil Nadu, 'Democratic Decentralisation of Power', Department of Rural Development, Chennai, 1999.

Government of Tamil Nadu, 'Democratic Decentralisation - Powers Entrusted to Panchayati Raj Institutions', Department of Rural Development, Chennai,1999.

Nilavalam, April, 1999.

Outlook, special number on Women.

Palanithurai, G., (Ed), *Contemporary Issues in Development Dynamics*, Kanishka Publishers, New Delhi, 1998.

Palanithurai, G., *New Panchayati Raj System : Issues and Prospects*, Kanishka Publishers, New Delhi, 1996.

Rural Industrialisation in India, Government of India Report, 1996.

Soundarapandian, M., *Industrial Resurgence in Rural India*, Kanishka Publishers, New Delhi, 2000.

Srivastava, S.R., *A Practical Guide to Industrial Entrepreneurs*, Sultan Chand & Sons, New Delhi, 1996.

The Hindu, January 3, 1994, Madurai

The Hindu, January 11, 1999, Madurai.

Thittam, March 1999.

Thittam, March 2000.

23

ENTREPRENEUR DEVELOPMENT PROGRAMME IN NATIONAL SMALL INDUSTRIES CORPORATION

— *M. Meenakshisundaram* and *E. Anand*

Introduction

Small Scale Industries play a vital role in the economy of India. These industries require comparatively a smaller investment and are generally within the means of entrepreneur with the support offered by various financial institutions. The small scale Industries can lead to a decentralised mode of production and therefore regional imbalances can be removed with the development of these industries. Considered from the point of views of employment, small scale industries create more avenues of employment and lead to an equitable distribution of wealth.

The role of socio-economic objectives of small scale industry are: 1. Creation of Employment opportunities. 2. Source of subsidiary employment. 3. Proper distribution of work force. 4. Raising the standard of living of weaker sections. 5. Faster women's liberation. 6. Capital light. 7. Import-light. 8. Skill-light. 9. Quick yielding. 10. Checks inflation. 11. Economic equality. 12. Decentralisation. 13. Use of latent resources. 14. Capital formation. 15. Less Administrative problems. 16. Promote talents. 17. Complementary to large small industry. 18. Agricultural Development. 19. Strengthen Democracy. 20. Rural Development. 21. Overall Industrial Development. 22. Contribution to export.

Small Scale Industries have been defined as an industrial undertaking engaged in the manufacture/processing preservation of goods/repairing/service operations with original investments in plant and machinery not exceeding Rs. 1 crore. And in the case of export unit up to Rs. 3 crores. In order to develop SSI the Government of India established NSIC.

The objectives of the study are: 1. To study the organisational structure of National Small Industries Corporation in Dindigul District. 2. To study the aim and functions of NSIC in Dindigul District. 3. To study the types of Entrepreneur training programmes of NSIC in Dindigul District. 4. To study the people who have utilised these training programmes of study area. 5. To study the problems as NSIC in conducting entrepreneur development programme, training programmes and the link between training and utility by trainees.

Research methodology refers to various segmental steps adopted by a researcher. Interview schedule, tables etc. Useful to this purpose of study. Studying the problems will determine the particular steps and order to be taken. The researcher had taken 25 respondents for the study. The researcher has used here the convenient sampling.

Organisational Structure and Functions of NSIC

The NSIC, which is a Government of India undertaking, has greatly been responsible for development of the SSI sector. The hire purchase scheme of NSIC provides preferential treatment to women entrepreneurs. While the earnest money required from entrepreneurs for supply of machines is 20 per cent of the value in non-backward areas, it is only 15 per cent for women entrepreneurs for machines. Similarly the rate of interest in 12-1/2 per cent upto the value of machines of Rs. 5 lakhs on timely payment of instalments, the normal effective rate of payment is 13-1/2 per cent. There is also lower service charges. NSIC also conducts Entrepreneurs and Enterprise building programme for women.

The sub-centre in Dindigul District started functioning from March 1987, under the head of the Director. It is primarily a training centre. This centre is imparting training in the areas of leather, machines of practice, leather garments, footwear and commercial practice apart from entrepreneurship development programme. This centre is having modern sophisticated machines in the respective areas. 50 to 60 trainees are being imparted training in the above fields.

Separate hostel facilities for ladies and gents are provided for outstation trainees.

Organisation Structure of NSIC

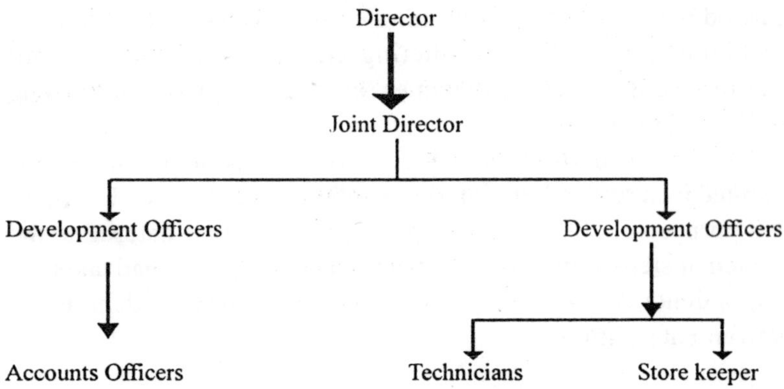

The National Small Industries Corporation conducts training to the interested persons, and who are enthusiastic to start leather-goods-making industry and lock section industry. The purposes of giving training are given below :

1. To give the employment opportunities to youths through training courses.
2. To develop the rural areas which promote the rural based industries.

3. To give the employment to women and promote their status.
4. Creating more entrepreneurs.
5. Motivating the women entrepreneurs and improving their business through training.

The National Small Industries Corporation imparts two types of training to the interested entrepreneurs. They are :

1. Lock section (for mechanical work).
2. Leather goods making (Footwear, bags and suitcases, gerkins and gloves).

Lock Section Training

In lock section the trainers are getting training about mechanical work, that is grinding, lathe, milling and surfacing of iron and machines. The training is given in two periods but continuously, that is normally three months training period.

Leather Goods Training Section

1. Only under age is rejected in this training, under age means below 18 years.
2. Educational qualification is 8th standard pass.
3. The age limit is upto 35 only.

There is no upper age limit to handicapped, widow and ex-servicemen.

Types of EDP in NSIC

The entrepreneurship oriented training in leather goods manufacturing is three pronged such as —

1. Leather synthetic products,
2. Gloves and Gerkins,
3. Chappals.

This is a three-month course where more emphasis is on the practical aspect of manufacturing. The students are given orientation towards entrepreneurship by way of lectures in the various aspects of entrepreneurship development like motivation, procedures in starting and manufacturing unit, management aspects people from various fields like bank officials, State Bank officials, and management experts are called to give lectures on the above subjects.

The students unlike the other programmes, where more emphasis is on theoretical aspects, is given an opportunity here to gain technical knowledge also because of the duration of the course is kept as three months. The students are also given opportunities to develop their marketing skills, leadership qualities and become a total manager by way of practical exercises and other opportunities. Those students belong to the Dindigul District are also given their provisional Small Scale Industries Registration Certificate by the DIC at the end of the course.

Results and Discussion

The field survey conducted from 25 trainees are analysed in this section. The sexwise classification is given in Table 23.1.

Table 23.1 : Sexwise Description of Respondents

Area of training	No. of Respondents		Total	%
	Male	Female		
1	2	3	4	5
Lock section	2	1	3	12
Leather	16	6	22	88
Total	18	7	25	100

Source : Data collected from NISC in Dindigul.

Table 23.1 deals with the sexwise description of respondents. Out of the total of 25 respondents, 3 respondents (12 per cent) only trained from lock section. In this lock section out of three respondents male respondents are two and the remaining one is female. And the remaining 22 respondents (88 per cent) are trained from the leather goods section. Out of them, the total number of male respondents is 16, and remaining 6 respondents are females. It also shows that the total number of male respondents are 18 (72 per cent) and the remaining 7 respondents (28 per cent) are females. Therefore more number of respondents are males.

Table 23.2 : Educational Qualification

Sl. No.	Educational Qualification	No. of respondents	%
1.	S.S.L.C.	7	28
2.	Hr. Sec.	5	20
3.	Degree	10	40
4.	Diploma	3	12
	Total	25	100

Source : Data collected from respondents.

Table 23.2 explains that educational qualifications of the respondents. In the total number of respondents (25), 7 respondents (28 per cent) are S.S.L.C. qualified respondents. 5 respondents (20 per cent) are having the higher secondary certificate, 10 respondents (40 per cent) have got degree, and the remaining 3 respondents (12 per cent) are diploma holders.

Table 23.3 : Reasons for undergoing Training

Sl. No.	Reason	No. of Respondents	%
1.	Own interest	22	88
2.	Compulsion	3	12
	Total	25	100

Source : Data collected from particular respondent.

The nature of interest for doing the National Small Industries Corporation Entrepreneurship training is shown in Table 23.3. Out of the total number of respondents (25) 22 respondents (88 per cent) have joined the training with their own interest and remaining 3 respondents (12 per cent) joined the training due to the compulsion of their parents, friends and officials.

Table 23.4 : Present Occupational Status

Sl. No.	Reason	No. of Respondents	%
1.	Employment	12	48
2.	Business	11	44
3.	Unemployment	2	9
	Total	25	100

Source : Data collected from respondents.

The employment status of respondents after completing the training programme is explained by the above table. Out of total number of respondents (25), 12 respondents (18 per cent) are employed and 11 respondents (44 per cent) are in business activities and the remaining 2 respondents living without any employment. The researcher understood from this table that more respondents got the employment or business activities.

Table 23.5 : Loan Borrowed

Sl. No.	Loan	No. of Respondents	%
1.	Yes	9	36
2.	No	16	64
	Total	25	100

Source : Data collected from the respondents.

This Table 23.5 shows the loan borrowed by respondents of the total number of respondents (25), 9 respondents to get the loan from commercial banks and remaining 16 respondents did not get any loan from Government or financial institutions.

Table 23.6 : Nature of the Financial Assistance

Sl. No.	Institutions	No. of respondents	%
1.	Syndicate Bank	2	8
2.	Canara Bank	7	28
3.	NIL	16	64
	Total	25	100

Source : Data collected from respondents.

Whether the respondents got any financial assistance from the commercial assistance from the commercial banks is shown by Table 23.6. Out of the total number of respondents (25), 2 respondents (8 per cent) got financial assistance from Syndicate Bank and 7 respondents got loan from Canara Bank and remaining 16 (64 per cent) respondents did not get any financial assistance from the banks.

Table 23.7 : Help obtained from National Small Industries Corporation

Sl. No.	Help from NSIC	No. of Respondents	%
1.	Yes	13	52
2.	No	12	48
	Total	25	100

Source : Data collected from the respondents.

Table 23.7 shows about the help obtained from the National Small Industries Corporation. Out of the total number of respondents (25), 13 respondents (52) got help from NSIC, in the form of order for manufacturing of leather goods and the information about the leather goods exhibition and the remaining 12 respondents (48%) did not get any help from the National Small Industries Corporation.

Table 23.8 : Benefited from the Training

Sl. No.	Benefited	No. of Respondents	%
1.	Yes	21	84
2.	No	4	16
	Total	25	100

Source : Data collected from the respondents.

This Table 23.8 shows the number of respondents benefited from their training. Out of the 25 respondents, 21 respondents (84 per cent) are benefited from their training and the remaining 4 respondents (16 per cent) are not benefited from the training.

Summary of Findings

An entrepreneur has a great social responsibility. An enterprise consists of not only those who manage it but a host of other segments of social workers, consumers, the State and the surrounding community.

1. In this study area, more number of respondents (18) 72% are males who are trained by NSIC.
2. Majority of the respondents (10) 40% are degree holders. It is understood by researcher that most of the respondents, have completed their degree. After completing the degree, the respondents joined the training courses in National Small Industries Corporation.
3. After completing the training majority of the respondents received the loans from commercial banks.
4. From the above analysis, it may be concluded that the trainees were not interested in getting financial assistance because of risk involved in self-employment enterprises to be borne by the entrepreneur.
5. The researcher understood that the 52 respondents have received help from the National Small Industries Corporation

at Dindigul. In the form of order for manufacturing of leather goods and the information about the leather goods exhibition.

6. More number of respondents have benefited from the training. This training is useful to trainees and it is life oriented, i.e. lock industries and leather industries.
7. The respondents who came forward to start new business enterprises obtained loans from various nationalised banks and financial institutions.

Suggestions

1. Give suitable instructions to the trainees. Some trainees do not know the value and details of this training. Therefore, motivate the trainees through detailed instructions.
2. Proper utilisation of time and materials as more number of trainees waste time and materials during the training period.
3. Give guidance to the trainees regarding how to get employment.
4. Improve the supply of raw-materials to the concerned industrial section in time.
5. Arrangement of loan and other financial facilities to the economically poor trainees.
6. Introduce the new training course such as coir industrial training, dyeing, industrial training and rural based industrial training courses.
7. NSIC should arrange for the employment information centre for the development of trainees and others.

Ever since its, establishment, there is no doubt that the NSIC has played a vital role in providing assistance to entrepreneurs in rural and backward areas. It has given momentum to industrial growth in the rural areas, attracted entrepreneurs and unemployed youths to self-employment opportunities. It has been supplying basic information for rural and urban entrepreneurs and has been contributing in implementation of special programmes like self-employment training and the training programme can be more meaningful if the above suggestions are implemented.

References

Balu, V., *Entrepreneurial Development*, Sri Venkateswara Publications, Madras, 1998.

Sherlekar, *Business Organisation and Management*, 1999.

Srivastava, *A Practical Guide to Industrial Entrepreneurs*, Sultan Chand & Sons, New Delhi, 1996.

Vasant Deszi, *Management of Small Scale Industries*, Himalaya Publishing House, New Delhi, 1995.

24

WOMEN ENTREPRENEURS IN COIMBATORE DISTRICT OF TAMIL NADU

— *G. Thenmozhi, J. Chandrakantha* and *S. Jayabalan*

"The greatest revolution in a country is one that affect the status and living conditions of its women."

— *Nehru*

Economic growth and development of a country is determined by human, physical and financial resources. An economy can move on to higher levels of growth either by acquiring a larger quantum of the factors of production or through technical progress. The objectives of any planned development is to develop human resources to their brimming utilisation. Therefore, industrialisation is one of the ways of bringing about socio-economic development in any country.

The economic development of a nation is sparked largely by its development in small-scale industries. India's economy is today poised for a flourishing entrepreneurial activity. It is also known that a healthy business environment is an essential requirement of entrepreneurial growth.

In India, entrepreneurial world is men's world predominantly. But today the trend is changed. Women can also contribute towards the economy of the nation. It demands the policy makers, planners and administrators to devise ways and means of promoting entrepreneurship among women.

Women entrepreneurs are playing a vital role in shaping the economy of a nation. In spite of the emergence of the women's liberation movement; this sector has not acquired its due importance significance in political, economic or social aspects of life.

It is misconception that women cannot be good managers. Because the complete manager in Indian society is the mother as she plans budgets, executes and shows results in the day to day life.

The government financial institutions have launched many schemes by which are exclusively meant for the development of women entrepreneurs. In spite of all these steps and efforts the development of women entrepreneurship is taking place at a snail's pace. This phenomenon is mainly due to the various problems faced by the women entrepreneurs. A field survey has been conducted in Coimbatore District and the opinion gathered from women entrepreneurs are analysed in this chapter.

Problems of Women Entrepreneurs

The entrepreneurial performance is affected due to various problems faced by the women entrepreneurs, namely self-sphere System Problems, Socio-Psycho Shpere System Problems, Resource System Problems and Support System Problems. It is explained in the following figure.

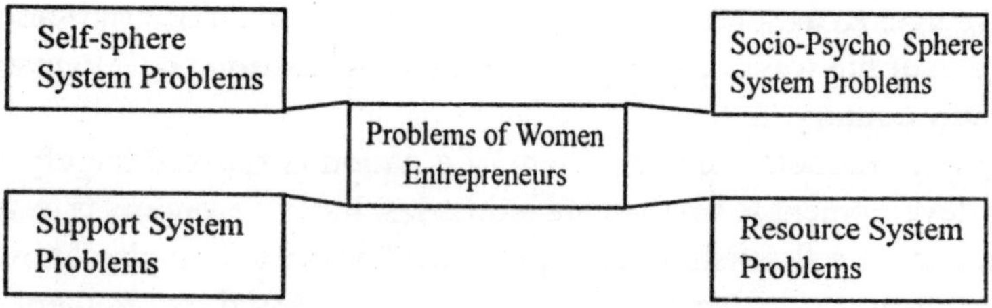

Self-sphere System Problems

Self-sphere system of a woman entrepreneur is composed of her personal characteristics, qualities and capabilities which can never be identical with other entrepreneurs. Self-sphere system problems encountered by the women entrepreneurs have been categorized into two, viz.

(a) General/Personal Problems, and
(b) Educational Problems

General/Personal Problems

Table 24.1 exhibits the various general/personal problems encountered by women entrepreneurs.

Table 24.1 : General/Personal Problems of Women Entrepreneurs

S. No.	Problems	Rank
1.	Poor-Risk-taking Ability	VI
2.	Lack of Proper Training	IV
3.	Lack of Leisure Time	III
4.	Lack of Systematic Planning and Working	VIII
5.	Health Problems	VIII
6.	Excessive Burden of Work and Responsibility	II
7.	Difficulty in Handling Technical Financial and Managerial Activities	V
8.	Excessive Tensions and Challenges	I

Source : Computed from Primary data.

It is clear from Table 24.1, among General/Personal Problems, excessive tensions and challenges, as endorsed by majority of the respondents, was the most common constraint. Many of the respondence expressed excessive burden of work and responsibility as one of the major problems followed by lack of leisure time.

Educational Problems

Table 24.2 shows that lack of knowledge about the various loaning schemes and procedures of financial institutions, about agencies and institutions working for women entrepreneurs and about the legal aspects are the most serious problems since these three problems have got the first-three ranks respectively.

Table 24.2 : Educational Problems of Women Entrepreneurs

S. No.	Problems	Rank
Lack of Knowledge About		
1.	The Legal Aspects	III
2.	The competitors	IV
3.	The Availability of Machines & Equipment's and various Improved Technologies	VII
4.	The agencies and institutions and procedures of Financial Institutions	II
5.	The various loaning schemes and procedures of Financial Institutions	I
6.	The Marketing	VI
7.	The availability of raw materials	V

Source : Computed from Primary data.

Socio-Psycho Sphere System Problems

Socio-Psycho system is conceptualised as a specific set of social conditions and particular psychological characteristics of women entrepreneurs. Table 24.3 shows the socio-psycho system problems of women entrepreneurs.

Table 24.3 : Socio-Psycho Sphere System Problems of Women Entrepreneurs

S. No.	Problems	Rank
1.	Lack of Self-confidence	X
2.	Lack of Encouragement, Recongnition and appreciation from Family and Society	VII
3.	Conflicts due to Dual Responsibilities	III
4.	Inconsistent to Traditional Norms	V
5.	Poor chance of Mobility for women	I
6.	Male Domination and No Equal status in Business	VI
7.	Lack of sufficient Time to look after Children/Husband, Household Activity and to attend Family functions	II
8.	Faculty Socialisation and Problems of Public Relations	VII
9.	Inferiority Complex	IX
10.	Society lacks confidence in women's ability	VI

Source : Computed from Primary data.

It could be inferred that women entrepreneurs in Coimbatore District face only a low quantum of Socio-Psycho Problems, poor mobility of women is the constraint mostly faced by the women entrepreneurs since it has the first rank. Apart from this, the women entrepreneurs have to look after their family members leading to dual responsibilities and ultimately resulted into family conflicts.

Resources System Problems

Resource system problems faced by the women entrepreneurs are grouped into five categories, viz., perception of opportunities and inception period problems, marketing, labour and raw material, technological and financial problems. Perception of opportunity and inception period problems of the women entrepreneurs are presented in Table 24.4.

Table 24.4 : Perception of Opportunity and Inception Period Problems of Women Entrepreneurs

S. No.	Problems	Rank
1.	Arrangement of Finance	I
2.	Lack of Information and Experience in the field	XII
3.	Selection and Installation of Proper Plant and Machinery	X
4.	Labour problems	VIII
5.	Location of site	IX
6.	Town-Planning Approval and Pollution Control Permission	VI
7.	Industrial Sheds provided by the DIC	V
8.	Obtaining Licence	IV
9.	Recruitment of personnel	VII
10.	Difficulties in obtaining and availing the subsidies and other facilities	III
11.	Inadequate Infrastructure	XI
12.	Power Supply	II

Source : Computed from Primary data.

It could be inferred that around 50 per cent of women entrepreneurs have suffered the perception of opportunity and inception period problems. Among these problems arrangement of finance is the major constraint followed by power supply. The Table

24.5 gives the various marketing problems faced by the women entrepreneurs.

Table 24.5 : Marketing Problems of Women Entrepreneurs

S. No.	Problems	Rank
1.	Lack of Transport Facilities	V
2.	Lack of Marketing Experience	III
3.	Competition from Established Large Entrepreneurs	I
4.	Slackness in Demand	IV
5.	Difficulty in getting Money from Buyer after Credit Sales	II

It could be inferred that marketing is a major constraint faced by the women entrepreneurs. Among the marketing problems, competition from established and large scale unit is the major constraint followed by lack of marketing experience. Table 24.6 exhibits the various labour and raw material problems encountered by the women entrepreneurs.

Table 24.6 : Labour and Raw Material Problems of Women Entrepreneurs

S. No.	Problems	Rank
1.	Absenteeism	X
2.	Labour Turnover	VII
3.	High Wage Rate	I
4.	Indiscipline	XI
5.	Frequent Work Stoppage	VIII
6.	High Training Cost	II
7.	Trade Unionism	IV
8.	Managing Male Workers	IX
9.	Non-availability of Skilled Workers	V
10.	Lack of Storage Facilities	III
11.	Lack of Supply of Raw Materials from Continuous Production	VI

Source : Computed from Primary data.

It is very clear from Table 24.6 that only very few respondents have labour problems. The women entrepreneurs appoint disciplined workers in their enterprises because this constraint has got the last rank. The constraint related to high wage rate and high training cost are quite heavy for some women entrepreneurs. They have revealed that trade unionism has no impact in their field and managing male worker is not an important constraint since it has got a low rank.

Table 24.7 : Technological Problems of Women Entrepreneurs

S. No.	Problems	Rank
1.	Lack of Technical knowhow about the unit	VII
2.	Inability to work in Project Round the year	III
3.	Non-availability of Modern Technologies	II
4.	Difficulty in Maintenance and Repairing Machinery	IV
5.	Availability of Technologies/Machinery and Equipment at Distant places	V
6.	Ineffective Consultancy Services provided by the Government Agencies	I
7.	Non-availability of Professional Managers	VI

Source : Computed from Primary data.

It is seen from the table that consultancy services provided by the Government agencies is ineffective. Further the table shows that non-availability of modern technologies related to their field is another most important constraint encountered by the women entrepreneurs.

Table 24.8 shows the financial problems faced by the women entrepreneurs.

Table 24.8 : Financial Problems of Women Entrepreneurs

S. No.	Problems	Rank
1.	Limited working capital	I
2.	Lack of funds for fixed assets	III
3.	Inadequate Assistance from Financial Agencies and banks	V
4.	Bureaucracy and Red-tapism of Government Institutions	IV
5.	Lack of Collateral Security	II
6.	Economic Incredibility of women	VI
7.	Inadequate Instalments for Repayment	VII

Source : Computed from Primary data.

It is clear from Table 24.8 that the limited working capital is a major constraint for almost all the women entrepreneurs since it has secured first rank.

Being a woman, she does not have enough collateral securities. But banks and financial institutions insist upon the women to produce collateral security for availing financial assistance. Hence lack of collateral security and lack of funds for purchasing fixed asset are also some other major problems of women entrepreneurs. Further it could be inferred from the Table 24.8 that 80 per cent of respondents in Coimbatore district are suffering from financial problems.

Support System Problems

The legal institutional and organisational measures initiated by the Government are designed to create a 'Support System' for developing entrepreneurship in all sections of society. The Table 24.9 gives support system problems faced by the women entrepreneurs.

Table 24.9 : Support System Problems of Women Entrepreneurs

S. No.	Problems	Rank
1.	Inadequate Incentives provided by the Government	VII
2.	Non-Co-operative Attitude of the employees	IX
3.	Time wasted due to visits to the financial Institutions	II
4.	Personal or political influences needed to avail Institutional Help quickly	VIII
5.	Bribing the Agencies Providing Subsidies/Loans/Incentives	VI
6.	Target/Oriented Approach and lack of Promotional Activities	I
7.	Inadequate Institutional Technical Training	X
8.	Lack of Effective Communication between Field functionaries and women entrepreneurs	III
9.	Harassment by Officials in Completion of Documents and other formalities	IV
10.	Lack of Communication and Co-ordination between Different Agencies dealing with small scale industrial units	V

Source : Computed from Primary data.

The above table exhibits that there is no proper support system for the Development of Women Entrepreneurship. Most of the entrepreneurs feel that the Government and other Financial Institutions make only target oriented approach and there is no real interest for the promotion of entrepreneurship development, because this constraint has got the maximum rank. They also feel, that there exists a lack of effective communication between field functionaries and themselves.

An attempt is also made to find out the most important system constraint by calculating the overall mean score for each and every system problems.

Table 24.10 : Overall Rank of various System Problems of the Women Entrepreneurs

S. No.	Problems	Rank
1.	Self-Sphere System Problems	II
2.	Socio-Psycho Sphere System problems	IV
3.	Resource System problems	III
4.	Support System Problems	I

Source : Computed from Primary data.

The table exhibits that the majority of women entrepreneurs have suffered the support system problems since it has got a top rank. Socio-Psycho Sphere System constraint has got the least rank.

Conclusion

Entrepreneurship is the only panacea for eradicating unemployment poverty; various problems of women entrepreneurs should be removed. The off-repealed lament amongst women is that there is no adequate national policy for development of women.

Women who are desirous of having economic independence enter the male dominated field of entrepreneurship for which they need guidance right from the formulation of the project till its execution. To enable women to break away from traditional activities like garments and food into more lucrative non-traditional areas, which need a much higher level of investment, the help of academic institutions, GOs and NGOs should be enlisted. Business training at college level and through EDPs, SIDO, as well as NGOs can impart information to a greater number of women as well as help them to make proper project reports and handle paper work. Once these women are equipped to cope with the formalities involved in formal borrowing they will succeed in broadening the base of their entrepreneurial activities, as credit will no longer be a limiting factor.

The existing government sponsored programmes and EDPs of non-government organisations have to be supplemented with efforts on the part of academic institutions and NGOs to tap the potential of even a reasonable number of perspective women entrepreneurs. Creation of entrepreneurial cells in colleges will go a long way in providing elementary business training, skill formation and information support system as to whom to approach for finance, technology, marketing problems, etc. Only then women will be empowered in the real sense to become both agents and beneficiaries of their country's development.

"When Women moves forward, the Family moves, the Village moves and the Country moves."

INDEX